FOREIGN JOINT VENTURES IN CONTEMPORARY CHINA

FOREIGN JOINT VENTURES IN CONTEMPORARY CHINA

Michael Franz Roehrig

St. Martin's Press
New York

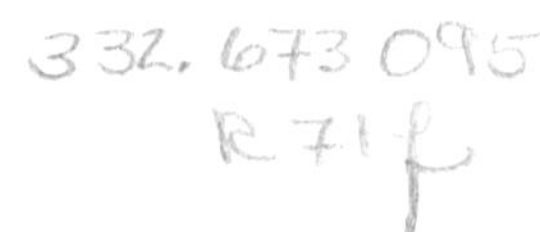

 For information, write:
Scholarly & Reference Division, St. Martin's Press,
175 Fifth Avenue, New York, N.Y. 10010

First published in the United States of America 1994

Printed in the United States of America

Book design by Acme Art, Inc., New York, NY

ISBN 0-312-12131-8

Library of Congress Cataloging-in-Publication Data

Roehrig, Michael Franz.
Foreign joint ventures in contemporary China / Michael Franz Roehrig.
p. cm.
Includes bibliographical references and index.
ISBN 0–312–12131–8
1. Investments, Foreign—China. 2. Joint ventures—Government policy—China. 3. International business enterprises—China. 4. Negotiation in business—China. I. Title.
HG5782.R64 1994
332.6'73'0951—dc20 94–11018
CIP

To my family

TABLE OF CONTENTS

ACKNOWLEDGMENTS

I acknowledge the East Asian Studies Program (EASP) of the Center for International Studies for its role in arranging my research trip to China on the OSU-Wuhan University Exchange Program, which allowed me to collect data that are central to this book. I also thank Wuhan University's Foreign Affairs Office for arranging and assisting in interviews with Chinese respondents and for the hospitality it extended to me while I lived there.

I thank Ryan McClay, Bob Loparo, and Eric Weston of Xavier University's Computer Support Staff who spent much time preparing the manuscript disk for the computer.

I thank Professor Kevin J. O'Brien who spent many hours instructing me in fundamental aspects of Chinese area studies research in the United States and in China while I was a graduate student. During the process of preparing this book, he continued in his role as adviser and teacher and was an invaluable source of insight and guidance.

I also thank friends and family. In particular, I thank Greg Levitt and Daniel P. Foley for encouragement and advice and Karim Massimov for valuable insight and data. I express gratitude to James Lee for assisting me with my research and teaching me much in the process. Finally, I had the steadfast and patient support of a loving family. My mother, Mary E. Roehrig, and my father, Helmut J. Roehrig, sacrificed greatly to extend the emotional and financial backing to see me through my studies and ultimately preparing this book. To my parents and family, including Helmut, Theresa, and Karl, I owe the greatest debt of all.

1

Introduction

In 1979, China began to introduce rules, regulations, and laws designed to regulate Sino-foreign joint ventures. This book explores how resident foreign businesspersons interact with Chinese associates and officials and how this interaction affects implementation of joint venture policies. In particular, it investigates bargaining between foreign joint venture managers and sub-national bureaucratic actors and focuses on the policy adjustments and legal innovations that grew from these interactions and the outcomes that have evolved despite conflicting objectives. Most notably, it examines policy implementers who strive to maximize and speed transfer of capital, technology, and management know-how while maintaining control over joint venture operations, and joint venture managers who develop countermeasures to maximize profit, including improving product quality and increasing autonomy from the state.

The objectives of the research are to identify bargaining occasions and strategies, to determine what laws were promulgated to address points of conflict, to identify factors that affect implementation, and to explain the ways foreigners bring to bear their influence on implementation. This book pays particular attention to strategies foreigners employ to circumvent local bureaucratic interference.

Through archival research and interviews with Chinese officials and business managers and foreign executives involved with joint ventures in China, this analysis suggests that the foreign presence in China has been an important factor affecting policy making and implementation; foreign investors bring to the bargaining table numerous resources, including capital, technology, and management know-how, all of which are needed for China's ambitious economic development. I argue that the context for implementation in China has exhibited both continuity and change when faced with an influx of foreign values and resources. The most vivid change in this policy context, for instance, has been the creation and evolution of a legal framework designed to address the concerns of foreign investors regarding a number of issues, including governing law, foreign exchange, labor relations, and taxes. Conversely, among the aspects of China's political system that continues to influence the policy process is the long-standing and all-important role of personal relationships to achieve goals (e.g., procuring resources outside the plan for production) outside of normal legal and administrative channels.

THEORETICAL OVERVIEW

The "hard core" of bargaining frameworks that analyze foreign direct investment (FDI) assume that multinational corporations (MNCs) and host countries bargain with each other to achieve their respective objectives.[1] MNCs invest in developing nations to earn a profit by taking advantage of cheap labor, natural resources, potential access to a new market, and various tax and other incentives that these nations offer. Host nations invite FDI to obtain capital, technology, and management training.[2]

Debate between proponents and critics of FDI has evolved for decades. Today, the two contending perspectives are represented by the bargaining school, favoring FDI, and the Marxist-Dependencia school, which is skeptical of the ability of developing host nations to bargain effectively with MNCs.[3]

During the 1960s and 1970s, these perspectives on FDI were rooted in "conventional" and "critical" schools of thought.[4] Dependency theorists of the critical perspective were pessimistic about the bargaining positions of developing nations vis-à-vis MNCs, while proponents of the conventional school argued that FDI contributed to the economic and political growth of developing host nations. In fact, proponents of FDI argued that in many instances the bargaining strength of host nations would increase over time.[5]

Critical theorists argued that FDI would leave developing nations dependent on the MNCs of the industrialized West for their economic and political development. Instead of FDI, the critical theorists supported alternatives, including state corporations, a private sector protected from the exploitative interests of Western nations and their MNCs, or a combination of the two.[6]

Conventional theorists, on the other hand, contended that MNCs could act as agents of development in the developing nations without creating a relationship of dependence. Among the positive contributions that MNCs would make were improved product quality, the promotion of competition, capital investments, and sophisticated management techniques.

A compromise between the contending schools of thought ultimately evolved in the form of joint ventures. It was hoped that this form of FDI would satisfy the concerns of both developing host nations and MNCs. Scholars also began analyses of this form of FDI to determine the relative benefits for MNCs and developing host nations. Ideally, joint ventures would afford the host nation at least limited control over these enterprises to discourage the negative aspects of FDI, while allowing it to enjoy the benefits that conventional theorists argued FDI would bring.[7] FDI literature began to contemplate whether joint ventures facilitated a more beneficial bargaining position for host governments or foreign investors.

Bargaining between host governments and foreign investors has been studied on a country-by-country basis, and bargaining strengths and weaknesses measured in relation to the unique characteristics of the individual nations.[8] FDI in China, for instance, has been studied in a variety of ways since the country opened its doors in 1979. China's evolving legal framework, central policies toward foreign investment, political culture, mood of the central authorities, and strengths and weaknesses of its socialist system have all been identified as factors affecting its bargaining capacity vis-à-vis foreign joint venture partners.[9] FDI literature frequently has been criticized for being "monolithic," pitting the host country as a whole against MNCs collectively.[10]

One prominent example is Margaret M. Pearson's 1991 book, *Joint Ventures in the People's Republic of China: The Control of Foreign Direct Investment under Socialism.* The author discusses bargaining in "monolithic" terms of the "foreign side" versus the "Chinese side." The analysis concentrates on interviews from China's most liberal economic zones, where laws and procedures have been evolving for well over a decade and where the Chinese have experienced most pronounced and prolonged exposure to foreign forces.

The bargaining strengths of local policy implementers and joint venture representatives may vary significantly in China's inland areas, where political conditions are more stringent and laws and regulations to govern FDI in joint ventures only recently have been passed. In this book, I will demonstrate that bargaining over the terms of FDI is only the first step of a long process of negotiation over implementation of joint venture laws and policies at the local level that is perpetual throughout the entire existence of the joint venture. Bargaining is not limited to the "foreign side" and the "Chinese side." In fact, foreign and Chinese joint venture representatives often work together to bargain with local authorities over implementation of rules and regulations that affect the joint venture from the outside, and among themselves over rules and regulations within the joint venture itself. This bargaining is not always explicit; bargaining results from legal ambiguities, foreign and Chinese legal ignorance, and cultural nuances that lead parties constantly to "feel each other out" to see what actions they can take and benefits they can extract without undermining business operations. Mutually acceptable innovations are often developed to circumvent local power authorities through such implicit bargaining. This book identifies the most salient factors that affect bargaining processes at local levels. Ultimately, it calls for more systematic comparisons of these local processes, where final policy and legal outcomes are often determined.

CONSEQUENT STUDY CONTRIBUTIONS

This study draws on legal analyses, as well as literature rooted in the social sciences. Legal analyses of reforms in China's foreign sector have focused on textual exegesis of laws and have highlighted gaps, ambiguities, and contradictions. These analyses often do not consider political (e.g., bureaucratic interference), economic (e.g., awkward dual-pricing system), and cultural (e.g., Chinese xenophobia) factors that may affect implementation of these laws, especially at the local level.[11] Implicit in many legal discussions is an assumption that cooperative government officials obediently enforce newly promulgated laws.[12] This study considers many of these important factors that legal analysts often ignore.

Social scientists have studied China's policy process for over 30 years. Sinologists in the 1960s characterized the Chinese Communist Party as a united body that promulgated policies that were implemented without obstruction by a responsive and cooperative hierarchy of party cadres.[13] The Cultural Revolution, however, revealed a party leadership plagued by factions, prone to bitter fights that fragmented policy making and implementation.[14] Subsequent literature introduced typologies of policy conflict that focused on line struggle,[15] tendencies of articulation,[16] factions,[17] and finally on system and bureaucratic factors.[18] Underlying much recent research is the assumption that China's policy process is "a complex bargaining process where policy implementation tends to be slow and incremental" and "outcomes . . . are often closer to bureaucratic needs than elite preferences."[19]

In recent years, attention has shifted from the policy process writ large to implementation of specific policies. Among the policies studied have been public health,[20] education,[21] water resources, the one-child policy, and election campaigns.[22] In 1991, Melanie Manion discovered that implementation of cadre-recruitment policy depended in large measure on bargaining between cadres and middle-level bureaucrats; she concluded that generalizability of such bargaining in other areas was "essentially an empirical question" that required further investigation.[23] This study responds to Manion's work by exploring how policy outcomes evolve from bargaining processes between joint ventures and local authorities.

This study also contributes to our understanding of the role of Chinese culture in China's foreign economic relations.[24] Bargaining as a cultural attribute of Chinese society is operative in implementation of joint venture rules and regulations.[25] This bargaining is used not only to bridge the commercial interests of the parties, but also to bridge the cultural differences between Chinese and foreign investors. For instance, I discuss how Confucian values in Chinese labor relations are reconciled through bargaining with conflicting foreign perspectives.[26] The study sheds light on how Chinese cultural values affect implementation of rules, regulations, and laws and, conversely, how the unique environment of the Sino-foreign joint venture has forced the Chinese to compromise some of their values and convictions. What, for instance, are the roles of patron-client relations and neotraditional values in the joint venture? Many have argued that these characteristics of Chinese culture would inhibit the evolution of a modern labor force.[27] It has also been argued that personalism and bargaining beyond legal boundaries would render laws only marginally effective at best.[28] My findings indicate that foreign values may have influenced the Chinese working within the joint venture. Several foreign managers, in fact, explained that it was their explicit intention to affect Chinese workers' attitudes toward management authority, responsibility, and product quality.[29]

This book also builds on other studies of Sino-foreign joint ventures. These enterprises have been considered in historical context, in legal analyses, in relation to China's Open Door policy, and in terms of U.S.-China relations in general, and have been analyzed to understand how China's socialist system has affected the country's bargaining position vis-a-vis foreign investors.[30] This book is unique in its treatment of bargaining between joint ventures and local policy implementers at the grass roots of the Chinese political system.

METHOD

During spring and summer 1989, I reviewed relevant journals and other source material dating from 1979 to become familiar with Sino-foreign joint ventures, determined what issues called for analysis, and assessed the feasibility of researching various topics. I also made contact with other scholars researching joint ventures and read Michael J. Moser's valuable contribution, *Foreign Trade, Investment, and the Law in the People's Republic of China.*

My first series of interviews took place in the United States in 1990 with several knowledgeable respondents. These interviews were arranged through private contacts and were conducted by telephone and in face-to-face conversations. In 1990-1991, while I was a Visiting Scholar at Wuhan University on the Ohio State University-Wuhan University Exchange Program, I conducted numerous interviews throughout China. In January 1991, for example, I traveled to Guangzhou, Foshan, and Shenzhen. During the course of this trip, it became apparent that many of my questions needed refinement. Respondents' interests varied: Some were managers, others were staffers; representatives came from contractual joint ventures as well as equity joint ventures; some respondents were from Special Economic Zones (SEZs), while others came from inland areas. Chinese management and staff exhibited particular interest in discussing labor issues. Foreign experts contributed considerable insight into establishment procedures and financial and operational concerns of ongoing enterprises, including foreign-exchange requirements, tax payments, procuring raw materials, and negotiating prices and various fee waivers.

I concentrated on question areas that fit particular respondents and avoided forcing them into answering prepared questions. In one interview, for instance, a joint venture staffer who had previously worked in a state enterprise provided (often in monologue form) valuable information on the role of bargaining by state enterprise managers, local labor officials, and joint venture representatives over transfer of a state employee to a joint venture. With little prodding, she also argued that neotraditional relationships characterize labor relations in state enterprises but are not as apparent in joint ventures.[31] In many similar encounters, I allowed respondents to relate personal experiences without locking them into a predetermined set of questions.

Interviews were the most important source of information for this book. They offered detailed insights into the inner workings of the joint venture, the human side of the multinational corporation as foreign managers grappled with issues of how to get things done in an alien culture with unfamiliar colleagues, and the bargaining strengths of various parties who battle for joint venture control to achieve their respective, often conflicting objectives.

There were 46 respondents. Twenty-seven were managers, staffers, and corporate executives from joint ventures. Five were Chinese government officials. Fourteen were people who had expert knowledge of the Chinese foreign- trade environment. Eight interviews took place in the United States. The rest took place in China. Most of the interviews were documented, and notes taken were read back to respondents. Some of the information was derived from numerous casual conversations with knowledgeable people throughout my research.

While in Wuhan, I obtained a copy of the Wuhan Local Laws governing Sino-foreign joint ventures that had been passed in 1988. I was able to relate information gathered in interviews already conducted to the rules and regulations outlined in this document and was able to use these laws to refine my questions for further interviews. Legally, power over almost all aspects of joint venture operations resides in the hands of local government authorities. However, through interviews, I discovered that most of these laws were negotiable. Joint venture representatives bargained among themselves and with local authorities over implementation. I concentrated on three issue areas: labor, taxes, and foreign exchange. Because my interviews were conducted with informants from joint ventures that were in operation, there was usually no interest in discussing dispute settlement or dissolution. Furthermore, informants seemed most interested in discussing the issues of labor, taxes, and foreign exchange. Laws that addressed these issues were identified, and I asked parties to explain whether they negotiated these terms and to describe the outcomes. Detailed responses often included explanations of strategies employed by various parties to influence bargaining for joint venture control.

This study did not aspire to be nor is it representative of all joint ventures in China. It is, however, representative of manufacturing joint ventures in Wuhan. Dozens of joint ventures have been established in Wuhan since China opened its doors in 1979.[32] My sources, however, universally agreed with the statement of one manager that "there are really only four major joint ventures in Wuhan."[33] Among the four are a brewery, a feed company, and a fiber-optic and cable company. The fourth is a joint venture located "about 150 kilometers outside Wuhan in the county seat."[34] I conducted interviews with personnel from all of these enterprises. I spoke with Chinese and foreign representatives from one enterprise on five different occasions, once with Chinese representatives from a second, twice with the foreign manager of a third, and once with a foreign representative of the fourth. The data gathered in these interviews are supplemented by interviews with three local government representatives and numerous casual conversations conducted with other individuals in Wuhan.

WUHAN AND FOREIGN INVESTMENT

Wuhan is an industrial city consisting of three parts: Hankou, Hanyang, and Wuchang. It is the capital of Hubei Province located approximately 1,200 kilometers south of Beijing, north of Guangzhou, and east of Shanghai. With a population of nearly seven million people, Wuhan offers an abundant labor force for both domestic and foreign-invested enterprises. Wuhan is a major center for industry and commerce throughout China, having been involved in international trade since 1858, "when it was designated a foreign trading port by Peking along with four other cities."[35] As one observer noted, however, the city "grew lazy under four decades of central planning and has lagged in recent years."[36]

Toward the end of the 1980s, Wuhan was granted special status by central authorities who believed that a prosperous Wuhan would increase the fortunes of its neighboring provinces and cities, thereby reducing "the growing disparity between the less dynamic inland provinces and the thriving coastal areas."[37] In 1988, Wuhan promulgated a comprehensive legal framework to encourage and protect foreign investment. Increased foreign interest in Wuhan has been largely a result of these new foreign- investment laws, which established three special zones and contributed to the development of the city's transportation and communication facilities. The three special zones are East Lake High-Technology Development Zone, Wuhan Economic Development Zone, and Yangluo Economic and Technology Zone.[38] Each of these zones has been granted special status to negotiate with foreign investors and to extend favorable tax and other incentives to encourage foreign investment.[39]

A major obstacle to economic and political development in developing nations involves inefficient transportation facilities. In the commercial sector, this leads to numerous supply problems, including shortages of raw materials and delays in delivery that can adversely affect product quality. Wuhan is strategically located in central China on the Yangtze River. Its "road, rail, and river networks connect it to more than a dozen provinces and 195 cities."[40] Since opening up, it is reported that Wuhan's municipal government "has renovated and extended over 30 roads and has established the Hankou railway station and the Qingshan foreign trade port"[41] and has also built new airports and bridges.[42] A substantial amount of Wuhan's infrastructure rehabilitation and construction is sponsored by the *Wharf Project,* which includes a new international airport, two passenger terminals (harbor and railway), three wharves, four railway stockyards, five high-grade highways, and a 600-line computerized telephone exchange."[43] No doubt, these infrastructure improvements will contribute to a much healthier commercial environment which will encourage confidence in Wuhan's foreign-investment community.

Wuhan has used foreign investment to improve its outdated and inefficient communications facilities. In 1992, it has been reported, the city "invested more than 35 million *yuan* in the construction of telecommunication projects," and "the number of the city's long-distance telephone lines increased from 105 to 300" while 9,000 "data-controlled telephone exchanges" were installed in the city's downtown districts.[44] Wuhan also has developed "160,000-line program-controlled telephone exchanges and established 145 post offices, through which contacts with more than 210 countries and regions can be made."[45]

One major foreign-invested project that has contributed to the development of Wuhan's communication facilities is the Changfei Optic-Fiber Cable Project, a Sino-Dutch joint venture between Holland's Philips Corporation and the Wuhan Optical Communications Technology Company and the Wuhan City Trust and Investment Company.[46] The company went into production in 1992 "and produced 60,000 kilometers of optical fibers, 5,006 kilometers of optical cables, and 65,000 kilometers of fiber wicks in the same year, exceeding the planned production quotas by 25 percent, 11 percent, and 80 percent, respectively," with sales that stood at 110 million *yuan* that year.[47] Japan's NEC corporation has also established a joint venture in Wuhan that began production of fiber-optic products in April 1992. These projects and Wuhan's commitment to becoming a major player in international trade are the impetus for further developing and perfecting the city's communication facilities.

Another attraction that Wuhan offers foreign investors is its history as a large industrial base with thousands of enterprises already established and in operation. Wuhan has been engaged in a campaign to decentralize decision-making authority in these enterprises and to encourage foreign investment in them to improve their productivity. "The government of Wuhan . . . has given local enterprises more freedom in their management so as to simplify its administrative structure and eliminate red tape."[48] As a result of this decentralization and administrative streamlining, which has given substantial freedom to enterprise managers and local economic bureaucrats to pursue foreign investments, there was a total contractual investment in the first ten months of 1992 that was double the total for the previous eight years.[49] In 1992, a total of 126 old enterprises were modernized with foreign investment, including the relatively well-known example of the No. 2 Dyeing and Printing Mill, which in 1991 was losing money until a joint venture was formed with the Hong Kong-based Hongtex Development Company.[50] After the renamed joint venture, Wuhan Cityford Printing and Dyeing, was granted freedom to operate as it saw fit, the enterprise soon became a highly profitable business.[51]

Wuhan's infrastructure development has proved to be a substantial incentive for foreign investment. Indeed, for infrastructure construction in one 4.4-square-kilometer area, "the builders have completed 12 kilometers of water pipes, an electric system, 2,000 program-controlled exchanges, over 10 kilometers of drainage pipeline and 12 kilometers of roads," with plans to build apartments, department stores, and more factory buildings.[52] This area has been dubbed Wuhan's "city of cars" in honor of a Sino-French joint venture with the Citroen Company that plans an annual production output of 300,000 automobiles.

As Wuhan speeds development of its infrastructure to contend with increased demand from foreign investors to enter its commercial sector,[53] it also has begun to market itself as a tourist town full of historical and cultural attractions[54] and has established an international futures and exchange market, "jointly founded by two companies from China and Canada . . . equipped with advanced telecommunication facilities including an information terminal system" that can "acquire directly through price and analysis systems information on futures markets in Hong Kong, Chicago, New York, and Tokyo."[55] Despite these impressive developments, the city does suffer drawbacks. It is an inland city where cultural differences between Chinese and Western societies remain pronounced. This book examines how these cultural nuances affect relations between domestic and foreign joint venture managers, negotiators, and local government bureaucrats.

Furthermore, the city continues to suffer from a cumbersome foreign-trade bureaucracy that may not easily be bypassed with even highly influential personal contacts. Also, its transportation facilities, while improving, remain inefficient, with "only a small amount of rail space available for freight," limited shipping options, and overcrowded flights to other Chinese cities and Hong Kong.[56]

As foreign interest and investment in Wuhan grow, however, it will be interesting to note how these outside forces contribute to the city's economic development and how the government responds to the problems inherent in its drive to enter the twenty-first century as a major player in the arena of international trade and commerce.

OTHER ISSUES

A more thorough treatment of local joint venture bargaining would have included greater attention to the role of local authorities. In Wuhan, I was not, for instance, able to arrange interviews with local labor bureau representatives.

The study does not sufficiently address the role of the Chinese Communist Party (CCP) in the bargaining process. In interviews, I normally phrased questions about bureaucratic involvement without reference to the party. Consequently, there was no differentiation between the roles of the party and the government in the bargaining process.[57]

A serious limitation of this and many other analyses is the virtual exclusion of important internal (*neibu*) joint venture policy documents. Ambiguities and issues not addressed in published laws may be addressed in internal materials. In reality, an internal law that neither I nor my interviewee knew about (or that a respondent chose not to discuss) may have determined the outcome of the negotiations. One manager explained that laws often changed and opined that local authorities frequently do not tell foreign parties about laws that have been passed.[58] However, even if internal laws were guiding the Chinese side in one or two of the instances of bargaining over implementation that I examine in this book, it does not diminish the fact that bargaining between foreign and Chinese parties over joint venture laws took place; it simply means that the Chinese side may have been constrained in the bargaining process by guidelines issued by the central authorities in Beijing.

PRINCIPAL FINDINGS

Large-scale bargaining between the Chinese government and foreign investors had numerous repercussions throughout the 1980s. Reacting largely to foreign pressure, the Chinese streamlined the foreign-trade bureaucracy to make it more accessible to investors and more efficient in meeting foreign needs, established a legal framework to encourage, govern and protect foreign investment, liberalized laws on three occasions (1979, 1983, 1986), and offered tax and other incentives and generally more liberal economic policies in SEZs, coastal regions, and other specially designated areas.

FDI bargaining theory and literature on Chinese policy implementation and culture suggest that policy outcomes will be determined at local levels through bargaining between foreign investors and local government authorities. FDI bargaining theory suggests that foreigners and host-country representatives will bargain with each other to achieve their respective, perhaps conflicting, objectives and that this bargaining is not limited to the monolithic host country and MNC but can involve numerous interested parties at the local level. We know that policy in China is bent and distorted at each level of the political system and that this tendency has increased substantially, as economic decision making has been decentralized from central authorities to localities. Therefore, it is hypothesized that joint venture policy also will be changed according to the needs of various actors at each level of implementation.[59] This expectation is heightened by cultural literature that stresses bargaining as a cultural attribute of Chinese society,[60] the general disdain among the Chinese for written law throughout their history and the resulting suspicion among many Chinese of the rule of law versus the rule of man.[61] In researching this book, I found that, in fact, implementation of joint venture laws and policies often is largely dependent on bargaining between joint venture representatives and local authorities. This bargaining, however, does not end after terms of the investment have been negotiated and agreed upon in the joint venture contract. Rather, bargaining for control over joint venture operations continues throughout the term of the enterprise. The principal parties involved in this process are Chinese managers, foreign managers, and local Chinese authorities. The bargaining is not, as often seems to be assumed, primarily between the "foreign side" and the "Chinese side." Numerous factors contribute to scenarios that involve foreign management and local authorities teaming up against Chinese management, foreign management and Chinese management bargaining on behalf of the joint venture with local authorities, and Chinese management and foreign management bargaining with each other over joint venture-related matters. Nor is bargaining always explicit. Often, foreign managers will recognize systemic and/or cultural factors in their environment that cannot be overtly challenged but must be overcome; implicit bargaining results when an innovation is developed and implemented without consultation or approval, but also without explicit disapproval from interested parties, including Chinese counterparts in management and local government. This study found examples of such implicit bargaining at each stage investigated.

Bargaining latitude of local authorities seems to increase with distance from the center. One American executive, for instance, who negotiated a joint venture in Guangdong explained that his company would not establish a joint venture in Beijing or anywhere in China if central bureaucracies were involved. In this case, there were two stages of negotiations for establishment of his corporation's joint venture. In the first stage, central authorities from Beijing were involved and made negotiations impossible; through personal relationships with Guangdong provincial authorities during a second stage, the company was able to eliminate Beijing from the negotiations, and agreement was reached "overnight."[62] Proximity to Beijing is only one of many factors that I identify in this book that may contribute to bargaining outcomes. Other factors include the personality of the foreign management, the geographic area of the joint venture's location, the length of time a joint venture has been in existence, the level of government of the Chinese partner, the joint venture type (e.g., export-oriented and/or technologically advanced), the nationality of the foreign partner, and the attitude of central authorities toward the outside world. This study does not contend that these factors are generalizable to all areas of local bargaining in China but, nevertheless, calls for more systematic investigations to determine their impact.

To overcome bureaucratic and legal obstacles of the Chinese political system, respondents explained that joint venture parties have developed numerous bargaining strategies. In both Tianjin and Wuhan, for instance, there are joint venture groups that meet to discuss problems they are having with local authorities, usually involving some sort of bureaucratic interference with joint venture operations. What has evolved is a form of collective bargaining between these organizations and local governments to draft and pass laws, change implementation procedures, and force local authorities to rescind or retreat from implementing laws.

Finally, this study finds that joint ventures can be agents of change in the personalities of the joint venture participants. This change is not limited to the Chinese but includes foreigners adapting behavior to accommodate the unique qualities of their new environments. Among the Chinese, from such superficial and ill-defined indicators as general appearance and style to more substantive measures such as their acceptance of culturally challenging processes and procedures in such sensitive areas as labor relations, it is evident that even in inland areas like Wuhan, change is occurring. Foreign managers also take into consideration cultural nuances of their Chinese colleagues, including the high value placed on consensus, status equality, and the Confucian value of harmony.

CHAPTER DESCRIPTION

Chapter Two, entitled "Joint Ventures in the Context of China's Modernization Program," discusses background information to China's joint venture policies as they relate to its larger modernization program begun in 1979. This section identifies the goals of China's modernization program and how the Chinese government hoped to use Sino-foreign joint ventures to achieve its aspirations. There are three types of Sino-foreign joint ventures (contractual, equity, and exploration) that are supposed to aid China in achieving its major objectives (obtaining foreign technology, capital, and management know-how) and simultaneously serve foreign joint venture investor interests as well. I will discuss legal frameworks that govern foreign investment and China's evolving joint venture laws in relation to the landmark years of Chinese foreign trade legislation, 1979, 1983, 1986, and post-1989, as well as problems that adversely affected FDI, including an insufficient legal structure, bureaucracy, and problems associated with decentralization, Chinese language, and culture. Factors that affected bargaining over joint venture laws between the foreign investment community and the Chinese government at the national level, as well as between local policy implementers and joint venture representatives, are identified and reappear thematically throughout the text.

Chapter Three, "Policy and Law Adjustments,"explains the evolution of national joint venture laws and policies that resulted from a process of bargaining between factions (conservatives and reformers) in the Chinese leadership and between the Chinese central government and foreign interests in the international political arena. The section focuses on issues of enterprise autonomy and finance. Issues of autonomy include resource procurement, joint venture management structure and division of power, and control of joint venture labor relations. Financial issues that this chapter addresses include valuation of in-kind contributions and profits and pricing, taxes, and foreign exchange. The discussion of national-level policy and law adjustments prepares the reader for Chapter Four, which focuses on local-level bargaining between local Chinese policy implementers and joint venture representatives over implementation of laws and policies designed to regulate these enterprises.

In Chapter Four, "The Objects of Bargaining," I identify and discuss the preconditions of bargaining in terms of foreign and host-nation interests, followed by a discussion of the objects of bargaining and strategies that foreigners employ to influence outcomes. Foreign investors want to maximize profits by acquiring as much autonomy from the state as possible and affecting changes in Chinese joint venture employee attitudes toward management authority, worker responsibility, and product quality. Local policy implementors want to maximize speedy transfer of capital, technology, and management know-how, maintain a high degree of control over joint venture operations, and prevent Chinese emulation of perceived harmful foreign cultural traits. The chapter focuses on the issues of labor, taxes, and foreign exchange.

Numerous scholars have identified reasons for variation in policy implementation. Susan Shirk, for instance, has argued that implementation depends on ministerial, bureaucratic, and geographic factors.[63] Personalism, proximity to Beijing, the power of the province, and the inherent role of bargaining in Chinese society have also been cited. This study builds on these works and identifies joint venture-specific factors that affect local joint venture bargaining processes. In Chapter Five, "The Primacy of *Guanxi* (Personal Relationships) and Other Sources of Variation," I explain the importance of personal relationships in affecting bargaining outcomes. The chapter is divided into three sections. In the first section, I identify the amount of time a joint venture has been in existence, joint venture type (export-oriented versus import-oriented), and the "mood" of the central authorities as factors that may affect positively or negatively local bargaining processes between local Chinese policy implementers and joint venture representatives, *depending on the nature of the enterprise's personal relationships* with relevant Chinese officials, managers, suppliers, and other relevant parties. In the second section, partner characteristics (level of government of the Chinese partner, corporate personality, and nationality of the foreign partner) are discussed as sources of variation in local joint venture bargaining processes, and in section three, I discuss geographic factors that partially determine bargaining outcomes between joint ventures and policy implementers.

Chapter Six is the concluding chapter of this book. It contemplates the factors that affect local joint venture bargaining outcomes, compares them to factors that have been identified as affecting domestic policy implementation, and identifies the ways the foreign element has affected the context for implementation with its numerous resources. It also reviews joint venture-specific factors that seem to determine bargaining outcomes and subsequently identifies those areas that require further systematic investigation.

2

Joint Ventures in the Context of China's Modernization Program

INTRODUCTION

China opened its doors to foreign investment in the form of Sino-foreign joint ventures in 1979 because the government believed it could acquire four items that the country desperately needed: capital, high technology, advanced management know-how, and access to international markets. If foreigners had limited control over the transfer of these items and the profits earned from them, it was believed, they would be more inclined to invest in China's socialist economy. Offering only limited control of the ventures was also a way for the Chinese to address economic, political, and cultural concerns that they had over the introduction of foreign businesses into their only recently opened society.[1] Among its economic concerns, China feared a loss of control over the direction of its economic development and domestic market to highly competitive foreign entities, a loss of capital to the outside world, an influx of obsolete technologies from dishonest foreigners, and a refusal among outside investors to use domestically produced supplies.

Politically, China feared that foreign economic power, once allowed to enter its borders, ultimately would turn into political power threatening Chinese sovereignty. Culturally, China's leaders identified "bourgeois liberalization," "spiritual pollution," and "unhealthy tendencies" as threats against the Chinese culture.[2] The Chinese also drafted laws and policies to create an environment favorable to foreign investment and to protect themselves from potential foreign exploitation and harmful foreign influences. In order to take advantage of the huge amounts of capital and technologies possessed by multinational corporations (MNCs), China would protect its sovereignty by "adopting planned controls over the activities of these multinationals and struggling to establish a new economic order based on equality and mutual benefit."[3]

ATTRACTING FOREIGN CAPITAL

China's Open Door policy was initiated in 1979 with a view to achieving the "Four Modernizations" in industry, agriculture, science and technology and military development. Opening to the outside world, China hoped, would allow it to use foreign investment in a variety of ways to achieve these objectives. Recognition of the value of foreign investment was accompanied by a determination to implement strict controls to prohibit foreign interests from extracting more from China than they invested.

Multinational corporations were viewed as a potentially substantial source of foreign investment. In 1979, the government began passing laws and promulgating policies to facilitate foreign confidence in China as a worthwhile place to invest capital and other resources. However, optimism about the role of these MNCs was tempered by doubts about problems they might also cause, most notably the possibility that, as a Third World developing nation, China would become dependent on the outside world for its economic development. Strict controls instituted through definitive laws and policies were needed to prevent MNCs from manipulating China's economic development. Among the fears enunciated about potential MNC misconduct were that they would try to "evade taxes, pull out capital, and adjust the rate of profits of their subsidiaries, as well as avoid remittance rates and other risks, and manipulate prices in their international trade to the loss of the government."[4] In order to take advantage of the huge amounts of capital and technologies possessed by MNCs, China would have to protect its sovereignty by "adopting planned controls over the activities of these multinationals and struggling to establish a new international economic order based on equality and mutual benefit."[5]

Functions of Capital Accumulation

One of the main objectives of the Open Door policy was to attract capital from abroad and to accumulate it at home. The Chinese government hoped that increased capital would have several positive repercussions. It would help the country to provide employment opportunities to its citizens, and numerous social benefits would be derived from an increased number of commercial and service centers.[6] Increased capital investment was also expected to provide incentives for managers and workers to make full use of and improve their technical knowledge of production and management techniques. In Shanghai, for example, it was reported that "more than 1,100 former industrialists and businessmen pooled funds to set up the Aiguo (Patriotic) Construction Company, and 100 of them took on such jobs as general manager, deputy general manager, adviser or plant director of the company and its subordinate units."[7] Attracting capital investment would also facilitate the utilization of local resources and the development of "sideline occupations and handicrafts."[8] New markets would be created, and the national socialist economy would be supplemented by new enterprises responding to new market demands. Finally, competition would be encouraged and management improved, as managers of new enterprises would feel compelled to study the relations between production, supply, demand, and marketing and the techniques best suited to respond to these indicators.[9]

Principles and Policies to Accumulate Capital

The principles and policies that the government promulgated to guide foreign borrowing emphasized China's determination to remain self-reliant, a theme that has resonated from the beginning of the nineteenth century to the beginning of the Open Door, through the 1980s and into the 1990s.[10] All foreign assistance must be supplementary to capital invested by domestic sources and should be used only insofar as China can absorb and repay it. The theme of equality and mutual benefit has also been stressed by the government in all of China's foreign relations. This theme was apparent in initial joint venture legislation, most notably "The Law of the People's Republic of China on Joint Venture's Using Chinese and Foreign Investment," promulgated in 1979. Largely in response to foreign fears that the government would nationalize foreign assets, equality and mutual benefit were emphasized "with a view to legally safeguarding the interests of foreign investors."[11] Furthermore, the People's Insurance Company of China (PICC) was granted power to sign reinsurance schemes with foreign insurance companies and individual enterprises to further protect foreign investments. The Chinese recognized that the evolving legal framework to govern foreign direct investment had many inadequacies and pledged to continue to work on laws that would guarantee protection to foreign assets.[12]

A third tenet of policies designed to attract capital from abroad was the creation of favorable conditions for foreign investment. To this end, the government established Special Economic Zones (SEZs) in the coastal provinces of Guangdong and Fujian, where numerous special incentives like tax rate reductions and import and export duty fee waivers are offered to foreign-invested enterprises, especially those categorized as "export-oriented" and "technologically advanced." China also made a special commitment to invest heavily in improving its infrastructure, offering special incentives to export-oriented and technologically advanced enterprises throughout the country, as well as to enterprises engaged in the production of goods and services that China needs. China also has been engaged in an ongoing process of simplifying its foreign trade bureaucracy and has established organizations like the China International Trust and Investment Corporation (CITIC) to guide foreigners through the process of investment.[13]

Another major aspect of policies towards foreign investment has been emphasis on economic results, repayment guarantees and equitable profits.[14] To this end, China named two project categories. The first category included "large-scale projects, requiring protracted construction, with low earnings or no foreign exchange earnings, such as port construction, railways, communications, power stations, farming, forestry, water conservancy, and educational facilities." The second category included smaller projects, "requiring a shorter construction period, or projects of scale which require[d] protracted construction, yet yield[ed] good earnings or foreign exchange earnings" in fields such as oil prospecting and exploration, coal mines, machinery, and chemical plants, light industry, and tourist industry.[15] Repayment of loans and distribution of profits would be based on enterprise earnings in line with the policy of using only that amount of capital that China could repay.[16]

China has also consistently emphasized priority areas for investments. These priorities were grouped into five general categories, and the objectives have remained generally the same throughout the era of the Open Door. The first has been to prospect for and exploit energy resources, including petroleum, coal, and electricity. Secondly, and in line with its objective to improve the conditions for foreign investors, China has emphasized the need for investment to build a stronger infrastructure in the urban and industrial areas where most foreign investments would be concentrated, including the construction of railways, ports, and telecommunications facilities. Smaller projects that would bring quick economic results were a third priority area for investment. Fourth, China emphasized improving the technological efficiency of enterprises using outdated equipment. Finally, China would try to shelve projects deemed less important to it's comprehensive modernization effort.[17]

Problems of and Prescriptions for Attracting Capital

Despite the many mechanisms established to encourage new enterprises and attract foreign capital, numerous problems plague foreign investment in China. The Chinese themselves recognized that modernization would be hampered by "Left Mistakes" of the 1950s and 1960s that led China to take on too many projects that demanded more investment and materials than were available.[18] Lack of experience with foreign investors often meant inadequate feasibility studies for projects, poor overall management and organization, a lack of rules and regulations for delivery procedures, failure to implement the responsibility system in management and building schedules, cost overruns, and little attention to product quality.[19] Other problems included backward equipment and technology, poor technical personnel and management, and insufficient funds. Furthermore, China's well-publicized abundant supply of natural resources was mostly underground and only a potential advantage, and although its huge population represented a potentially strong labor force, training and mobilizing it to meet international standards would require many more resources than China possessed.[20]

Several areas required improvement, and foreign investment was perceived as a necessary vehicle to achieve these objectives. Implementation of the responsibility system in management was to be stressed consistently. Feasibility studies for proposed joint ventures and domestic enterprises were required, with special attention to be paid to preparatory work, including "site selection, designing equipment purchase, land acquisition, and rehousing persons displaced by the acquisition."[21] The responsibility system was to be implemented in survey and design, construction scheduling, and loans and deliveries: "Those who delay delivery or overrun their budget will be charged double interest or their loans will be stopped."[22] Policies toward foreign investment stressed expansion of exports, especially mineral products, nonferrous and rare metals, machines and electrical appliances, textiles, light industrial products, "art and handicraft products," and "local specialties, including tea, medicinal herbs, animal products, famous wild vegetables, and fruit."[23] Policies emphasized importing the most advanced science and technological know-how in the form of "equipment, accessories, high-quality materials, new principles, data, and formulas," and "new technical processes and scientific procedures of operation, and advanced management methods."[24] Streamlining the foreign trade bureaucracy to make foreign investment procedures less confusing and emphasizing product quality were also meant to increase foreign willingness to invest capital in China.[25]

Attracting Foreign Capital: Conclusion

A major motivation of China's Open Door policy has been to attract foreign capital. An increase in capital investments was expected to serve several functions, including encouraging implementation of the responsibility system among enterprise managers, contributing to the well-being of host industries that would service and provide goods to joint ventures, creating new markets, and generally improving the quality of enterprise management and production through increased competition.

The government promulgated policies and drafted laws to create a favorable environment for foreign investment, as well as to institute strict controls to regulate the capital influx. Through the policies, China sought to ensure equality and mutual benefit, stressing equal protection of Chinese sovereignty and foreign interests, to remain self-reliant by borrowing from abroad only to supplement domestic capital and only that which could be repaid quickly, and to continue to draft laws that would favor foreign investors who wanted to establish enterprises that would contribute to China's designated priority areas for foreign investment. Legislation was designed to attract foreign investment while vesting considerable decision-making authority in the Chinese joint venture representatives and local officials.

Problems that have plagued capital-investment projects include a lack of experience, inadequate feasibility studies, poor management, poor product delivery and distribution, and a lack of attention to market values and product quality. Although China made efforts to create a favorable investment environment, these and other problems often hampered foreign investment.

ATTRACTING HIGH TECHNOLOGY

In addition to attracting capital, another purpose of China's Open Door policy has been to attract high technology from abroad. In the early 1980s, Premier Zhao Ziyang enunciated the Chinese government's belief that modernization depended largely on China's ability to develop rapidly high technology: " 'In order to realize modernization, reinvigorate the economy, and quadruple the total industrial and agricultural output value, we must rely on the progress of science and technology.' "[26] Technological development was expected to play several roles in China's economic development program. The quality of labor and management was expected to improve as personnel responded to the pressure of becoming familiar with new technologies and their applications; levels of production and labor productivity were expected to increase as high-technology equipment replaced obsolete, technologically backward equipment; product quality was expected to improve; and, consequently, competitiveness on the international market would increase. The effort to advance technologically was led by the "Three Policies of Technological Enhancement":

1. First, China must develop its technical and professional resources; because higher education in China is scarce, personnel often do not meet the requirements of modernization, hence; an effort to train people in operating technologically advanced equipment was required;
2. various departments must decide individually what technologies to import, because it is at these levels that officials know best what their localities and, therefore, China needs;
3. an effort to transform existing enterprises into technically advanced producers, rather than establishing new ones against which the old will not be capable of competing, is also an objective of the initial policies toward technological import and development.[27]

Before promulgation of the "Four Modernizations" in 1978, China imported complete sets of equipment and new factories.[28] This led to a "polarization" in industrial production, with a small number of enterprises possessing high-technology modes of production and a greater number of enterprises with little or no high-tech characteristics.[29] Since the 1979 Joint Venture Law and subsequent legislation, importing technology has been "integrated with the work of attracting foreign direct investment," based on "licensed trade," and there has been a drop in import of complete sets of equipment.[30] The purpose of the legislation was to encourage China's technological development. "Generally speaking," one author noted, "a relatively successful project can narrow a 20-30 year gap in output level in about three years."[31] Furthermore, education of domestic managers, workers and researchers would also be encouraged with the introduction of "new ideas . . . on product design and operational and managerial skills."[32] Technological imports were expected to be a catalyst for the domestic development of new technologies and distribution of new knowledge in a horizontal (lateral) direction throughout Chinese industry.[33] However, just as policies to attract foreign capital were designed to protect China from foreigners extracting more capital from the country than they invested, laws and policies toward the import of foreign technology embodied recognition of past dealings with unscrupulous outside investors and encouraged caution in future foreign economic relations. The most significant warning to the

Chinese was to beware of overpriced technology, especially in joint ventures where foreigners valued it as an in-kind contribution; as a result, foreigners generally were not able to value technology at more than 20 percent of their total capital contribution to a project.[34] The Chinese also routinely insisted on "broad-use" rights to the technology, which often meant that foreigners were contractually required to provide education and training to Chinese labor and management.[35] Also, the Chinese placed great emphasis on documentation proving that the technology was state-of-the-art and generally insisted on ten-year licensing agreements for technology, after which all rights to the technology would revert to their side. Finally, strict performance requirements, government approval and supervision procedures involving tedious feasibility study requirements, and recognition of Chinese rights to compensation if a technology did not live up to Chinese expectations were also embodied in legislation controlling technology imports.[36]

Despite these controls, China has faced substantial obstacles in technological development.[37] Decision-making decentralization that was supposed to empower localities to make judicious decisions about importing only technology that they needed often meant the import of redundant technologies. One Chinese observer called the situation "planless and chaotic."[38] For instance, hundreds of assembly lines for the production of such items as televisions, refrigerators, and washing machines were imported, defying the policy of trying to import parts rather than whole equipment lines, and consuming huge amounts of foreign exchange.[39] Although the intention of decentralization was to promote competition, it was also expected, ironically, to lead to diffusion of technology imports in a lateral direction. What has often resulted, however, is departmentalism and compartmentalism; hence, a flow of information along vertical rather than horizontal lines.[40]

Planning has also been an impediment to technological diffusion throughout Chinese society. Departments in charge of approving projects have consistently been criticized for not differentiating between enterprises requiring the import of the same and/or similar technologies. In one case, two different departments imported basically the same technology for producing a fireproof material used in smelting furnaces. For this reason, some people said that was a case of duplicate imports. However, the two projects were approved by the same commission one after another at short intervals and were undertaken by two different bureaus of the same commissions.[41] In fact, competition between bureaucratic agencies often has been a catalyst for the approval of redundant projects. Indeed, although Western observers often have cited tedious feasibility-study requirements as an obstacle to reaching agreements on technology transfers, Chinese observers have criticized and consistently called for improvement of these procedures. Local authorities, it is argued, become mere formalities in approval procedures governed by bureaucrats who have vested interests in importing wares for their constituencies and clients. One author, in fact, wrote that "senior personnel of several American companies indicated that if China does not take some measures to protect the fruit of technology imports, they will no longer be interested in transferring technology."[42]

This sentiment has been echoed in many Western critiques of Chinese legislation that is supposed to be designed to protect the interests of both Chinese and foreign joint venture partners. In February 1991, the International Intellectual Property Alliance (IIPA) urged the Office of the U.S. Trade Representative to name the People's Republic of China, Thailand, and Indonesia as "priority countries for failing to provide either adequate protection to U.S. copyrighted works or market access to U.S. copyright industry firms."[43] Indeed, in April of 1991, the U.S. Congress named China as a "'priority country' for violation of intellectual property rights under Section 301 of the 1988 U.S. Trade Act."[44] China traditionally has viewed intellectual property rights (*zhishi chanquan*) as conflicting with socialist values that regard advances in science and technology as the property of the entire society and, therefore, not subject to such capitalist manifestations as patent and trademark laws.[45]

As an incentive to foreign investors, however, over the 1980s and into the 1990s, Chinese reformists succeeded in drafting and promulgating new patent and trademark legislation.[46] In March 1984, the Chinese government adopted The Patent Law of the People's Republic of China, hailed by foreign observers as a significant step in the effort to meet their expectations for protection of technological imports.[47] Further legislation included the 1985 "Regulations for the Administration of Technology Import Contracts," the 1987 "Implementing Rules of the Ministry of Foreign Economic Relations and Trade for Examination and Confirmation of Export-Oriented Enterprises and Technically-Advanced Enterprises," and the 1988 "Detailed Rules for the Implementation of the Regulations on the Administration of Technology Import Contracts," which were not designed specifically for joint ventures but often applied to them.[48] In June 1991, a new copyright law went into effect that handled "disputes arising from copyright infringements."[49] By the end of 1990, the State Patent Bureau of China had granted 63,000 patents on inventions, and 270,000 trademarks with valid registration were in existence.[50] Furthermore, China "acceded to the Berne Convention for the Protection of Literary and Artistic Works on July 31, 1992, and the Universal Copyright Convention on October 30, 1992," with the "Regulations for the

Implementation of International Copyright Treaties" going into effect on September 30, 1992, reportedly "bringing China's copyright and software rules largely in line with international practice."[51]

Among other signs of good faith shown by the Chinese government with regard to its commitment to establishing a solid foundation for the protection of intellectual property has been its participation in several international property rights treaties and organizations, including the United Nations World Intellectual Property Rights Organization, the Paris Convention on Protection of Industrial Property Rights, the International Permits and Traders Association, the Madrid Agreement on International Registration of Trademarks, and the Treaty on Intellectual Property Rights for Integrated Circuits.[52]

Although observers note that "failure to follow the law and lack of structures in enforcing the law are new problems" in this area, "China's first and only law court specializing in intellectual property disputes is highlighting a nationwide campaign to shape an extensive legal framework in the fight against patent and trademark violations."[53] The ten-person Beijing Collegiate Bench on Disputes over Intellectual Property, established in January 1991 under the Beijing People's Intermediate Court, heard that year over 55 domestic cases and two foreign cases. One of the cases involving a Chinese and a foreign entity was that of the Beijing Haidan Tuozhan Company, which "sued the American Far Era Trading Limited over transfer of technologies and a Chinese professor [who is] seeking damages from the American DEC company for violation of his patent over a computer technology."[54]

Attracting Technology: Continuing Problems, Goals, and Policy Prescriptions

According to China's 1986 *Science and Technology White Paper*, China experienced substantial improvement in ten areas of technological development:

1. large-scale integrated circuit
2. computers
3. computer software
4. telecommunications
5. biological technology
6. new materials
7. space technology
8. remote sensing technology

9. laser technology
10. isotope and radioactive technology.[55]

In attempting to create a more favorable environment for foreign investors, China has passed a series of landmark laws for the protection of intellectual property rights. Also, as a sign of good faith, China began establishing judicial structures to implement high-tech rules and regulations. Special Economic Zones, Economic Development Areas, and High-Technology Development Zones have also been established throughout the country. These zones offer preferential tax and customs duty rates for high-technology enterprises, thus further encouraging potential high-tech investors from abroad.

Bureaucratic pitfalls, poor quality standards, awkward pricing, and inexperienced personnel have hampered China's plans for technological development and the import of high technology. Decentralization of decision-making authority has meant competition between administrative units and geographic regions for the same types of technology, sloppy planning, and projects that have not contributed to China's overall modernization drive. Inexperienced personnel have often meant that negotiators are overcautious in their demands on foreigners to provide technological documentation, state-of-the-art technology, and performance guarantees. Inexperience has also hampered Chinese application of imported high-tech processes and procedures. An irrational pricing system has compounded Chinese inexperience in the valuation of in-kind contributions; they routinely overvalue their contributions and engage in endless bickering over the worth of foreign contributions in the area of science and technology. A general lack of experience with free-market economic principles and marketing procedures often has meant that Chinese advances in science and technology have not translated into the development of products that could be sold at home or on the international market. The problem has been exacerbated by China's long-standing problems with poor quality-control processes.

To correct these problems, several policy goals have been included in the eighth Five-Year Plan. China seeks to industrialize and commercialize its new high technologies, integrate technological developments under the guidance of the plan with market demands, and internationalize its high-tech industries.[56] Improving the education of managers and other personnel involved in high-tech applications is a major step in achieving these objectives. Also, implementation of the responsibility system among researchers and managers dealing with high-tech development is an objective. An example of carrying out this policy can be seen in the recently passed

"Measures for the Implementation of the Responsibility System for Directors of Research Institutes Owned by the Whole People in Xinjiang Uygur Autonomous Region," which requires research institute heads to design research projects in such a way that they will contribute products to be sold on domestic and international markets.[57]

Further strengthening of science and technology legislation is also an objective. Macroeconomic restructuring and planning are also recognized as keys to implementing laws and guiding principles. However, overcoming the obstacles associated with decentralization of decision making will continue to hamper these efforts, and it is unlikely that this situation will change in the near future, as participants in the modernization process, including foreign investors, local and national policy-makers and implementers, and Chinese managers and employees, bargain over implementation of laws and regulations to meet their own individual needs and desires.

Attracting High Technology: Conclusion

Attracting high technology has also been an objective of the Open Door policy. However, poor organization and management have often meant the import of redundant technologies as decentralization has encouraged bureaucracies to compete for the same types of projects. A lack of appreciation for the value of technology and intellectual-property rights has also been a hindrance to foreigners interested in transferring technology to China. To correct these and other problems, the government has promulgated numerous policies, joined several international property-rights organizations, and drafted trademark and patent laws to encourage foreigners to invest in technology transfers to China. Although problems remain, foreign pressures have moved the Chinese government in the right direction in this area.

ATTRACTING MANAGEMENT KNOW-HOW

One of the main objectives of China's modernization program has been enterprise-management reform. Reforms in this area have encouraged the establishment of private enterprises and improvement in state-enterprise operation "to meet the demands for goods and services that the state-owned economy had failed to provide."[58] In 1980, the State Council issued guidelines for enterprise transformation: (1) goods produced should meet market demands; (2) profits should be used, in part, to expand and improve enterprise facilities; and (3) enterprises should recruit their own workers and take responsibility for discipline and dismissal.[59] In general, decision-making authority was to be decentralized from government and party administrative organs to individual enterprises, where managers would take responsibility for day-to-day operations and ultimate enterprise success or failure.

In order to improve management, several objectives were enunciated. In contrast to the 1960s and 1970s, when enterprises were managed by "revolutionary rabble-rousers," managers, it was stressed during the Four Modernizations policy, should be better-qualified, possessing skills acquired through technical and university training. One author in 1983 noted that reforms in this area had already meant that the average age of enterprise managers had declined to 53 and at least one-third had higher education.[60]

Introduction of the responsibility system was another major aim of reforms in this area. Under this system, the manager is responsible for the direction and management of production. Technical aspects of the enterprise are supervised by a technical engineer, while all financial aspects are managed by a chief accountant. Labor specialization was also stressed, with defined responsibilities assigned to different levels and jobs. In contrast with the values of traditional enterprises in socialist China, where "collective responsibility (and punishment) was stressed along with unquestioning obedience to higher authorities," reforms encouraged individual initiative and responsibility.[61] In order to compete successfully in a free market and especially on the international market, poor product quality and inadequate accounting had to be rectified; hence, improved attention to quality and accounting practices also has been stressed throughout China's era of reform.

A major task for reformers was the implementation of policies designed to separate the responsibilities of the government and party from enterprise management, which met with numerous problems. Finally, workers congresses were to be established, so workers could "exercise their democratic rights as masters of their own affairs."[62]

Throughout the 1980s and into the 1990s, substantial obstacles have hampered enterprise-management reform. Leaders who favored reform of the economic system constantly had to contend with conservative leadership factions who opposed radical economic reform. These conflicts often sent mixed signals to the administrative hierarchy charged with implementation of reforms. They often exacerbated the problem of convincing party bureaucrats to relinquish power to individual enterprise managers who were expected to take responsibility for success and failure of enterprises without offending their party superiors: "One factory director told how his company superiors had pushed his factory into cooperation with another factory, despite the fact that it had already entered into cooperation with yet another one. The director could do nothing but hand in his own resignation."[63]

Interference from local bureaucrats is also common in the area of employee relations. Although managers are supposed to enjoy decision-making authority over worker recruitment, discipline, and dismissal, local authorities have been loathe to give up these powers. Consequently, managers have reported endless approval procedures to make these decisions and constant bureaucratic interference after controversial decisions have been made. The political culture of labor further hampered manager decision making in this area. Having traditionally been guaranteed employment by the state without threat of firing or dismissal, fired workers often relied on party bureaucrats to force reinstatement and even threatened managers and their families with retaliation, including physical violence.[64]

Problems in the education of managers and workers also have been evident, and, as one writer observed, they often had to do with more than just finding the right teachers and facilities: "Standing in the way of enterprise-management decentralization and its concomitants . . . is the Chinese bureaucratic and educational tradition. Recent teaching experiences in China . . . suggest that there is a long way to go to move the education system so that it encourages individual thought and action."[65] Although Chinese scholars stress the importance of quantitative methods in teaching economics, marketing, and accounting, a "severe underrepresentation of nonquantitative methods, particularly in the engineering-based management programs in China," has also been noted.[66] Finally, poor product quality control continues to impede enterprise improvement, and sloppy accounting procedures have remained prevalent.

The Chinese government expected Sino-foreign joint ventures to supplement domestic efforts to improve enterprise management. Joint ventures represented foreign capital and technology, as well as a training ground for managers and labor in the application of technology, marketing techniques, personnel administration, financial management and managing production, and other operational issues. These enterprises were granted considerable decision-making freedom but, just like domestic enterprises, found themselves in a political and economic context fraught with substantial obstacles. Overcoming cultural obstacles amplified the difficulty foreigners would face in labor relations, especially teaching Western management techniques that embodied values contrary to traditional Chinese management approaches. Indeed, foreign managers found that they not only had to engage in bargaining with local policy implementers to overcome economic and political obstacles, but also had to bridge substantial cultural gaps between diverse and seemingly highly incompatible management strategies derived from conflicting cultural values.[67]

Just as legislation to attract capital was also designed to protect China from becoming dependent on the outside world and legislation to attract technology also made heavy demands on foreigners for state-of-the-art technology and grueling performance requirements, legislation to grant substantial power over employee relations to individual joint ventures also sought to protect Chinese labor from foreign exploitation and inculcation of perceived harmful foreign cultural traits. Among the major pieces of this body of legislation have been the 1980 "Regulations on Labor Management in Joint Ventures Using Chinese and Foreign Investment," the 1981 "Provisional Regulations on Wages in the Enterprises in the Special Economic Zones in Guangdong Province," the 1984 "Provisions for the Implementation of the Regulations on Labor Management in Joint Ventures Using Chinese and Foreign Investment," and the 1987 "Interim Provisions Concerning Ideological and Political Work for Chinese Staff and Workers in Chinese-Foreign Equity and Cooperative Joint Ventures."[68]

This legislation sought to check labor management by delegating substantial power to various Chinese units within the joint venture, including Chinese management, the local labor bureau, joint venture labor unions, and party cells. Hiring and firing routinely requires the unanimous consent of Chinese management.[69] Labor regulations also require a labor plan and system of labor employment contracts that address issues such as "employment terms, dismissal and resignation, wages, working hours," social welfare benefits, and labor insurance.[70] Local labor authorities have the power to approve or disapprove these documents and control the distribution of the wages and social welfare benefits.[71] Laws require the establishment of unions in all joint ventures; they are "the formal extension" of the CCP into the enterprise.[72] Unions must be consulted on all dismissals and may object to dismissals with the board of directors. Furthermore, joint ventures are required to make monthly payments of "2 percent of the total amount of wages paid to the staff and workers into a labor union fund" completely controlled by the union and provide office space for union use.[73] Party cells are charged with the responsibility of "ideological and political work," often sponsoring political study meetings, which were required after the June 4, 1989 incident at Tiananmen.[74]

In addition to abiding by labor laws that vest considerable authority in Chinese units, joint ventures are also required by law to abide "by common Chinese labor practices."[75] This phrase implies that foreigners must appreciate cultural nuances of Chinese labor management, especially in the areas of hiring, discipline, and firing. Among the values that must be recognized by the foreign partner in labor relations are consensus building, the Confucian value of harmony, an iron rice bowl mentality (this term originated after 1949, when the Chinese Communist Party guaranteed that all Chinese, irrespective of background would enjoy a variety of welfare benefits, wages, and salaries, despite work performance), economic egalitarianism, respect for the aged, and Chinese xenophobia.[76] Encouraging partners, bureaucrats, and personnel to cooperate in decision making is a hallmark of Chinese joint venture legislation. In dismissing a worker, for instance, the need to build consensus among numerous people and groups, including foreign and Chinese management, the labor union, and the local labor bureau, is crucial and usually required by law.[77]

The Chinese political culture places great emphasis on the Confucian value of harmony and despises chaos (*luan*). Any dismissal of an employee threatens enterprise harmony and causes both manager and subordinate employee to "lose face." For this reason, dismissal is avoided and even discipline must be handled carefully, "with criticisms disguised as suggestions for improvement, for example."[78]

In Chinese society, a citizen's work unit (*danwei*) is more than just his place of employment; it is the worker's lifetime source of income. It provides health and welfare benefits and a variety of other subsidies. It is also a primary source of personal connections (*guanxi*), a vital component of any Chinese citizen's prospects for social mobility. Dismissal has been almost unheard of in state enterprises since 1949, and workers have become accustomed to receiving employment benefits, despite work performance. This aspect of traditional Chinese labor also hampers the implementation of novel management techniques that stress worker performance.[79]

The Chinese sense of economic egalitarianism for workers and managers in state enterprises has translated into demands for wages for Chinese joint venture employees two to three times higher than wages earned by comparable state employees. The Chinese insistence on management salaries paid to foreign managers is also related to this sense of economic egalitarianism. This value also inhibits management from dominating labor and from exercising options of harsh disciplinary measures or expulsion.[80]

A common theme in discussing enterprise-management reforms in China has been the difficulty of persuading older managers and officials to accept the novel ideas and methods that have been introduced by these policies. Furthermore, a respect for the aged has inhibited replacing these personnel with younger, better-educated managers who are more open to new ideas.[81]

Finally, Chinese xenophobia intensifies any characteristic of Chinese political culture that hampers implementation of new procedures in Sino-foreign joint ventures. Employee dismissal, for instance, is already a harmony-threatening act that can cause those persons who are involved to "lose face," a particularly dramatic and humiliating experience. Should such an act be perpetrated by a foreign manager (especially one without an appreciation for the fact that, as initiator of the act, he would also "lose face" in the eyes of the other employees), it would take on an even starker, more disturbing complexion.[82]

Attracting Management Know-How: Conclusion

The government hoped that China's Open Door policy would attract foreign management training to improve China's overall enterprise management. In particular, it hoped to see advances in the implementation of China's responsibility system for managers, appreciation for product quality, and limitation of party and government involvement in enterprise operations. Legislation over joint venture labor relations was designed to give the units autonomy over labor decisions but granted substantial power to various Chinese groups, including Chinese management, the local labor bureau, the joint venture labor union, and party cells. Ultimate decision making concerning labor and management issues is often the result of bargaining between the Chinese and the foreigners in the joint venture.

CONCLUSION

Among objectives of China's Open Door policy were to attract capital, and to acquire high technology and advanced management know-how. The Chinese government believed that foreign investors would be more willing to invest these commodities in joint ventures where they would enjoy some control over earning profits. The government promulgated policies and drafted laws to create a favorable environment for foreign investment. However, this legislation also granted ultimate decision-making authority over joint venture operations to Chinese. The lack of foreign legal control over investments in China was compounded by a multitude of other problems often associated with socialist economies and the decentralization of decision-making power within these economies. Foreign investors ultimately asserted their presence by using their access to capital, technology, and management know-how to pressure the Chinese into relinquishing some joint venture control. The Chinese, in turn, were able to use their resources to gain cooperation from foreigners on a number of issues. Indeed, the conflicting objectives of both the Chinese and the foreigners were often resolved through bargaining.

3

Policy and Law Adjustments

INTRODUCTION

Bargaining over Chinese joint venture laws and policies occurs at the beginning of the policy formulation process and continues throughout the various stages of implementation. At the national level, this process is influenced by both domestic and international factors. In the domestic arena, joint venture laws and policies resulted from a process of bargaining between two leadership factions—namely, the reformers and the conservatives.[1] Internationally, the Chinese policy formulation process for joint ventures was influenced substantially by the foreign-investment community. Thus, the formulation of national-level laws and policies concerning Sino-foreign joint ventures evolved from a process of bargaining between reformers and conservatives in China's leadership and between the Chinese government and investors from the outside world.

The Chinese government has made policy and law adjustments in many areas of concern to the foreign joint venture investor. Foreign investors made demands on China to correct inadequacies in its foreign-trade system, and the government responded with new laws and policies that, in turn, made demands on foreigners to make various concessions and to abide by China's desire to maintain ultimate decision-making power over joint venture operations.

The topics discussed in this chapter (including issues of autonomy like joint-venture resource procurement, management, and labor, as well as financial issues like profits and pricing, valuation, and taxes) represent only some of the issues that have been objects of bargaining between the Chinese government and the foreign-investment community since the beginning of the Open Door in 1979. Other areas include lending from the Bank of China, feasibility-study costs, domestic sales versus exports, early termination, governing law, the threat of expropriation or confiscation, profit distribution, dispute resolution, and dissolution.[2] Mapping the evolution of the laws and policies that addressed these various issues of concern to the foreign joint venture investor will demonstrate the role of bargaining at the time of policy formulation and will set the stage for more detailed analysis of the role of bargaining between joint venture representatives and local Chinese policy implementers at the grassroots of the Chinese political system, where policy outcomes are ultimately created.

RECENT DEVELOPMENTS IN CHINESE POLICY-MAKING

Foreign investors in China must be aware of the pendulum-like nature of central policies in Beijing and of the constant behind-the-scenes activities that are undertaken by both reformers and conservatives to wrest power from each other. One major question for policy analysts and foreign investors concerned who won the ideological battles fought during the 14th Congress of the Chinese Communist Party in October 1992. On the surface, many agreed that Deng Xiaoping accomplished a great deal to further his liberal, reformist agenda. Among his achievements were to place key reformers into powerful positions in the Chinese policy-making apparatus. One important success involved Vice-Premier and economic chief Zhu Rongji, who became a full member of the Standing Committee of the Politburo, jumping the usual step of serving a term as a full member of the party's Central Committee.[3] Deng was also successful in removing eight older members of the Politburo and adding 14 younger members, "including party secretaries from coastal cities and provinces that have been in the vanguard of economic reform."[4] He was able to remove Yang Baibing as secretary general of the Central Military Commission whom he viewed along with his brother, Yang Shangkun, as potential political adversaries.[5] In addition to these important personnel changes, one report indicated, the 14th Party Congress "set out to enshrine Deng Xiaoping's market-oriented 'reform and opening' policy line for one hundred years."[6]

With these successes, China's reformers were able to end a three-year austerity program and begin to campaign for foreign funds to rehabilitate and improve the nation's infrastructure.[7] In addition to attracting foreign investment for infrastructure, Deng led efforts to establish stock exchanges in China's major cities, to grant more administrative autonomy to local governments to attract foreign investment, to lift price controls on "most agricultural commodities, including staple foodstuffs, such as grain and oil," and to initiate managerial reforms to make individual enterprises responsible for profits and losses, and, ultimately, to create a convertible *renminbi* (RMB).[8]

A year after reformers began to make a comeback against conservatives and only seven months after Deng's impressive showing at the 14th Party Congress, however, the pendulum had already started to swing back in the direction of the conservative faction of the CCP. One report, in fact, suggested that Li Peng and his "conservative allies may have been staging a comeback in response to the recent reformist victories."[9]

Liberal Zhu Rongji was charged with overseeing "a series of measures to curb credit and cool down overheated investment," while Li Ruihuan, known as a supporter and "protector of artists and intellectuals against Marxist witch-hunts," was "calling for intensified ideological study and attacking 'money worship, egoism, and hedonism.' "[10] Cadres were warned not to accept gifts, while editorials in newspapers condemned "money worship," and networking, reminiscent of the days of the Cultural Revolution, was revived as a means of keeping track of the whereabouts of citizens.[11]

On the economic front, Zhu Rongji, a long-time supporter of liberal economic reforms, urged that investment be redirected away from "property development and toward government-approved infrastructure projects."[12] Among his other objectives were to "dampen speculation, curb inflation, and promote savings . . . rein in provincial authorities, prevent local governments from raising money for pet projects, [reduce] People's Bank financing for the fiscal deficit," bring the money supply under control, and "to close the gap between the country's rich coast and poor interior."[13] For foreign investors in 1993, the reemergence of conservatives in the Chinese leadership has meant tight new monetary policies that make borrowing on the Chinese side a far more difficult enterprise than it traditionally had been, putting the onus of responsibility for arranging capital financing on the shoulders of the foreign investors.[14] Quite simply, banks are out of money in China, and Chinese investors are asking foreign partners to invest more capital even as "many foreigners are backing away from equity investments."[15] As part of their program, there was a *renminbi* devaluation, which stunned foreign-invested companies at the end of 1993, resulting in many delays in real-estate projects, especially in the face of Vice Premier Zhu Rongji's campaign to cool down [an] overheated economy.[16]

At the end of 1993, the CCP Central Committee Plenum stressed several areas that required continued reform, including state-enterprise reform, market reform, tax reform, and banking reform.[17] There was little mention of the 16-point austerity program that had been launched over the summer.[18]

It was feared that abandoning the austerity drive in a highly visible public forum might have made the center look weak in relation to the provinces, could have led to uncontrolled growth, inflation, and the "Three Crises" in China's "primitive capital market," involving chaos in "interinstitutional lending, fund-raising, and setting up financial entities."[19] The Plenum featured a book of Deng's speeches urging rapid economic reform, as a sign of Deng's emphatic commitment to the efforts of China's reformers as well as his apprehension over a possible comeback by conservatives.

Foreign investors and analysts of Chinese economics and politics should take note of these developments. Not only are they instructive in understanding the different agendas of the two factions in China's leadership, they give insight into how quickly changes in the policy orientations of the Chinese leadership can take place. In this largely unpredictable environment, caution and prudence must be utilized when attempting to predict and analyze changes and developments in Chinese policy making.

ISSUES OF AUTONOMY FROM THE STATE: MANAGEMENT POWER, LABOR RELATIONS, AND RESOURCE PROCUREMENT

Throughout China's Open Door policy, foreigners have pressured the Chinese to relinquish at least some control over joint venture operations to the foreign side. The government responded to foreign demands by liberalizing some areas of foreign direct investment, but always on condition that certain of its own demands be met by foreign investors. Three areas of control over which the two sides bargained at the national level were management structure, labor relations, and resource procurement; Chinese tax and foreign-exchange policies represent financial issues over which the government and foreign-investment community bargained. This chapter examines how bargaining between the two sides led to policy and law adjustments that sought to satisfy foreign demands while simultaneously inducing foreigners to make certain concessions to Chinese demands as well.

Joint Venture Power and Labor Control

Traditionally, a two-tiered management system has been utilized in equity joint ventures. The first tier is the board of directors (BOD), which is defined as "the highest organ of authority of a joint venture." The second tier is the management staff, which is "responsible for the daily operational and managerial work."[20] It has been a priority of the Chinese to maintain control of joint venture management and operation by vesting power in the hands of Chinese managers and local authorities. It has often been a difficult task for the foreign managers to assert their presence and to implement their strategies for joint venture operation and management. The result has frequently been a battle for joint venture control between a number of actors inside and outside of the enterprise.

In the early 1980s, foreigners usually did not enjoy majority ownership in Sino-foreign joint ventures or majority representation on the boards of directors.[21] Decision making was a process to be stipulated in the joint venture contract. However, the 1979 Joint Venture Law stipulated that the following decisions had to be made by consensus: (1) revisions in the joint venture articles of association; (2) joint venture termination; (3) increase, transfer, or mortgage of joint venture capital; (4) merger with another enterprise. All other decisions could be made by a two-thirds vote or by a majority vote. In practice, however, majority voting did not work because the two sides usually voted in blocks against each other on contentious issues, effectively leaving consensus the only viable alternative for successful decision making.[22] Indeed, one observer thought decision making by consensus to be so crucial to the success of the joint venture that if an important decision lacked consensus, early termination would threaten the enterprise.[23] The Implementing Act for the Law of the People's Republic of China on Joint Ventures Using Chinese and Foreign Investment, promulgated in 1983, legally required the major decisions to be made unanimously, but it suggested that all other voting requirements should be outlined in each joint venture's articles of association.[24] Ultimately, decision making concerning all major issues is achieved through consensus, while everyday operational matters are left to the management staff.

The Chinese have instituted numerous safeguards against foreign domination at the management level as well. Foreign decision-making autonomy is limited by a "shadow management" system that provides for a Chinese deputy for each management position in the joint venture. This bifurcated structure has encouraged bargaining, as "managerial decisions must generally be based on agreement between the expatriate manager and his deputy."[25] Major decisions (e.g., hiring and firing) that are not addressed by the BOD are supposed to be approved by the general manager and the deputy general manager, according to the "Sample Articles of Association for Joint Ventures Using Chinese and Foreign Investment" promulgated by the Laws and Regulations Bureau of the Ministry of Foreign Economic Relations and Trade (MOFERT) in 1983.[26]

Although laws generally reserved decision-making powers for Chinese joint venture partners, practice has indicated that the parties often compromise on day-to-day operational issues through bargaining. Overall, in fact, one observer discovered three trends in joint venture management since the beginning of the Open Door as a result of this compromise: (1) Foreigners increasingly held general manager positions; (2) The Chinese recognized benefits of foreign managerial guidance and began to press for more expatriate managers to be sent by parent companies to China; and (3) foreigners discovered informal methods to influence joint venture operations as they learned about their environments.[27] At the national level, the Chinese government responded to foreign concerns about decision-making autonomy in the joint venture by passing laws and promulgating policies designed to give more power to individual joint ventures. However, they also instituted safeguards to ensure that foreigners would not dominate joint venture management and that ultimate control would remain in the hands of the Chinese.

Labor Relations

One of the major operational areas, for instance, that the Chinese wanted to control was hiring, firing, and terms of employment of joint venture employees. The government was also determined to prevent Chinese joint venture employees from absorbing foreign habits perceived by the government to be unhealthy.[28]

Although the cost of the total labor package was decided through bargaining between foreign and Chinese joint venture representatives and local government officials, the 1979 Joint Venture Law stipulated that wages would be higher for Chinese in joint ventures than Chinese working in similar positions in state enterprises and that the joint venture would be responsible for social welfare benefits, including labor insurance, medical care, and numerous subsidies.[29]

The "Regulations on Labor Management in Joint Ventures Using Chinese and Foreign Investment," which were promulgated on July 26, 1980, stipulated regulations and procedures to be followed in hiring and dismissing joint venture employees. Although this law allowed free hiring and screening procedures with the consent of the local labor bureaus, in practice foreigners were forced to accept the recommendations of their Chinese colleagues without "instituting formal selection procedures."[30] Dismissals were also allowed but required the approval of the labor union, Chinese management, and local labor bureau; furthermore, protests could be lodged against dismissals, and, ultimately, a dismissed employee could request arbitration or bring suit in a Chinese court.[31] The complexity of these procedures, combined with a severe cultural aversion to harsh disciplinary measures in China, discouraged joint venture management from dismissing even very poor employees.[32]

The 1983 Implementing Act and the 1984 "Provisions for the Implementation of the Regulations on Labor Management in Joint Ventures Using Chinese and Foreign Investment" clarified wage and welfare benefit schemes, labor protection, training and discipline.[33] This legislation required joint ventures to submit a labor plan with the local labor bureau and to recruit employees from localities stipulated by the local labor bureau, and limited the conditions under which an employee could be dismissed.[34] This legislation responded to foreign concerns regarding a lack of definition of wage and welfare requirements; it also provided a framework of conditions for employee dismissal, indicating at least a grudging acceptance of the foreign practice of dismissing uncooperative and/or unproductive employees.

The 1986 Provisions extended special privileges in labor relations to joint ventures that were termed "export oriented" and/or "technically advanced." These provisions explicitly explain that Export-Oriented Enterprises (EOEs) and Technically-Advanced Enterprises (TAEs) are not required to pay Chinese labor more than wages plus labor insurance, welfare expenses, and housing subsidies.[35] At local levels, furthermore, authorities drafted even more specific provisions. In Guangzhou, for instance, it was stipulated that welfare and insurance benefits should match state-enterprise payments but should not exceed them by 27 percent of total wages and benefits. Beijing established a rate of 60 *yuan* per month (half of which constituted the housing subsidy) for staff and workers in all foreign-invested enterprises other than TAEs and EOEs which were required to pay only housing subsidies.[36] Thus, the 1986 Provisions sought to create a more favorable environment for foreign investors by systematizing wage and welfare benefits paid to Chinese joint venture employees, extending more favorable benefits to the EOEs and TAEs and generally clarifying issues addressed insufficiently by previous legislation.

The Implementing Regulations for the 1986 Provisions included the "Provisions of the Ministry of Labor and Personnel on Employment, Wages, and Welfare in Foreign- Invested Enterprises," promulgated on November 24, 1986.[37] Although the 1979 Joint Venture Law and the 1980 Labor Regulations gave joint ventures the right to hire on their own, in practice the foreign side was usually pressured to accept recommendations by the Chinese side without any screening procedures like examinations and interviews. The 1986 Provisions codified the joint venture's right "to independently recruit and hire workers by conducting examinations for qualified personnel."[38] This legislation legally granted permission to the joint ventures to recruit from other parts of the country if the localities could not provide the right personnel, and ordered the transfer of technical personnel from state enterprises to joint ventures if the joint enterprises required them.[39] Other advances over previous labor regulations included an explanation of more specific conditions for dismissal, extension of the right to determine independently wages, bonuses, and allowances, and clarification of the enterprise's right to tie raises to the economic performance of the enterprise.[40]

In May 1988, the State Council passed the Ministry of Labor and Personnel "Opinion on Further Implementation of the Right of Autonomy of Enterprises with Foreign Investment in the Hiring of Personnel." These regulations addressed a number of issues, including recruitment, labor disputes, what Chinese units may not do to undermine transfers of employees from state enterprises to joint ventures, conditions for dismissal, and protection of senior Chinese management away from FIEs.[41] Although a "step in the right direction," Chinese units often ignored the regulations, forcing joint ventures to spend substantial time and energy bargaining "to resolve what should [have been] relatively simple labor matters."[42]

Labor legislation concerning Sino-foreign joint ventures was the outcome of a bargaining process between the Chinese government and the foreign-investment community. The legislation responded to foreign concerns in several ways. First, this body of legislation granted substantial autonomy to joint ventures in the areas of recruiting, hiring, disciplining, and firing employees. It also clarified conditions under which employees could and could not be dismissed and called for approval of such decisions from Chinese management, labor unions, and local labor officials, thereby prohibiting foreign representatives from unilaterally deciding these issues. The legislation also sought to systematize wage and benefit amounts paid to employees. Implementation of these regulations, however, depended largely on bargaining between foreign joint venture representatives and their Chinese counterparts in the enterprise as well as in government at local levels and other Chinese state enterprises.

Control Over Resource Procurement

One of the most prominent concerns of foreign joint venture investors in China has been the amount of autonomy from the state they would enjoy in running their enterprises. Although laws and policies have been designed to extend greater decision-making authority to joint ventures over their operations than, for instance, is enjoyed by state enterprises, foreign investors found that ultimate power remained in the hands of the Chinese and that decision-making latitude was further limited by domestic political factors, including irrational pricing and supply shortages.[43]

Although China boasts a rich supply of natural resources as an attraction to foreign investors, access to raw materials has been a major problem cited by foreign joint venture managers since the beginning of the Open Door policy in 1979. In reaction to foreign frustration in this area, the Chinese government has attempted to fashion laws to accommodate foreign demands without relinquishing control over joint venture resource procurement.

Resource shortages are a chronic problem for enterprises in centrally planned economies. State-enterprise managers in China, for instance, often must bargain for resources with a variety of actors, including suppliers, black market sources, other enterprise managers, as well as party and government officials. "Decision makers," one expert notes, "at all levels must decide how to allocate exceedingly scarce resources with few, or no, market signals. Not surprisingly, they respond to political pressure and pecuniary opportunity. Scarcity that cannot be resolved becomes the grist for the bargaining mill."[44]

Major sources of frustration in resource procurement in China include the country's irrational pricing structure, its poor transportation and distribution facilities, and local bureaucrats who inflate prices for foreign investors. Undervalued energy prices, for instance, lead to enormous consumer waste that translates into energy shortages that often lead to electrical blackouts and brownouts during joint venture operations.[45] Even if a resource is available, the foreign investor often must contend with late deliveries caused by poor communication, transportation, and distribution facilities.[46] Also, at the beginning of the Open Door policy in 1979, joint ventures were required to be incorporated into the state plan, which strictly regulated the resource procurement procedures of the enterprises, severely limiting joint venture autonomy.[47] Furthermore, gouging by local officials in charge of resource distribution also has been a common obstacle haunting the Sino-foreign joint venture.[48] Foreign joint venture representatives found this environment particularly difficult to contend with and immediately began lobbying the Chinese government to liberalize its policies in the area of procurement. The two sides have continued to bargain back and forth over these requirements; the evolution of government policies toward joint venture resource procurement can be traced over several stages.[49] During the first legislative phase (1979-1982), the government maintained strict control over joint venture access to and procurement of raw materials. Generally, joint ventures were required to operate within the bounds of the state plan, were allowed to sell to other enterprises only what they produced in excess of the plan, could export products only through China's Foreign Trade Corporations, and were required to estimate the prices of their goods according to the prices of similar state-produced products.[50]

In the mid-1980s, the 1983 Implementing Act, the 1984 urban reforms, and the 1986 Provisions contributed to a more liberal environment for joint venture resource procurement.[51] By 1986, only 20 major commodities were distributed exclusively within the state plan (down from 256 in 1978), joint ventures enjoyed greater autonomy in developing production plans, and they could sell products on their own rather than relying on permission from China's foreign-trade bureaus.[52]

The benefits of central policy adjustments in this area, however, often did not outweigh the disadvantages that accompanied autonomy from the state plan:

> In an economy where the shortages of materials are common and distribution channels are unestablished and unreliable, the relative security of being able to procure materials through the plan was for most ventures desirable. In this context, the function of the central and local plans was more facilitative than restrictive, as had been acknowledged earlier by a MOFERT official: "with the guarantee of the plan, investment projects will have a dependable foundation."[53]

Foreign recognition of the negative results of operating outside the plan was accompanied by Chinese frustration with problems of decentralization, "such as the duplication of projects and poor coordination among agencies."[54] In 1987, consequently, China's leadership began "to apply the plan more vigorously."[55] Quite simply, the foreign-investment community learned that it could not enjoy a more liberal investment environment until problems involving infrastructure, local bureaucratism, and, most important, I believe, irregular pricing could be corrected.

After conservatives in China's central leadership consolidated their power and took control of the direction of the nation's economic policy making after the Tiananmen incident in June 1989, the government called for the dual-track price system to be replaced by more stringent government controls over commodity prices,[56] rather than continuing the liberal price reforms favored by Zhao Ziyang, which conservatives blamed for high inflation rates.[57] However, in the country's eighth Five-Year Plan, promulgated by the National People's Congress in March 1991, there seemed to be a move away from conservative prescriptions for price controls "back toward the program of decontrol and reduction of state planning that was a central element of Zhao Ziyang's reform program."[58] While foreign investors may welcome this news, a more liberal environment for resource procurement, for which they have bargained with China's leadership in the past, will continue to be hampered by the systemic problems that have plagued decentralization of decision-making autonomy throughout the 1980s. Until domestic leadership factions can bargain successfully with each other for solutions to the problems of decision-making decentralization, the foreign-investment community may want to wait until it attempts to bargain with leaders for autonomy from the plan.

Throughout the 1980s, China's policies on joint-venture resource procurement were adjusted and readjusted largely in reaction to foreign concerns over decision-making autonomy. However, foreign desire for independence in this area was tempered when liberalization of those policies demonstrated the advantages of being included in the plan and the many disadvantages joint ventures experienced outside the plan. Neither inclusion in nor exclusion from the plan, however, precluded the need to bargain at local levels for resources among a variety of actors. Indeed, the uncertainty of both liberal *and* highly regulated environments increased the need to find personal local contacts capable of arranging resource procurement irrespective of central-leadership policies.

ISSUES OF FINANCE: VALUATION AND PRICING, TAXES, AND FOREIGN EXCHANGE

Valuation and Pricing

Among the most difficult problems that foreign joint venture managers and negotiators face in China is the valuation of various commercial items, including in-kind contributions and the products produced by the enterprise.[59] During the joint venture negotiations, each side estimates the dollar value of the contributions it will make to the enterprise. These contributions may include cash, machinery, equipment, and intangibles, including technology, trademarks, and industrial-property rights; the Chinese may also make contributions in the form of the joint venture site.[60] Having been accustomed to a state-controlled price system that traditionally precluded commodities from having a market value in China, a general suspicion of such capitalist concepts as intangible property rights, and a lack of appreciation for the increased value Western investors attach to items of better quality, the Chinese often have had difficulty in estimating the value of their in-kind contributions and accepting the valuation of the in-kind contributions of their foreign counterparts. Chinese negotiators were reported routinely to allow their foreign counterparts to estimate the value of their contributions first. The Chinese would then estimate their contributions at 50 percent or more of the total value of the joint venture, regardless of the market value as perceived by the foreign negotiators.[61]

The lack of systematized procedures for the valuation of in-kind contributions was an impediment to foreign investment in China: "U.S. investors have told the Chinese time and again that the enemy of a healthy investment climate is unpredictability and that one of the quickest and most efficient ways of doing away with it is the systematic issuance and implementation of trade, economic, and commercial laws."[62]

The most trying objects of negotiation have been the valuation of technology and land. Especially during the early years of China's Open Door, the Chinese were deeply suspicious of the value of the technologies that foreign investors wanted to sell. Restrictions on the purchase of technologies from abroad included the following guidelines: (1) The technology had to contribute to the production of goods that China "urgently" needed or that were suitable for export; (2) the technology should increase the quality of products and/or raise productivity; and (3) the technology should "contribute to the conservation of energy and raw materials." Convincing Chinese negotiators that technology served these purposes, however, was a difficult task. It was exacerbated by Chinese suspicion that the technologies that foreigners wanted to sell were obsolete and Chinese insistence on only the best whether or not they had the sophistication to apply the best of Western technologies or understand the monetary value of such commodities: "It is paradoxical," noted one observer, "that the Chinese should place a high value on 'only the best' but have almost no appreciation for the monetary value of knowledge."[63] Indeed, in the early 1980s, the Chinese imposed a regulation that allowed a foreign corporation to value its technology at only 15 percent of its total contribution.[64] Consequent to this lack of understanding of the market value of Western goods and technologies, the Chinese openly admitted that "whenever possible they [would] ignore patents and, after paying for only a single model, [would] try to copy it."[65]

Chinese valuation procedures have thus been an object of bargaining between the Chinese government and the international-investment community. Foreign investors have stressed their concern over this issue, and the Chinese government has responded by trying to systematize the procedures taken to value technology and land. In order to alleviate foreign concerns over technology transfers to China, numerous policy and attitude adjustments have been made since the beginning of the Open Door policy. For instance, in order to make it possible for foreigners to value their technology contributions at more than 15 percent of their total investment, the Chinese government in 1985 passed the Import of Technology Law of the PRC, which allowed foreigners to supplement joint venture contracts with separate technology-transfer agreements.[66] As was explained in Chapter Two, China has also joined a series of international property-rights organizations, passed numerous laws for the protection of industrial property, indicating a changed attitude in government toward crucial technology-transfer issues, and in 1983 began extending tax and other special incentives to those enterprises that qualify as Technically Advanced Enterprises.[67] As I discussed in Chapter Two, numerous problems in the transfer of technology still exist, but the advances briefly outlined here indicate a move by the central leadership in China toward a better understanding of the valuation of foreign technologies.

Numerous strides have also been made in the area of land valuation. The 1979 Joint Venture Law granted foreign entities fixed-term land-use rights.[68] The Foreign Land-Use Measures of 1980 established a wide-ranging set of land-use fees from five *yuan* to 300 *yuan* per square meter without an effective set of guidelines on how to implement them. In the early 1980s, it was reported that land-use rates were decided locally, but because of the ambiguity of the guidelines for deciding land-use rates, price gouging by local officials was quite common. Because local authorities had the power to decide exact land-use rates, the foreign partner often negotiated the terms so that the final outcome depended on a process of bargaining between the parties. The result of this process was often an agreement on annual leasing and rental fees that varied widely from one joint venture to another all over China.[69] To alleviate the inconsistencies in this free-wheeling system of land-use management, the government in 1982 began to create a land-management system with the drafting of a new law that "effectively expropriated the privately owned residential plots of millions of peasants and urban families" in exchange for land-use rights for the homeowners.[70] This change "paved the way for the creation of a national land- management system based on exclusive public ownership and mixed public and private use."[71] The 1982 legislation was followed in 1986 by the Land Management Law, which set up a Land Management Bureau (with local branches) under the State Council and a national regulatory system for land-use rights "to allow accurate assessments of land-use fees and other taxes and provide clear statements of ownership (and leasehold) for purposes of mortgages and sale."[72] Power to determine land-use fees was delegated to the Land Management Bureau, and land-use fee incentives were codified in the 1986 "Provisions for the Encouragement of Foreign Investment."[73] Although rates still varied considerably, bargaining between the Chinese government and outside investors led to more explicit and systematized procedures for the valuation of land.

In 1990, the Chinese government further sought to systematize the valuation of land for foreign-investment purposes with two new sets of interim regulations: The "Interim Regulations of the PRC on the Sale and Transfer of Land-Use Rights in State-Owned Land in the Cities and Towns" (the land-conveyance regulations) and the "Interim Regulations of the PRC Concerning Administration of Investing, Developing, and Managing Sizeable Land Areas by Foreign Investors" (the land-development regulations). These laws served the purposes of codifying the ways foreign interests could acquire land for development projects while clarifying that ownership of the land did not transfer to the foreign party with the land-use rights.[74] This legislation defined four methods that foreigners could utilize to acquire land: grants, transfers, leases, and appropriations.[75] The legislation also required foreigners to fulfill the following three requirements: (1) to develop a Land Development Plan, which is negotiable, but which often has required substantial investment in infrastructure construction; (2) to define the purpose, time frame, and overall goals of each stage of land development; and (3) to gain approval at local and provincial levels.[76]

The outcome of bargaining over technology- and land-valuation procedures between the Chinese government and the international investment community evolved in the form of efforts by the Chinese government to systematize the valuation of land and technology. The Chinese designed laws to gain international cooperation in return for its efforts in investing in land development-projects that the government favored and transfers of technologies that China needed. Thus, national legislation concerning land development and technology transfers was, in large part, the outcome of bargaining between the government and the world investment community and sought to achieve three objectives: (1) to respond to foreign concerns about Chinese inconsistency in the valuation of in-kind contributions; (2) to ensure that Chinese authorities retained control of implementation of fee assessments and valuations; and (3) to codify responsibilities of foreign investors to transfer only those technologies that would benefit China's overall modernization objectives and to contribute to the building of China's infrastructure as a prerequisite to acquiring land-use rights for land development. Although China has made progress in these areas, problems still remain. China's dual-pricing system and lack of appreciation for product quality continue to undermine attempts at accurate valuation. These systemic characteristics encourage bargaining between local policy implementers and joint venture representatives not only over valuation of in-kind contributions but also over profits and product pricing.

The 1979 Joint Venture Law did not specifically address the issue of how much autonomy joint ventures would have to set the prices of their products. Products for sale in the international market need to be priced in line with those market prices in order to be competitive.[77] Often, products for sale on the domestic market are priced by the State Price Control Commission "in light of the state's economic plans affecting a given product and current production conditions relating to the product."[78] The 1983 Regulations extended formal pricing autonomy to joint ventures (with some restrictions), but convincing the Chinese how to price products has been a difficult task that continues to plague joint ventures today.[79] One of the last issues addressed by the local laws for the East Lake High-Technology Development Zone (ELHTDZ) in Wuhan, passed in 1988, is pricing.[80] The trial sales price of newly developed products may be set by the enterprise itself, and "high-tech products for which there is no unified state price" can be priced independently by the enterprise itself.[81] The tendency among the Chinese toward overvaluation, however, is also apparent in product pricing.[82] In one instance, the Western marketing manager of a joint venture in the ELHTDZ explained that he was discussing pricing strategy with one of the venture's Chinese representatives who was preparing to conduct negotiations with a potential buyer. The foreign manager instructed his colleague to ask for a certain amount but not to allow the price to be negotiated down more than 3 percent. His colleague's response was to ask for an original price 15 percent higher than was suggested and then to allow the price to be negotiated down 18 percentage points, if necessary. According to the foreign manager, common international practice dictates that 3 percent is the most a "discount" should be, and he hoped to instill this value in his Chinese counterparts in the joint venture. He compared the experience to the Chinese marketplace where "everything is negotiable" and explained that although there is industrial negotiation everywhere in the world, "the degree of negotiation here [in China] is much greater."[83]

A confusing dual-pricing structure, years of buying state-subsidized goods on the domestic market, a lack of understanding of the market value of products and raw materials, little appreciation for why higher market prices are attached to products of better quality, and a cultural tendency to bargain about the pricing of everything with wild abandon are some of the factors that plague attempts to establish rational pricing structures for goods produced by Sino-foreign joint ventures. Even if the foreign-investment community is successful in bargaining for legislation that grants greater autonomy to joint ventures in the area of product pricing, foreign investors will be hampered by these characteristics of the Chinese political system. Managing joint ventures in this complex environment is a difficult task, especially when the foreign manager constantly must battle for even limited power over joint venture operations with numerous actors, including Chinese management, CCP representatives in the joint venture, union officials, and local authorities.

Taxes

The Income Tax Law of the PRC Concerning Joint Ventures Using Chinese and Foreign Investment was promulgated in September 1980 to address joint venture issues that were left previously unanswered by China's Foreign Enterprise Income Tax Law (FEITL).[84] The 1980 joint venture tax legislation contained four new major features: (1) lower tax rates if an enterprise was deemed "reasonably profitable"; (2) more generous tax holiday provisions; (3) tax refunds for enterprises that reinvest profits; (4) provisions for enterprises equipped with up-to-date technology to apply for tax reductions.[85] Problems with this original joint venture tax legislation concerned the wide-ranging interpretations of the various tax laws by local authorities charged with implementation.[86]

In the 1983 Implementing Act, the Chinese government attempted to "compensate for the law's failure to thoroughly address taxation of joint ventures."[87] Tax exemptions were extended for imported machinery, equipment, parts and construction materials that were either contributed as part of the foreign partner's equity share, imported with capital funds, or unavailable domestically, and for some items imported for export and/or the production of items for export.[88] As part of its effort to create a more favorable environment for foreign investment, China, in addition to trying to clarify various issues, also granted more tax breaks. Originally, joint ventures, for instance, enjoyed a 100 percent tax exemption in the first profit-making year and a 50 percent reduction in the second and third years, under the 1980 Joint Venture Income Tax Law.[89] The 1983 amended version of this law extended the 100 percent exemption for the first *two* profit-making years and granted 50 percent reductions in years three, four, and five.[90] The 1986 Provisions exempted EOEs from taxes on remitted profits and income taxes and gave a three-year extension on a 50 percent tax-reduction holiday.[91] If a joint venture received EOE or TAE classification, based on the "MOFERT Rules on the Confirmation of Export Oriented Enterprises and Technically Advanced Enterprises with Foreign Investment," the 1986 Provisions exempted it from all non-housing subsidies, extended the reduction period for the joint venture income tax, and granted a host of additional tax benefits for reinvested profits.[92]

On April 9, 1991, the National People's Congress (NPC) passed the Income Tax Law of the PRC for Enterprises with Foreign Investment and Foreign Enterprises, popularly known as the Unified Income Tax Law. It was followed by State Council approval for the "Detailed Rules and Regulations for the Implementation of the Income Tax Law" on July 30, 1991. This legislation has been hailed by foreign experts as containing "much clearer guidelines" on Chinese tax policy, and by Chinese as a law that is "more attractive to foreign investors" because it has "unified the income tax rate, making it simpler, clearer and more convenient for foreign partners operating in China to calculate and pay income tax."[93] The new law boasts both administrative improvements in the tax system and advances in the incentive structure for foreign-invested enterprises.[94]

This tax legislation "stipulates that all foreign investments be taxed under one system, eliminating prior distinctions between equity joint ventures and other foreign enterprises."[95] As of 1991, there were two categories of foreign enterprises: "enterprises with foreign investment" and "foreign enterprises." The first category includes joint ventures, cooperative joint ventures, and wholly foreign-owned enterprises; the second category includes management branches, representative offices, factories involved in foreign licensing arrangements, places for exploitation of natural resources, contracted project sites, companies providing labor services like contractors and consulting firms.[96] Generally, this is a distinction between manufacturing enterprises and independent-contracting enterprises. Previously, independent agents did not have to pay taxes on profits and sales, but under the new legislation, this situation may change.[97] In fact, the wording of the law is ambiguous, and implementation is yet to be seen in practice. Another administrative change concerns the method the authorities will use to determine resident and nonresident companies. Under previous legislation, this question was not explicitly addressed. The new law explicitly stipulates that residence depends on management, control, and registration ("incorporation"). Effectively, resident enterprises will be considered Chinese legal entities "subject to treatment as Chinese resident companies," while nonresident enterprises will be taxed on only the income that they derive in China.[98]

A flat tax rate of 33 percent of taxable income has been introduced to replace a progressive rate that ranged from 20 percent (plus a local 10 percent tax) to 50 percent (combined local and state taxes); depending on the type of enterprise, this change may mean higher or lower taxes.[99] Under the new legislation, a previous requirement to pay a 10 percent withholding tax on profits remitted outside China has been eliminated, tax holidays previously available to only specially designated enterprises are now available to all "productive foreign-invested enterprises with contracts of at least ten years," and tax refunds for reinvestment are extended to more enterprises.[100] The 1991 tax law also allows foreign companies with many businesses in China to file a single tax return.[101] Also, the State Taxation Bureau will accept "dual pricing" for products that have varying prices on the international and national markets, which, one specialist observed, indicates a recognition by the Chinese that joint venture pricing policies should be controlled by business sense, not taxes imposed by the government, and that "lower prices are often required for joint venture-produced products to be competitive on the international market."[102]

China has also used this legislation to flex its administrative muscle by prohibiting transfer pricing and maintaining strict penalties for late tax payments in reaction to perceived foreign abuses in these areas:

> It is common practice internationally that related enterprises evade tax by the method of assigning profits through the transfer of list price. In China, this problem is becoming increasingly serious. Some foreign investors evade taxes and make profits by raising the prices of imported materials and forcing down the prices of products to be sold abroad or readjusting the standard for other charges.[103]

The legislation allows the State Taxation Bureau to apply this regulation concerning transfer pricing retroactively, since China has no statute of limitations.[104] Penalties for late tax payments are reduced from 0.5 percent to 0.2 percent per day, but this is still a harsh 73 percent per year and is not tax deductible. Officials recognize the stringency of the regulation but contend that first-time offenders will be assessed by local authorities who will have the alternative not to impose the entire amount.[105]

A major overhaul of China's tax system was expected to take place in early 1994. The reforms were expected to affect personal income taxes and value-added taxes, while creating "unifying rates for domestic and foreign businesses."[106] Objectives of tax-system reform include broadening "the tax base and increas[ing] revenues, while simplifying the existing hodgepodge of levies."[107]

Among expected changes in the system are the introduction of a "single-rate system for foreign companies" that will increase their rates without eliminating tax breaks or discouraging investment, a "tax declaration system" that will set reasonable thresholds for income tax liability and require stricter enforcement, increased manpower in the Finance Ministry to enforce and make more efficient the procedures for collecting taxes, and a uniform value-added tax (VAT) that will allow companies to "receive tax credits for all inputs, and pay tax only on the value they add to a product or service."[108] Ultimately, proponents of tax reform hope to establish a simplified and more efficient program for assessing and collecting taxes from participating actors in foreign-invested enterprises.

Since 1979, China's tax legislation has evolved considerably. The Chinese government has sought to make laws more explicit and thereby limit the rather substantial variation in official interpretations of the laws, to create favorable conditions for foreigners engaged in the types of production desired in China, to recognize common international practice regarding tax legislation, and, finally, to streamline the varying tax structures into one unified system. My research indicates that despite these advances, ambiguities remained apparent, and the power vested in local authorities to implement tax regulations has meant bargaining over the tax legislation between them and joint venture representatives.

Foreign Exchange

Legislation for foreign investment was designed to guarantee the principle of equality and mutual benefit in China's foreign economic relations. This theme was used to stress the protection of foreign assets from nationalization and Chinese losses of capital to outside investors. Foreign-exchange requirements were imposed on joint ventures to guarantee and protect China's accumulation of foreign currency through legislation: "The government wished to avoid the experience of those countries where foreign- investment projects spend more on foreign exchange to import parts and materials than they earn through exports, thereby creating a drain on hard currency, exacerbating debt problems, and threatening economic dependence."[109]

There have been three major phases of legislation since the beginning of the Open Door in 1979, marked by the years 1979, 1983, and 1986, as well as numerous advances since the incident at Tiananmen Square in Beijing in June 1989. In the 1979 Joint Venture Law (and the "Provisional Regulations on Foreign-Exchange Control of the People's Republic of China"), the Chinese required all Sino-foreign joint ventures to maintain a positive balance between foreign-exchange expenditures and revenues.[110] For many of these enterprises, obtaining the necessary high-quality inputs needed for production meant importing goods that could be bought only with hard currency.[111] Furthermore, paying expatriate salaries and dividends to foreign shareholders also required hard-currency payments. Balancing foreign exchange quickly became and, despite liberalization of some restrictions, has remained the biggest obstacle facing the Sino-foreign joint venture.

In the early years of 1979-1983, the only viable way to balance foreign exchange was by exporting the goods produced by the joint venture. However, with no assistance from the state, "higher-than-anticipated labor costs," poor product quality, lack of skilled labor (which often meant higher production costs), high import costs due to import duty fees, as well as innumerable bureaucratic obstacles to gaining approval to export, this option was often unattractive and impractical.[112]

In 1983, largely in reaction to foreign criticisms, the Chinese government passed new laws and issued new regulations to encourage foreign investment by easing the foreign-exchange requirements. The 1983 "Implementing Act for the Law of the People's Republic of China on Joint Ventures Using Chinese and Foreign Investment" (Implementing Act) and the "Rules for the Implementation of Exchange Control Regulations," as well as regulations issued at local and provincial levels, gave joint ventures more freedom in deciding how to go about meeting foreign-exchange requirements.[113] These regulations gave local governments the power to lend money from their own foreign-exchange reserves to import-substituting joint ventures, "MOFERT was directed to incorporate the foreign-exchange needs of the venture into the state plan," and joint ventures were allowed to sell their products to qualified domestic enterprises for foreign exchange.[114] Though the new regulations were seen by the international investment community as progress, acquiring import-substitution status required tedious bargaining with local authorities, was generally available only to a narrow range of joint ventures, and even if import-substitution status was achieved, there was no guarantee that domestic enterprises would provide the necessary markets for joint venture goods.[115]

In 1986, the "Regulations on Foreign Currency Balance of Equity Joint Ventures" (Foreign-Exchange Balancing Provisions) went into effect. These regulations amplified some of the provisions of the 1983 legislation. This new legislation allowed joint ventures to buy and sell foreign exchange with other joint ventures (which led to the establishment of swap centers in all major cities and provinces in China), gave primary responsibility to aid joint ventures with foreign-exchange problems to the central government and, in 1987, encouraged domestic enterprises to buy joint-venture-produced goods with their foreign-exchange reserves.[116] Strict requirements to achieve import-substitution status, lack of purchases of joint venture products by the government, and difficulties obtaining approval to cxport goods unrelated to the joint venture product line (for foreign-exchange purposes) continue to plague the foreign-exchange balancing processes.

In 1992, there was a growth in foreign-exchange swap centers across China as foreign-exchange income continued to grow, albeit at a slower rate than in 1991.[117] Foreign-exchange balancing remains the greatest challenge to the foreign-invested enterprise (FIE) in China. According to one survey, most FIEs rely mainly on swap centers to obtain foreign exchange.[118] However, this method of foreign-exchange generation is plagued by numerous problems. In 1993, for instance, volatile exchange rates meant a decrease in the "availability of hard currency."[119] Most FIEs have been forced to use several methods to attempt to meet the stringent foreign-exchange requirements imposed by the central government. Until convertibility of the RMB is achieved, in fact, FIEs will continue to be forced to be creative in utilizing all of their resources to meet their foreign-exchange requirements.

Overcoming the foreign-exchange dilemma is a difficult task, fraught with numerous political obstacles and stringent legal requirements. However, joint ventures are able to overcome these obstacles by bargaining with local policy implementers for favorable and/or relaxed implementation of these regulations. Without diminishing the difficulty of trying to meet China's foreign-exchange legal requirements, I have found that it is possible for joint ventures to bargain around these otherwise strict laws and policies. This position is supported by the fact that most joint ventures remain in operation despite an inability to meet foreign-exchange requirements. Those that do remain in operation have developed strategies to meet, bargain over, and, in some instances, evade the regulations.

CONCLUSION

At the national level of the Chinese political system, conservative and reformist factions of the Chinese leadership bargain with each other over the formulation of economic policies in general and joint venture policies in particular. The Chinese government responds to numerous factors in drafting the laws and promulgating the policies, including, most notably, concerns expressed by the foreign-investment community. Throughout the 1980s and into the 1990s, Chinese joint venture laws have evolved largely through the process of bargaining between the Chinese government and foreign investors. These laws were designed to serve the functions of creating a favorable environment for foreign investment while requiring that foreign investment not threaten Chinese sovereignty and that it contribute to achieving China's modernization goals. This legislation addressed issues of joint venture autonomy, including management structure, labor relations control, and resource procurement. It also addressed financial issues, including valuation and profits and pricing, taxes, and foreign exchange.

Final policy outcomes did not result from this national-level bargaining alone. Provincial and local governments crafted laws in line with national regulations and policy goals, as well as in consideration of special local conditions. Furthermore, both national-level laws and provincial and local-level legislation were ambiguous and open to wide-ranging interpretations from both the Chinese and foreign sides. Decentralization of decision-making authority to local levels meant that these legal ambiguities would be resolved by local-level bureaucrats who subsequently bargained with Sino-foreign joint venture representatives who sought to acquire the most favorable interpretation of the rules and regulations possible. In order, then, to appreciate fully the role of bargaining in the implementation of joint venture laws and policies, it is necessary to investigate the ways local policy implementers and joint venture representatives resolved issues through bargaining and to identify specifically the outcomes of this complex process.

4

The Objects of Bargaining

INTRODUCTION

The preconditions of bargaining are understood in terms of the conflicting interests of foreign joint venture representatives and their Chinese counterparts in the enterprise and bureaucracy. The profit motive is the single most important reason that a foreign party will invest in a joint venture. The Chinese objectives are to maximize the speedy transfer of foreign capital, technology, and management skills. To achieve these objectives and to deter zealous foreigners from extracting undue profits from China, the government has passed numerous regulations covering such areas as imports and exports and foreign-exchange earnings. These regulations have been impediments to foreign earning power, often involving excruciatingly difficult foreign-exchange requirements and exorbitant Chinese valuation of their in-kind contributions.

Foreign investors often battle with Chinese authorities for autonomy in controlling enterprise operations. From the board room, where decision-making negotiations follow a pattern of Chinese voting in "blocks" against foreign board representatives, to enterprise operations, where the Chinese and foreign sides struggle for control, there exists a perpetual game of tug-of-war.

The foreign investor has three types of profit-related objectives: market-related, production-related, and special incentive-related.[1] Ultimately gaining access to China's potentially enormous markets is also a principal attraction for the foreign investor. A presence in China will allow the foreigner to learn about potential markets and to establish important contacts that will be of value in the future as policies become less stringent.

Production-related objectives include "access to new or cheaper raw materials, labor, transportation routes," and inexpensive land (site)- use fees.[2] Special incentives in the form of tax breaks and other preferential treatment are available to enterprises in the SEZs and to export-oriented and technically advanced enterprises in other areas (e.g., East Lake High-Technology Development Zone and Tianjin Economic Development Area).

Chinese laws, systemic constraints and cultural values severely limit the extent to which the foreign investor can take advantage of the benefits of investment in China. The ability of the foreign party to take advantage of sales to the domestic market has been undermined by heavy import and export duties, rules that exclude the sale of products that China does not need or that are not high-tech, and stringent foreign-exchange requirements that amplify foreign inability to convert *renminbi* to hard currency (to pay expatriate salaries, buy imported materials and equipment, and to remit profits abroad).

Production-related benefits like inexpensive land (site)-use fees are tempered by the costs of technological innovation (e.g., improving outdated facilities and equipment). China's poor economic and industrial infrastructure (which makes shortages of "strategic goods"[3] like coal, oil, and electricity a constant problem), poor distribution facilities, and irrational pricing, the competition with state enterprises, and contention with bureaucrats who respond to political pressure and monetary rewards for distribution of goods have made the well-publicized attraction of cheap raw materials much less attractive in reality. The production-related benefit of cheap labor has also been more expensive than expected. Chinese law requires that joint ventures pay their employees 120 percent to 150 percent more than comparable state enterprises pay their employees and subsidize them for an array of social welfare benefits. Culturally, China's iron rice bowl (which guarantees employment despite performance quality) and the Confucian value of harmony (which inhibits discipline and dismissal of employees) have inhibited state managers from exercising authority in labor relations. Foreign authority is limited by these factors, as well as a number of Chinese bureaucratic structures that have power in such matters as labor relations (including Chinese management, the local labor bureau, the union, and party cells). Productivity, as a result, is often poor, and, ultimately, labor costs are "not especially low [even] when compared with wages in Indonesia, Thailand, or Malaysia."[4]

Foreigners have a wide variety of resources to induce concessions from the Chinese on many of these issues, including access to capital, technology, and management training techniques. The Chinese also possess many mechanisms to influence the foreign partners, including laws, common cultural values, and a host of official bureaus and units inside and outside the joint venture. These instruments of control can be used both to create a comfortable environment for foreign investors and to exert pressure on them to abide by Chinese laws and customs that may be inconvenient. The Chinese may enter into negotiations with foreigners over inconvenient rules and regulations and try to help them with tedious tasks like resource procurement and getting special preferential treatment on taxes and import and export duties, for instance. Autonomy over joint venture operations does not belong exclusively to one side or the other but rather is shared and bargained over throughout the existence of the joint venture.

OBJECTS OF BARGAINING IN LABOR

In this section, I will discuss the items over which Chinese and foreigners bargain. There are three major issue areas: labor and personnel, taxes, and foreign exchange. At both national and local levels, laws have been passed to address these issues. However, foreign parties are often able to bargain with the Chinese over implementation of regulations that these laws outline.

Recruitment and Hiring

Article Ten of Wuhan's local joint venture laws states that "the selection process is only the best (qualified) are hired."[5] The power to decide who are "the best" formally resides with local authorities who have ultimate decision-making power over whom enterprises can and cannot hire. Throughout the 1980s, more and more foreign partners introduced screening procedures in hiring, despite local resistance, to wrest control over hiring from Chinese labor authorities. Screening procedures are now common practice, and foreign power over hiring is increasing.

One corporation, for instance, has recently begun a process of recruitment on Chinese college campuses in Guangdong.[6] There has been no interference by government bureaus with the recruitment, and the company hopes to begin the process in other parts of China.[7] As of June 1991, this company was the only foreign corporation known to be engaged in this method of recruitment.[8] As always, a personal relationship with someone in a position of power must be established before such an activity can be initiated. In this case, forging a relationship with university central administration (e.g., university vice presidents) is the key to obtaining approval.[9] After these formalities, information about the corporation and application materials are distributed to students in their dormitories.[10] If no one is in a room, then the materials are slipped under the door.[11] My informant believed that it was strictly up to the university to allow such recruiting activities and that local officials did not have any input.[12]

Joint ventures have been guaranteed by local authorities that "only the best will be hired," but determining who are "the best" is a power that remains in the hands of the authorities. By negotiating permission to recruit on college campuses, this foreign company has been able to circumvent local authorities and decide on its own which students it believes to be "the best." Foreign joint venture partners in this case are able to exploit their relationships with university officials to speak with potentially valuable employees (the students) before they graduate and are assigned to jobs by Chinese authorities. If a student is able to make a good impression on a foreign recruiter and the recruiter expresses interest in hiring her or him, the student can begin the process of negotiating with relevant contacts to arrange for employment with the joint venture. The foreign company, likewise, has the opportunity to express interest in the prospects it finds most interesting to its relevant contacts who may be instrumental in arranging the student's first job. Thus, the joint venture partner must try to obtain employees who possess the necessary skills valuable to the enterprise, often avoiding meddling local bureaucrats who want to maintain control of the process of employment assignments, perhaps, without concern for the particular needs of diverse enterprises.

Indeed, the lack of qualified on-site Chinese personnel to receive advanced management and technical training has been a major concern to foreign investors. Article Seven of the Wuhan Local Laws responds to this concern by allowing joint ventures to "employ special technologists, operation and management personnel, and workers in the society on its own. If the personnel aren't enough for the employment, after the approving of the municipal labor bureau, the enterprise can recruit personnel from other parts of the country."[13] The law goes on to vest power over these *transfer procedures* in the hands of local authorities. This has effectively prohibited joint ventures from hiring "in the society on [their] own."[14]

A manager in Wuhan, for instance, explained that his joint venture could not hire from the countryside and would not try to test the law's flexibility.[15] However, if a person from the countryside could obtain a work permit, then the joint venture could hire that person.[16] The intricacies of obtaining a work permit were not discussed, but this was identified as a possible point of bargaining.[17] No doubt, for instance, if a peasant from the countryside had the necessary wherewithal to bargain with local authorities or had a relative with an inside track to a joint venture job, that peasant would be in a relatively good position to arrange such a transfer.

In special cases, the local labor authorities will get involved in the transfer of personnel whom a joint venture needs from a state enterprise but whom the state enterprise does not want to let go.[18] In one Wuhan joint venture, for instance, management needed to acquire engineers from a local state enterprise that did not want to release them.[19] They went to the local labor authorities, who ordered that the necessary arrangements for the transfers be made.[20]

In Tianjin, an official explained that hiring from the countryside and from other provinces was a process controlled by the labor authorities.[21] In the case of one Sino-foreign joint venture that needed to hire extra workers, the personnel bureau in Tianjin had to contact the personnel bureau in Shaanxi Province and make arrangements for the transfer of 20 employees. Hiring from the countryside in Tianjin is controlled by the local labor bureau. Peasants may be chosen but are never coerced into taking joint venture employment. In fact, it was reported to me, they are always very willing to move to the city because of the better wages and high prestige of joint venture employment. Although enterprise autonomy has increased, support from local authorities is still crucial to initiate activities like hiring from other areas of the country, including the countryside and other provinces.[22]

Generally, arranging for the transfer of a management-level employee from a state enterprise to a joint venture is a complex process that involves numerous actors. Because staff-level positions may not be considered important by local authorities, they are less inclined to expedite the process of transferring personnel holding these jobs. These joint venture positions, however, are considered very valuable by Chinese workers; therefore, competition for them is fierce, and a substantial amount of bargaining may be involved in trying to obtain one. The bargaining is initiated by the prospective employee and may ultimately involve government bureaus, state enterprises, and the joint venture.

A former state-enterprise employee in Beijing explained that she had to ask for a transfer (*yaoqiu*) to a joint venture and had to negotiate with the state enterprise's personnel department to let her go.[23] Because she had been a valuable employee, the personnel department was reluctant to grant her permission to leave. Her chance to move on depended on a large network of influential personal contacts. This process is common for staff-level employees who want to move from state enterprises to joint ventures. One manager explained that "if they [the employee's superiors in the state enterprise] don't want to let you go, you're dead."[24] One of his employees had been involved in such negotiations before coming to work in his joint venture. During the process, this employee responded to inquiries regarding how it was going with the response, "Trying to move over there" (*diao dio zhebian*) [25] In fact, this response has become a popular catchphrase among state employees who are in the midst of negotiating transfers from their enterprises to joint ventures.[26]

The difficulty of arranging a transfer can be exacerbated if a prospective employee wants to move from one part of the country to another for permanent joint venture employment. Although many managers are allowed to move to other parts of the country for temporary joint venture employment, it is difficult to arrange a permanent transfer. A Chinese employee's place of residence is largely defined by the location of his household registration (*hukou*).[27] Obtaining permanent joint venture employment in another part of the country depends on arranging the transfer of the account. One manager explained that he had worked in Harbin for a state enterprise and then the Bank of China for several years, when he was offered a temporary management position in a joint venture. After working there for some time, he subsequently was offered a permanent position. He wanted to take the position but first had to arrange approval from the relevant authorities for transfer of his bank account. His boss in the joint venture utilized contacts in the Shenzhen government, who used contacts in Harbin, and together they expedited the transfer of the account, enabling him to become a resident of Shekou and permanent employee of the joint venture.[28]

The value of joint venture employment makes it an object of bargaining. The practice is common and seems accepted but can also become corrupt. In the view of one foreign joint venture manager in Wuhan, the hiring practices of a former personnel manager were undeniably corrupt and good reason for dismissal.[29] Having discovered that the personnel manager had embezzled 5,000 *renminbi* from the union retirement fund, the foreign manager initiated an investigation of his other dealings and found that among employees he had hired were friends and relatives, including the ex-mayor's son, the relative of a high-ranking official from the Ministry of Foreign Economic Relations and Trade, and the relative of a public-security bureau official. The personnel manager had been "loading the place with his own people," trying to create his "own little kingdom" within the firm.[30] This manager and the employees whom he had hired were dismissed. The ex-personnel manager promised retaliation with the support of local labor authorities.[31] However, when the authorities arrived to discuss the matter, it was not about reinstating the former manager but rather about the possibility of the joint venture bringing criminal charges against him in court.[32]

The process of recruitment and hiring confirms that the battle for power in the joint venture is not always between the "foreign side" and the "Chinese side." Rather, it can involve Chinese and foreigners inside and outside the joint venture working together to influence the decision making of Chinese authorities. The battle for power can also involve foreigners working with local Chinese authorities to wrest power from other Chinese. Although ultimate decision-making authority over hiring and transferring of employees resides with local authorities by law, their decisions often result from a long, complex process of negotiation among a number of interested actors. The authorities are more likely to arrange transfers of special personnel that local enterprises must have, whether they are from local state enterprises, from other provinces or from the countryside. If the opening to be filled is a relatively minor staff-level position, then the prospective employee (especially if considered valuable by the state enterprise for which she or he is working) will have to initiate a long consensus-building process to arrange permission to transfer. Similar to the case of the graduating university student or the peasant from the countryside, the state employee who wishes for a transfer to a joint venture must utilize personal contacts to jockey for an effective position from which to bargain for such an opportunity.

Labor: Employee Discipline and Dismissal

According to relevant Wuhan Local Laws, and in conjunction with national regulations, a system of labor employment contracts must be established in all joint ventures:

> In accordance with the law and regulations of our country, the equality and voluntary principle of unanimity through consultation, a Sino-foreign joint venture signs the labor employment contracts with the staff and workers and formulates definitely in the contracts about the two parties' rights, duties, time limit, pay, insurance, welfare, labor conditions, labor discipline [responsibilities] and other things that both sides think need to be formulated.[33]

The purpose of this regulation is to protect Chinese labor from exploitation and to vest control over labor in the local authorities.

In one Wuhan joint venture, there are two documents that embody the contract system: individual labor contracts and the company's *Rules and Procedures Manual,* which includes many items that do not appear in the contracts.[34] The individual labor contract is a short "one- or two-page document" that specifies the responsibilities of the joint venture, the staff, and its employees.[35] The manual includes a much more detailed explanation of employee and joint venture responsibilities. If there is ever a misunderstanding about responsibilities, the standardized individual contracts may be changed to include or elaborate items in the manual. The manual may address "treatment," salary, housing, and the possibility for training in China, as well as in the foreign partner's country.[36] There are different sets of standardized contracts for different classes of employees.[37] According to my informants, there is no interference from local labor bureau officials with the formulation and implementation of the contract system, and filing the contracts with the local officials seems to be a routine procedure.[38]

Article Six of the Wuhan Local Laws specifies that the "change of the contracts must be agreed by both sides through consultation" and that "the contracts can be renewed through the agreement of both sides when the contracts expire."[39] The reasoning behind a short, general, standardized contract, then, is to avoid specifics that may be misinterpreted and have to be changed and approved.[40] The *Rules and Procedures Manual* will clarify meanings and, if insufficient, can be changed quickly without requiring approval from the local authorities.[41] This innovation was created by the foreign partner to give it a greater degree of power over a labor contracts system that, by law, is ultimately controlled by the local labor authorities.[42] Although they have power to approve and disapprove the labor contracts, their jurisdiction does not extend to the labor manual.[43] Because the labor manual is under the domain of the joint venture and does not require approval from local authorities, foreign managers are able to use it as a rule book by which employees must abide. It therefore gives managers more autonomy in monitoring and controlling the behavior of joint venture employees that they would otherwise not have under the comparatively ambiguous labor contracts that are under the ultimate control of the local Chinese labor authorities. Nevertheless, even when a Chinese employee does not live up to the expectations of joint venture management, discipline and dismissal can be a severely difficult task; it is especially arduous for the foreign joint venture manager who is unfamiliar with Chinese values and the numerous problems that accompany the introduction of new management concepts into Chinese industry.

A common complaint of foreign managers, for instance, has been China's collective lack of concern for product quality.[44] Systemic and cultural factors have been attributed to this problem. Among systemic factors are China's awkward pricing system, a preoccupation with meeting state-mandated production quotas irrespective of quality, and deficient distribution methods. Cultural factors include China's iron rice bowl, which guarantees employment despite productivity, and a Confucian desire for harmony, which inhibits discipline and dismissal of even very bad employees. Contending with the systemic nuances of China's economic system, as well as the cultural attributes of Chinese labor and management, has proved to be a major challenge to the foreign joint venture partner. One representative's assessment seemed to reflect a common attitude among expatriate managers:

> One of the greatest needs is that Chinese begin to turn out products of better quality. In order for this to occur, a cultural transformation is needed; that is, Chinese have to become cognizant of the fact that according to international standards, their products are generally mediocre. Somehow, they have to have instilled in them a sense of pride in the nature of their production and this involves psychological change.[45]

In a closed society, structured by a command economy that has been protected domestic industries from international competition and a labor system that disallowed employee dismissals, the challenge of trying to alter Chinese attitudes was one of mammoth proportions. This challenge was exacerbated by Chinese determination to avoid exploitation of Chinese for cheap labor and to prohibit Chinese inculcation of harmful foreign cultural traits. What has resulted from these conflicts is a process of negotiation for control of labor, involving foreign managers, Chinese management, party cells, unions, and local labor bureaus. Attitudes on both the Chinese and the foreign sides have changed throughout this process, with obstacles diminishing in quantity and intensity in the liberal areas of the Guangdong SEZs over the 1980s. In inland areas like Wuhan, where joint venture regulations were passed as recently as 1988, cultural differences are still pronounced, and bargaining over implementation of labor regulations remains evident.

In the mid-1980s in Guangdong, it was reported that in cases of dismissal, the local labor bureau had little incentive to extend approval, because it was then required to continue to pay wages to the dismissed employee until it could arrange alternative employment.[46] Recent interviews suggest that implementation of labor regulations has become less trying in general and that, in particular, there is little interference with dismissals. Joint venture representatives in Guangdong expressed no legal or cultural problems dismissing employees. It is normally done by the general manager after consultation with other management personnel. The labor bureau normally does not interfere with dismissal and is not responsible for the worker after she or he is dismissed. A Chinese manager in Foshan explained that it is best to wait until the term of a worker's contract is up before one lets the employee go.[47] Otherwise, the manager may be expected to find another position for the employee within the firm until the contract expires.[48] This manager had fired several employees and expressed no feelings of cultural embarrassment associated with losing face for disrupting enterprise harmony or social responsibility for the dismissed employee.

Difficulties in dismissals may arise if an employee has good contacts inside or outside the firm. One manager explained that "the workers who have connections will be less likely to put forth the effort of a peasant from the countryside without the right ties and protection."[49] It becomes difficult to discipline or dismiss these workers—despite low productivity or heinous behavior—-precisely because of their contacts.[50] Generally, however, there seems to be no local interference, and the managers express few of the cultural inhibitions associated with dismissals in China, especially in the less liberal inland areas like Wuhan.

Joint venture laws concerning employee dismissal in Wuhan follow a pattern similar to those in the Guangdong SEZs. However, interviews with joint venture managers in Wuhan suggest that dismissing an employee is still a very difficult task that must be handled with delicacy. One foreign manager explained that "firing an employee should not be a problem technically or theoretically," but that "personally, it was very disturbing to have tested the freedom of firing."[51] He expressed a feeling of "moral and social responsibility" that he had not felt elsewhere.[52] He did not detail the dismissal but indicated that he would not fire as readily in Wuhan as he would in other areas of the world (including Europe and Peru) where he had managed enterprises.[53] The dismissal was handled without consultation with the local labor bureau (earlier, he emphasized that he would not tolerate involvement from local authorities), which violated the law.[54] This, however, was not a concern. Rather, he expressed distress and sadness to see the effect of the dismissal on the rest of the employees: They became frightened that they might be next to be let go.[55] In fact, he believed that this one incident of dismissal "had really backfired."[56]

Another foreign joint venture manager in Wuhan suffered repercussions for the way he handled the dismissal of four of his employees. He consulted none of the other managers or the union. Without consensus, such an act becomes legally and culturally unacceptable. Furthermore, in dismissing them, he used the most radical language one can use to describe the act: *kaichu.*[57] The shock that resulted from the use of this term inspired him to use it as a threat to any employee who was uncooperative.[58] Soon, his company's headquarters in Beijing contacted him and explained that Wuhan authorities were concerned about his frequent use of the term and asked him to "please, stop using it."[59]

The experience led the manager to change his approach. After the firings, he restructured the employment contracts system and the firm's labor manual.[60] Unlike his approach to the dismissals, he sought the approval of a number of units inside and outside the joint venture through a "long process of consensus building," which he "hated."[61] Also, in order to avoid the obstacles involved in firing an employee, he established an "information area." If, after being warned, an employee continues to be problematic, the employee is sent to a dorm room, stripped of all responsibilities, and receives a substantial cut in salary.[62] The intention is to make the employee "lose face" and subsequently "just kind of disappear."[63]

Fundamentally differing values between Chinese and foreign parties concerning labor discipline and dismissal are evident in the inland city of Wuhan and throughout China. Although joint ventures are allowed to dismiss employees with the approval of a number of Chinese parties, in practice, differences between Chinese and foreign value systems concerning enterprise management in general and employee relations in particular often have precluded joint ventures from exercising that option. Instead, the situation has led to behavioral change among joint venture management and innovations like "information areas" that allow both sides to express dissatisfaction with an employee without enduring the face-losing, harmony-threatening act of dismissal. Indeed, the information area is a compromise between Chinese and foreign value systems. Rather than abruptly dismiss an unwanted employee, which is accepted as common practice in the West but is perceived in China as a rash act that threatens the harmony of enterprise operations, the joint venture management is able to ease a worker out of a particular position and indicate with the stripping of responsibilities, a forced change in residence, and significant cut in pay that the employee's presence in the enterprise is no longer desired.

Although employee dismissals seem still to be taboo in many parts of China, the practice has become more prevalent over the last few years, especially among older, inefficient state enterprises that are taken over by foreign interests. "Workers and cadres are finding themselves sacked or redeployed as the regime struggles to rationalize its bloated state-sector industries and 'Smash the Three Irons' (guaranteed employment, pay parity, and perks of position) in the workplace."[64] In the case of Wuhan's No. 2 Printing and Dyeing Company, for instance, which formed a joint venture with the Hongtex Development Company of Hong Kong, a new management team was given permission to run the enterprise as it saw fit and subsequently "layed off 1,200 of the factory's 1,900-strong workforce."[65] As reforms continue and the foreign-investment community grows in China, it will be interesting to observe the evolution of worker and management attitudes in Chinese industry.

Bargaining Over Social Welfare Benefits: The Union Retirement Fund, Insurance, and the Union

The local labor authorities are charged with the responsibility of collecting and distributing social welfare benefits. "Although the precise terms of the benefits are subject to negotiation, Chinese negotiators insist that the benefits provided in joint ventures must be at least as good as those in comparable state enterprises."[66]

One joint venture manager in Wuhan explained how he had bargained over a number of social welfare benefits. The bargaining did not always involve face-to-face negotiations between the two sides. Indeed, bargaining may only involve independently finding a way to avoid an inconvenient rule or regulation; if a joint venture is able to evade successfully an inconvenient rule or regulation without explicit disapproval from local authorities, or perhaps even with the silent cooperation of local authorities, one can conclude that a bargain has been struck. The tradeoff in its most basic form is that the joint venture remains in operation because the two parties are able to avoid a struggle over interpretation of an inconvenient rule or regulation by working out a way to ignore it without either side losing face in the process. In dialogue form, this process might, ideally, evolve this way:

> *Foreign Investor:* "As a foreign corporate representative, I have a management method that I must implement in the joint venture but that will conflict with one of your joint venture regulations; if I am not able to implement this strategy, managing the joint venture will be terribly difficult. Is there any way to accomplish my objective without violating your regulation and engaging in a struggle with you over it?"
>
> *Chinese Policy Implementer:* "Because I have the power to interpret this regulation and you have approached me in a nonadversarial manner, and a struggle between us would end up with both of us losing face, thereby causing strains in our relationship which will be crucial for the future success of the enterprise, you may implement your strategy without undue concern over interference from me or my colleagues, provided you meet this or that condition."

This interaction might occur implicitly, without the two sides ever openly discussing the conflict; thus, a solution to a conflict would have been struck through implicit bargaining.

In the case of the joint venture manager in Wuhan, his company had contracted to provide housing to its permanent employees.[67] However, it was becoming virtually impossible to provide the benefit due to a number of problems, including incompetent senior Chinese management, lack of space, and expense.[68] The solution that this foreign manager decided on was not to renegotiate the contracts but to stop hiring permanent employees and begin hiring lesser-paid, harder-working, temporary employees who do not receive the benefits that permanent employees receive.[69] Although his joint venture was under the restrictions of a labor plan, the foreign manager was able to implement his strategy without interference from the local labor bureau.[70]

Other examples of social welfare benefits that this manager bargained over were expatriate salary contributions to the union retirement fund, another requirement for additional contributions to the retirement fund, and insurance.[71]

Articles Twenty-one and Twenty-two of the Wuhan Local Laws specify the amount of and procedure to disburse welfare appropriations.[72] These funds are to be based on the enterprise's profit and used for the welfare of staff and workers.[73] The foreign manager had been told by local authorities that 2 percent of expatriate salaries had to be earmarked for the retirement fund.[74] The manager saw to it that this amount was paid until he learned from another local joint venture that it was not required to make payments from the expatriate salaries.[75] At the time of this revelation, the manager had already invested 20,000 *renminbi* from funds that included the expatriate salaries into the retirement account.[76] He planned to wait for the amount of time to pass that it would take for the percentage of wage contributions to equal 20,000 *renminbi* and then would resume 2 percent wage payments from the Chinese salaries only.[77] At the time, the local authorities had not responded to the stop in payments.[78] Nevertheless, he expected a battle when they discovered he was not making payments from the expatriate salaries.[79]

While the government feared the negative influences of foreign investment, their campaigns against bourgeois liberalization, spiritual pollution, and Westernization also encompassed crackdowns on Chinese bureaucratism and corruption that led to arrests and executions of tens of thousands of Chinese officials suspected of such crimes as bribery and embezzlement. It is no surprise, then, that foreigners seemed to be able to co-opt the support of Chinese authorities against rules, regulations, and other bureaucrats that were believed to be making unfair demands on joint ventures. Indeed, the evolution of the joint venture groups to contend with perceived unfair implementation of laws and policies was, in part, facilitated by an *ad hoc* recognition on the part of China's power authorities that the foreign investor sometimes required protection from unfair treatment by Chinese.

The foreign joint venture manager from Wuhan also explained that the local labor authorities attempted to make his joint venture pay it for unemployment insurance.[80] This manager insisted that there was no requirement that a company had to "buy into the insurance scheme of the city" and refused to pay.[81] Following the example of another local joint venture, he decided to purchase insurance directly from the People's Insurance Company of China, circumventing involvement from the local labor authorities.[82] No settlement had been reached at the time of this discussion.[83]

Foreign managers generally have no objection to paying for social welfare benefits. Although the collection and distribution of these benefits are controlled by Chinese authorities, the exact terms are often the objects of bargaining. Foreign innovations like the Joint Venture Organization give foreign managers considerable leverage to bargain with local authorities over terms that they perceive to be unreasonable.[84]

The Labor Union as an Object of Bargaining

Although the provisions of the 1983 Implementing Act vested substantial power in joint venture labor unions, they have not exerted much influence over joint venture affairs in day-to-day operations.[85] They have, in fact, become objects of bargaining that have allowed foreigners to negotiate "omission of contractual provisions" that extend to them a great deal of decision-making authority.[86]

The foreign general manager of a Wuhan joint venture refused demands by the local labor bureau for the establishment of a union in his enterprise.[87] He and the labor bureau negotiated the issue, and he finally agreed to allow the bureau to take an independent survey of the enterprise workers.[88] The bureau informed him that the results of the survey indicated that the employees wanted a union, and he agreed to allow them to establish one.[89] He remained skeptical of the union but hoped that he could use it as a tool of communication with the workers.[90]

The Chinese personnel manager of the joint venture saw the union's purpose to be to arrange activities for the workers.[91] The perception of this manager and his secretary (who was translating) was that the unions in China were much different from the unions in the United States. They perceived labor unions in the West to work against management through big strikes. Unions in China, they explained, wanted to work with management, to arrange activities for everyone in the enterprise.[92] In fact, he chuckled, the president of the union would serve concurrently as a manager in the company.[93]

Foreign managers expressed disdain for unions as a potential threat to management control of labor. The Chinese viewed them as benevolent mechanisms to unite management with labor through organization of various social activities. These fundamentally differing perceptions led to bargaining over the roles of unions. Ultimately, this process of negotiation led to the establishment of unions in joint ventures that did not exercise the considerable authority vested in them by law. A complacent and nondisruptive union is the compromise struck between the Chinese, who wanted institutions of administrative control in joint ventures to check foreign behavior and to act as potential barriers to foreign domination of joint venture management and exploitation of Chinese workers, and foreign investors concerned about having enough autonomy from the state to implement necessary operating and management procedures that would improve the chances of earning a profit. The complacent union satisfies the Chinese wish to have an administrative safeguard against foreign domination and the foreign desire to have enough control over operations not to have to go constantly to the union for approval or to have to worry about interference from the union every time a decision has to be made.

As of the end of 1993, there were indications that the roles of unions in joint ventures may have evolved somewhat from the time of my research in 1990–1992. It has been reported, for instance, that many partly foreign-owned factories were "increasingly beset by wildcat strikes," and that "in Tianjin alone, a dozen Japanese and South Korean-owned factories" had endured employee walkouts due to "poor working conditions."[94] Cognizant of the fact that "barely 30 percent of foreign joint ventures have been unionized," the *All China Federation of Trade Unions* (*ACFTU*) has initiated a call "for accelerated unionization of foreign joint ventures."[95] Whether these organizations grow stronger and evolve into powerful units that engage in collective bargaining with their Chinese and foreign managers is yet to be seen.

OTHER OBJECTS OF BARGAINING: TAXES AND FOREIGN EXCHANGE

Since 1979, the Chinese government has passed numerous tax laws for joint ventures. Implementation of these laws depends on bargaining between foreign partners and local policy implementers:

> Foreigners quickly learned that the Chinese would not necessarily interpret their tax laws in the same manner as a Western-trained lawyer. Rigorous statutory construction, no matter how logically impeccable or internally consistent, was not always persuasive in dealings with tax officials, nor was it necessarily probative in predicting a transaction's treatment.[96]

Bargaining over implementation of tax laws between foreign joint venture representatives and local officials became the norm during the 1980s.

The most liberal tax breaks in China are extended to export-oriented and technically advanced enterprises (EOEs and TAEs). Legislation at the national level has defined the requirements that an enterprise must meet to enjoy EOE and TAE classification, but power to grant this status often resides with local authorities. It is, therefore, at the local level where bargaining for EOE and TAE status between the Chinese and foreign sides takes place.

Negotiation for high-tech status is most apparent in Guangdong. Hong Kong investors know best how to elicit favorable tax treatment from local officials and all joint ventures enjoy control over their capital (especially their foreign exchange), and this allows them to entertain and reward local policy implementers on a much wider scale than, for instance, state enterprises. A frequent example of the joint venture type that will enjoy TAE status without being technically advanced is the joint venture that is involved with computer sales. Although many of these enterprises do not produce computer-related products, they are often able to obtain the "necessary paperwork" to warrant the special status.[97]

In Wuhan, bargaining over tax rates between local authorities and joint ventures is also common. Discussions with joint venture managers and local tax officials yielded insight into these bargaining processes. The experience of one manager, in particular, was quite revealing. The 1983 Implementing Act contained provisions that allowed joint venture exemption from the Commercial and Industrial Consolidated Tax (CIC).[98] One foreign manager in Wuhan has had a difficult time obtaining this benefit. He understood this tax of 5.05 percent of yearly profits to have "been on the books forever" when he discovered that another joint venture in the city had not been paying it since the early 1980s.[99] Local authorities repeatedly demanded that he pay the tax, but he refused: "I told them 'No! Take me to jail.' They hated me and later would not talk to me."[100] The manager went away for vacation, and while he was gone, the Chinese management buckled under local pressure and began paying the tax.[101] He "knew" that had he approached the authorities with a "wine them, dine them" attitude, he would not be paying the tax today.[102] That is, had he offered incentives in the form of gifts, he would have received the tax break without any problems.[103]

His strategy now would be to use official channels to obtain the break.[104] He submitted an application with the local tax authorities and hoped that they would apply for the tax break on his behalf with the central authorities in

Beijing.[105] However, relations between his firm and the local authorities had been damaged during their first exchange and had not yet been fully repaired. One of the officials refused to cooperate, although his superior and subordinate pledged their support for the manager's request.[106] Until a consensus was reached that included the middle bureaucrat, however, the tax would have to be paid.[107]

About one month after our first discussion, the manager attended a large meeting with officials from all over the city, including the mayor and the middle-level tax official.[108] At this meeting, the manager publicly criticized the tax authorities and made specific reference to the middle-level tax representative, making him "lose face . . . really big face."[109] Responding to this public criticism, the mayor subtly pledged his support for the manager's position by directing a comment at the tax official that included the admonition, "We have to be better than other areas of China with respect to our joint venture policies."[110] The manager believed it would be only a matter of time before the tax authorities cooperated.[111]

The process of bargaining in which this manager engaged indicates the willingness of Chinese authorities to recognize when foreigners are being treated unfairly by local rules and regulations and to extend support to the foreign partner as that partner tries to influence implementation of the regulations. However, it also suggests the importance of maintaining good relations with local authorities and how strains in these relationships may adversely affect a venture's chances of receiving favorable implementation of a certain rule or regulation. Although there was wide agreement that such bargaining occurs frequently, it was interesting to hear a different perspective from an official representative of Wuhan's local tax bureau.

Generally, high-technology enterprises will be granted TAE status without question. In Wuhan, the decision to grant tax benefits to joint ventures rests with the Wuhan Municipal Tax Bureau.[112] Their decisions are based on recommendations made by the Foreign Economic Commission in conjunction with the State Scientific Commission and their branch offices in Wuhan.[113] The tax bureau official dismissed the joint venture manager's assertion that a "wine them, dine them" approach to the tax authorities would lead to tax breaks.[114] Rather, the law makes provisions for bargaining for TAE status.[115] Also, the local tax authorities see their first responsibility as helping local joint ventures and are, therefore, always willing to negotiate tax breaks with enterprises that need them.[116]

The official explained that bargaining for high-tech status is not uncommon.[117] There are 11 industry types designated by the State Scientific Commission as high tech:

1. high technology: special science
2. electronic information testing
3. optical fiber
4. biological
5. natural science
6. energy
7. environmental
8. earth science
9. physical science
10. medical science
11. other[118]

The eleventh category is open for joint ventures that wish to negotiate for TAE status but that do not fall into any of the other ten categories.[119]

If an enterprise is having problems earning a profit or paying taxes, the local authorities may go to Beijing at the bureau's own expense to discuss the problem with the State Taxation Bureau.[120] The State Taxation Bureau may contact the joint venture directly or through official channels to get more details and subsequently make a decision on the request.[121] Furthermore, the government wants to know about problems enterprises are having and, therefore, holds a meeting every third month with local officials and joint venture representatives (it was in this forum that the joint venture manager criticized local authorities for not cooperating with his request for help with the application for exemption from the CIC tax) to proffer complaints.[122]

The Chinese see taxes as a source of capital, while foreigners view them as obstacles to earning a profit. These conflicting views, combined with innumerable legal ambiguities, result in considerable bargaining over tax terms. The most important factors in bargaining with authorities are good personal relationships and a need for help with paying taxes. Chinese laws have been drafted to accommodate demands for negotiation over taxes, and government-sponsored forums have been established to hear the demands of joint ventures concerning implementation of tax laws. These innovations satisfy foreign parties who may believe that they are being treated unfairly and Chinese who want to maintain control over the process of negotiating taxes. Not only do these innovations shed light on the ways foreigners bargain with the Chinese over implementation of tax laws, it is indicative of the willingness of both parties to compromise on the conflicting objectives they have in investing in joint ventures. The Chinese use taxes as a tool to obtain foreign capital, to control the amount of capital the foreign party is able to extract from China, and to prevent the joint venture from earning too great a profit. Foreigners, however, are able to utilize their resources to pressure the Chinese to extend special tax benefits that ease the financial burden of both parties in the enterprise and afford the joint venture a greater opportunity to earn a profit in a highly restricted commercial arena where achieving this objective requires a herculean effort.

Bargaining over taxes between local-level policy implementers and Sino-foreign joint ventures is the likely result of several factors. Differing views of taxes and conflicting objectives between the Chinese and foreign parties have been the source of bargaining over national-level formulation of tax legislation *and* local-level implementation of the consequent tax regulations. Decentralization and legal ambiguities have meant that provincial and local governments deviate from the national laws and draft legislation that fits their own unique objectives. Legislative ambiguity and decision-making decentralization have also meant that bargaining between interested parties (most notably, local Chinese policy implementers and joint venture representatives) over interpretation of tax laws substantially influences implementation of these rules and regulations.

Foreign Exchange Requirements as Objects of Bargaining

The Chinese objective of attracting hard currency and the conflicting foreign objective of earning a profit are most evident in negotiations over foreign exchange. Although foreign-exchange regulations have been liberalized since the 1979 Joint Venture Law, they are generally strictly enforced, with official recommendations for balancing foreign exchange precluding substantial explicit bargaining over the terms. Considering the number of joint ventures that are not able to meet the Chinese foreign-exchange requirements but remain in operation, it is not surprising that enterprises have devised numerous methods to negotiate the foreign-exchange terms.

As of 1988, 4,000 foreign-invested enterprises were in operation, but only about one-third were "maintaining a positive balance between foreign-exchange revenues and expenditures," according to MOFERT.[123] Because of the inconvertibility of the *renminbi,* foreigners are hard-pressed to come up with the hard currency required to pay expatriate salaries, buy raw materials and equipment, and remit profits abroad. Officially recommended solutions include: making contractual commitments to export in the future,[124] trading currencies with other joint ventures or at other recently established swap centers, developing import-substitution products, engaging in direct foreign exchange sales, investing in other foreign-exchange-rich enterprises like hotels, and buying Chinese goods for exports.[125] At the end of 1993, foreign-invested enterprises continued to face foreign-exchange problems. Most relied on several methods to obtain foreign exchange. Especially important have been local swap centers where foreign enterprises can exchange *renminbi* for hard currencies.[126] However, volatile exchange rates and unpredictable monetary policies mean that hard currencies are often in short supply, so foreign-invested enterprises must be constantly aware that their cash supply lines are never completely reliable.

Two MNC representatives explained that they overcame their foreign-exchange dilemmas using aspects of several of the above solutions.[127] They established *two-tier joint ventures.*[128] In one case, the top tier is a 70 percent-30 percent joint venture with a Western trading company in China, with the MNC as the majority holder.[129] The role of the trading company is to raise the necessary amount of foreign exchange required by Chinese law.[130] The manufacturing joint venture (which represents the second tier of the two-tier joint venture) is one established between the top tier (55 percent) and a factory in Guangzhou (40 percent) and the city of Huangpu (5 percent).[131] The structure of the joint venture leaves the MNC with a share of less than 50 percent, but with majority holdings in the top tier.[132] The relationship has worked well, with a representative of the Western trading company on the board of directors with the responsibility of raising the foreign exchange.[133] This MNC representative also stressed the importance of good relations with local suppliers.[134] His corporation contracted a local supplier (a soft-drink can factory) to install a line for the production of plastic bottles to package the product.[135] The arrangement allows the MNC to boast its contribution to the local economy while also establishing an important source of savings on foreign-exchange expenditures.[136] All firms, however, have not been as successful as this MNC in creating methods to meet foreign-exchange requirements.[137]

In many other instances, officially recommended prescriptions may actually encourage legally ignoring foreign-exchange requirements until an unspecified future date. The solution of contractually pledging to export in the future is one such example. One representative explained that in his joint venture's contract they included a phrase that closely approximated the following: "It is the intention of this joint venture to export x percent in the future."[138] However, this joint venture had been established to manufacture a product explicitly for sale to a city in China, and at the time there was no intention to export in the future.[139]

Constraints associated with China's political system may also encourage local policymakers to be lenient in implementing foreign-exchange regulations. The most prominent example was a recently established joint venture in Wuhan that had been rocked by unpredictable monetary policy in the form of a *renminbi* devaluation in June 1990.[140] Everything in the contract, including raw materials and production costs, had been specified when the *renminbi* devaluation was announced.[141] This forced the foreign partners to make adjustments in the original plan, including new price estimates that skyrocketed and shocked their Chinese colleagues inside and outside the firm.[142] The enterprise had planned to sell its product to the Ministry of Water Resources and Production in Wuhan.[143] If they now decided to buy much cheaper products from a local state enterprise, the joint venture would collapse.[144]

Firm Chinese commitment to foreign-exchange requirements precluded explicit bargaining over them. However, the Chinese encouraged implicit bargaining in the form of officially prescribed solutions that allowed enterprises to delay balancing their foreign exchange until unspecified future dates. In cases when the Chinese political system adversely affects the foreign-exchange plans of a joint venture, local officials may be lenient in implementation of the foreign-exchange requirements. Together, the parties have developed these innovations to satisfy the Chinese demand for foreign capital and the foreign desire for at least limited access to the Chinese marketplace.

BARGAINING STRATEGIES

Successful bargaining may depend on the strategies one employs. Throughout my research I found that foreign representatives often relied on good personal relationships, a sensitivity to Chinese cultural values, effective lawyers, and joint venture groups to increase their bargaining strength vis-à-vis the Chinese political system.

Personal Relationships

The most important strategy for Sino-foreign joint ventures to elicit favorable implementation of laws, rules, regulations, and policies from local authorities is to establish good, personal relationships with strategically located individuals in business, government, and bureaucracy who may be able to influence outcomes of questions and disputes in favor of the enterprise. Throughout my research on Sino-foreign joint ventures, personal relationships were found to be crucial in accomplishing several objectives, including obtaining permission to recruit potential employees on college campuses, making official arrangements to move a temporary employee's household registration from one part of the country to another, obtaining necessary permission to change employment from a state enterprise to a joint venture, negotiating tax breaks, procuring resources, getting a job in a joint venture, and marketing joint venture products.

For the foreign manager, establishing these all-important ties depends largely on finding a Chinese manager in the firm who can be considered a trusted friend. Indeed, one foreign joint venture manager wrote that one should "ensure that among . . . local management staff there is one individual who has maturity, experience dealing with the bureaucracy, good people and business instincts, and is completely trustworthy."[145] This echoed the sentiments of numerous foreign representatives with whom I spoke. In one joint venture, the foreign manager's secretary represented the trusted confidant.[146] In a second, all members of the Chinese management team seemed to be deeply trusted, while the security manager seemed to have become a good friend of the foreign management team.[147] In another case, a foreign corporate representative explained that in negotiating a Sino-foreign joint venture in China, his negotiating team placed a great deal of trust in a MOFERT representative who guided them through China's complex bureaucracy, assisted in interpreting various joint venture rules and regulations, and ultimately overcame numerous obstacles for the foreign negotiating team.[148]

Relationship Maintenance in the PRC

Lampton has demonstrated that it is often difficult to differentiate between legal and illegal bargaining activity.[149] It is, therefore, imperative that the foreign investor understand that as crucial as personal relationships are to business success in China, it is critical to use discretion in nurturing and cultivating these associations.

When foreign investors establish joint ventures with Chinese partners, it is likely that the foreign parties are comparatively rich and their colleagues comparatively poor, although this situation is one that is in constant evolution as more and more Chinese entrepreneurs become China's wealthy *nouveaux riches*. It is important that foreign partners, in exchange for the generous hospitality that they likely will receive while in China, be prepared to reciprocate proportionately the Chinese investment in the relationship. Depending on the nature of the venture and the financial wherewithal of the foreign partner, a highly appropriate sign of good faith is to sponsor a representative or delegation of representatives from the Chinese side to visit the foreign party's home country. Officially, the purpose of the trip must contribute to the success of the joint venture (e.g., management training, attending trade shows, etc.); unofficially, however, the foreign side should make arrangements for the Chinese to enjoy as many recreational activities as possible (e.g., sightseeing, trips to different cities, etc.). These trips may last a few weeks or a few months. In the case of a small 11-year joint venture, initial trips made by Chinese representatives lasted only a few weeks,[150] while another American corporation hosted delegations for six-month management-training periods.[151] Whether the trip is intended more for pleasure or business, most Chinese rarely even have the chance to go abroad and, therefore, will cherish any opportunity to do so. Such trips are not only worthwhile investments in valuable relationships with Chinese colleagues, but also will help to solidify a foundation of trust that will lead to introductions to other valuable contacts, who will also contribute to achieving commercial objectives in an environment where personal relationships are crucial for achieving business success.

The most extravagant gift-giving should be reserved for primary Chinese contacts associated with the joint venture. Relationships with secondary contacts in the government and bureaucracy are also important and, therefore, also require nurturing. Although bribery is neither suggested nor condoned, it is apparent that gift-giving in the form of outright cash payments is an effective way for foreign investors to elicit cooperation and, perhaps, extra effort from bureaucrats charged with assisting the foreign investor with any number of tasks. In winter 1993, I observed a series of meetings between Chinese managers of a joint venture and the enterprise's foreign investor (who is a native Chinese), as well as representatives from a local government branch who were supposed to assist the joint venture with some important business-related activities. During the course of one of these meetings, one of the bureaucratic representatives spoke of bribery (*huilu*) on several occasions, bluntly explaining that in order to carry out several assignments within the time frame expected, not only would they (the bureaucrats) require financial incentives, but so would a number of other parties who would be involved in the processes. Later, the foreign investor explained that the amount of money required to obtain the *timely* cooperation of the bureaucrats was only a few hundred *renminbi* and that this should be expected in the same way that a government agency in a so-called legal-rational society might charge an extra fee for expediting a task. In the unique context of the Chinese socio-economic realm, "bribery" may not connote an illegal activity but, rather, a legitimate fee for the extra services of a local bureaucratic agency.[152] One primary example, discussed earlier, regarding the damage that can be done to a relationship if a foreign partner does not understand the cultural nuances of conducting business in China concerns the foreign joint venture manager who undermined his firm's relationship with local tax authorities by refusing to pay a particular tax from which the firm should have been exempted by law.

Although bargaining and gift-giving remain important ways to maintain relationships in China, the foreign investor must beware that the style employed is not offensive to Chinese colleagues and does not create the impression that the boundary between legitimate and illegitimate bargaining is crossed. It seems that gift-giving becomes bribery when the size of the gift is relatively substantial and, more importantly, relevant authorities *perceive* a crime to have taken place.[153]

Even if one is cautious not to cross these subjective boundaries between legitimate and illegitimate bargaining, however, other considerations are also important. Chinese expectation of reciprocation for special efforts undertaken on behalf of the joint venture or foreign partner will not be stated as overtly as the local bureaucrat who suggested bribery (*huilu*) to accomplish a particular objective.[154] Because perception is so extremely important, it is crucial that the process of relationship creation and maintenance *never* appear shady. In fact, a tactless approach by a foreign partner is precisely what might lead a local official or business contact to reject a request for a favor by a joint venture representative.[155] Foreign investors must assume that when a Chinese colleague makes special arrangements on their behalf, the colleague goes into debt to any number of parties who contribute to the effort. Foreigners must be highly cognizant of subtle suggestions offered by Chinese counterparts indicating the level of difficulty involved in performing a special task and should be willing to offer compensation or to entertain suggestions for compensation before and after the task has been completed. Also, one must be careful to choose at least one dependable contact. Time and again, foreign joint venture representatives (especially those with little previous experience in China) stressed that it is critical to have at least one person who is completely trustworthy and through whom other important contacts can be made.[156] By limiting one's trusted personal contacts, one does not risk becoming indebted to numerous persons who believe they have established long-term relationships with an investor only to find out that their time and energy have been wasted on a socially overextended foreigner. Sincerity and cultural sensitivity are also important. If, for whatever reason, foreign investors have no intention of nurturing and sustaining a relationship with a Chinese counterpart after a certain short-term task has been completed, they should make clear what their intentions are, and arrangements on compensation should be negotiated and reached. If there is a *sincere* desire to establish a long-term, fruitful, and mutually beneficial relationship with a Chinese counterpart, the parties may enjoy countless personal and professional rewards over a long period of time. However, these relationships require constant attention and cultivation; foreigners must exhibit scrupulous cultural sensitivity when establishing relationships and must use discretion when bargaining over perceived fair compensation for Chinese efforts on their behalf.

At a time of increasing government attention to corruption, a changing view of customs surrounding bargaining and gift-giving, and the lack of definitions of what exactly constitutes illegitimate activity (i.e., bribery and embezzlement), foreign investors must prepare themselves well before entering a very complex Chinese commercial arena.[157]

Sensitivity to Chinese Values

Establishing a personal relationship (*guanxi*) is the first step in an ongoing process that requires constant nurturing and cultivation. Consciously or not, foreign corporations have developed means to achieve this end. One representative of a Western corporation that has had enormous success in joint venture operations and sales in China stressed that sensitivity to Chinese values is important to overcome obstacles in bargaining and gave two examples, in particular, that highlighted this sensitivity.

Throughout China's history, a major concern has been to deflect foreign interference in its internal affairs.[158] In June 1989, responding to international outcries against the incident of June 4 at Tiananmen Square in Beijing, the Chinese leadership warned against foreign meddling in China's internal affairs. Despite assurances by the government that foreign investments were not in danger, foreign companies withdrew personnel and, fearing damage to their international reputations, remained distant until the political winds had calmed.

One Western corporation, however, followed a different policy. In July 1989, confident of local assurances that investments would remain safe and operations would continue without central interference, the corporation sent a delegation to China to assure its joint venture partners that it would not back out of the project and that production should proceed as planned.[159] The Chinese were thrilled with the company's willingness to remain in China at a time when others were leaving and agreed to the following conditions for the delegation's trip: (1) no press coverage; (2) no official banquets;

and (3) the Chinese side would take all blame for delays that resulted from the Tiananmen incident and its ensuing political turmoil.

Originally, the parties had been able to arrange sufficient foreign exchange to establish the joint venture and to begin production, while provincial authorities would allocate the necessary funds to cover a subsequent shortage of local capital. The relationship between the foreign corporation and provincial authorities was good, but, after Tiananmen, provincial authorities were unable to procure the promised capital—perhaps, the corporation's representative speculated, as a result of a lack of cooperation from central authorities.[160] Provincial authorities in Guangdong proceeded to work with Hong Kong officials and eventually succeeded in arranging the necessary financing for the project. The representative believed that the persistence of the provincial authorities, despite possible disapproval from central authorities, was due, in part, to the company's policy of separating politics from business and trying to keep things moving according to plan even during the tumultuous months of spring and summer 1989.[161]

A recognition of the values of consensus and status equality between foreign investors and Chinese counterparts is also a crucial ingredient in maintaining good relationships. The foreign corporation undertook a conscious and determined effort to include the Chinese at every step of the negotiation and establishment process for a joint manufacturing venture as well as a joint technology-transfer agreement, which called for two groups of four management trainees and an interpreter to come to the United States for two months of advanced technical training. For practical business reasons that were compatible with important cultural concerns, the corporation called for increasing the managers' training time to six months. Stressing the importance of appreciating the Chinese values of consensus and status equality,[162] the representative explained that including the Chinese side at every step of the process was necessary.[163] Therefore, the foreign side sent a delegation to explain the decision for increased training time in great detail. The representative reported that including the Chinese side in this manner made a good impression on them and was an important ingredient in developing trust in the relationship. Another practical advantage of the decision was that the increased training time allowed the foreign corporation to house the Chinese in apartments where they felt at home and enjoyed such benefits as doing their own cooking.

Gaining knowledge about the Chinese marketplace and culture takes time and hard work. The corporation hired a Chinese-American who had lived in China for 18 years, before moving to the United States, to offer cultural and linguistic advice to the delegations. Also, the representative with whom I spoke made the decision to take Chinese classes at night at a local university for two years while he was engaged in market research and negotiations in China.

A sensitivity to Chinese cultural values is imperative for successful relationship maintenance and bargaining in China. Before going abroad, many foreign executives must participate in seminars to learn about the intricacies of conducting business in the countries where they are going. These programs aim to suppress "a conditioned propensity on the part of . . . personnel to think in ethnocentric or geographically nearsighted terms."[164] Even if one is well-prepared for the cultural nuances of local commercial bargaining in China, however, at least one completely trustworthy personal contact is crucial for thoroughly accurate interpretation and understanding of the economic and political environment. Ultimately, one's bargaining success will depend on one's preparation and the strength of one's personal contacts.

Lawyers

During negotiation, one representative said, "the biggest mistake you can make is to stop in Hong Kong and pick up a Chinese-speaking lawyer."[165] It was instructive to note, he explained, that Japan still requires visiting foreign lawyers to obtain visas before entering the country. It is a fundamental reality of Asian culture in general, and Chinese culture in particular, he insisted, that one can negotiate a deal most effectively when there is enough trust between the parties that a verbal agreement is as good as a written contract.[166]

Another representative believed that his company should have consulted more with a Chinese legal expert in private during the negotiation stage of his joint venture.[167] However, he said, bringing a Chinese-speaking lawyer to the negotiating table inhibited the prospective partners from speaking freely. The company's Chinese-speaking lawyer proceeded to engage the Chinese delegation in debate over a number of minute details. The Chinese became very frustrated, and, he continued, "the arrogant bastard almost scuttled the deal."[168] The best use for a lawyer at the negotiation stage is for consultation away from the bargaining table. If the lawyer is present at the negotiating table, one foreign representative suggested, the individual should be introduced as a representative of the company and should act as a negotiator and consultant, not a litigator.[169]

One joint venture manager, in particular, stressed that every joint venture should have a Chinese lawyer "if for no other reason than to supervise the hundreds of contracts you go through here."[170] The contracts this manager signed with the city government have been no problem, with each side living up to its responsibilities. Contracts with other units, however, "are usually not worth the paper they're written on," and for this reason many disputes arise.[171] In one instance, this manager signed a contract with the "mayor" of a small village that adjoined the city property where his joint venture was located. The contract called for the village to allow the construction of a water pump on its land for a certain sum of money. The pump had been built and was operating when the official who had signed the contract died. The new village mayor demanded extra money to keep the pump running. The joint venture manager explained that a contract had been signed with the former mayor, but the new mayor responded that since the other had died, the contract was no longer valid. The manager refused to pay the extra money, and the township shut down the water pump. Soon thereafter, the manager hired an experienced lawyer to negotiate a settlement. The problem had not been solved at the time of our last conversation, but the manager has used this lawyer since to supervise the formulation and implementation of contracts signed between his joint venture and other units. The role of the lawyer in the joint venture is to advise the foreign partner and to bargain on the joint venture's behalf.

There are numerous reasons why the role of the lawyer in China is often limited to consultation and bargaining on behalf of the joint venture. First, foreign (especially Western) investors must appreciate the difference between the roles of Chinese lawyers and of those trained in an Anglo-Western tradition. The most appreciable difference is that Chinese lawyers, by and large, "practice within a collective work system,"[172] where they "represent the facts not the client" and "are the legal workers of the state."[173] It is precisely due to their obligation to the state, one American negotiator explained, that Chinese lawyers are very hesitant to get involved with China's legal system, especially on behalf of a foreign corporate interest.[174] Indeed, in this environment, another Chinese manager insisted, the chances for a foreign corporation to win a suit against a Chinese entity are slim.[175] This does not mean that a foreign party cannot win in China; however, it *is* required that the parties try conciliation before litigation, largely due to questions concerning a foreign party's chances of getting a fair trial in a Chinese court.

The Chinese court system often, in fact, is not sophisticated enough to render competent decisions concerning joint venture disputes. The Chinese courts are often unable to award lost profits because they lack an appropriate system of calculation.[176] Furthermore, trials can last a very long time, and even after judgement is rendered, the parties are allowed to appeal, at which time they inevitably will be ordered by the court to attempt to solve disputes on their own through conciliation.[177]

The importance of personal relationships and of achieving ends through the "back door" (*houtai*) in order to avoid Chinese legal and administrative channels is also a reason that the lawyer's role is one of consultation and bargaining. One Chinese manager, for instance, explained that to obtain resources that were unavailable to the joint venture through the central economic plan, it might have to negotiate a deal with another enterprise that has the necessary documentation (*piwen*) to purchase the goods.[178] Such a transaction may be undertaken by a lawyer with the necessary connections to make the appropriate arrangements.

Legal connections also may be crucial in understanding important internal (*neibu*) laws that are concealed from foreign eyes and in working out legal ambiguities in favor of the joint venture. A manager in Shekou explained that the foreign and Chinese sides in a board of directors meeting in her joint venture each had a lawyer taking notes.[179] When the two lawyers read their notes at the end of the meeting (to write the minutes), their versions were completely different. The manager, who had a master's degree in law from a Chinese university, was asked to present her notes, and the two sides accepted her version as the basis for the minutes of the meeting. This example highlights the very different perceptions that Chinese and foreign partners might have concerning laws and the importance of someone with substantial judicial knowledge who can bargain effectively for legal interpretations that favor the joint venture.

Collective Bargaining: The Evolution of the Joint Venture Group

An effective bargaining strategy that foreigners developed over the course of the 1980s involved the creation of joint venture groups that make demands on local authorities to respond to their needs. These groups consist of foreign and Chinese representatives of local joint ventures who meet on a regular basis to discuss issues and problems of common concern, make demands on local authorities to respond to their inquiries and complaints, and attempt to influence the policy process at the local level.

As foreigners grew weary of gouging by local officials and frequent inaction to remedy the situation by central authorities, they took action independent of the government, teaming up with each other to create joint venture groups which collectively make demands on local authorities to recognize and correct improper treatment of foreign investors. Not only does this indicate a recognition on the part of the foreign investor that one must be prepared to mobilize resources to bargain with shrewd and cautious local authorities, it also indicates a willingness on the part of the Chinese to compromise their own commitment not to allow foreigners to turn their economic power into political power; that is, using their resources to influence Chinese policy making and political decisions that serve foreign interests at the expense of Chinese interests:

> [This] broad concern, which grew out of the legacy of anti-imperialism, was that foreigners, through ownership of assets located in China, would be able to translate control over investments into political power. Once in such a position, foreigners might deprive the government of its authority to direct the economy toward its own goals, and possibly even threaten its political authority. Conservative leaders in particular worried that neither the times nor the country had changed drastically enough to eliminate concerns about foreign domination. Reformist leaders countered this with their argument that China's socialism, and its ability to protect China's political independence, rendered foreign political intervention unlikely.[180]

In Wuhan, there are two joint venture groups. One is the Organization of Joint Ventures and the other is a "sort of chamber of commerce in Hankou."[181] The Organization of Joint Ventures consists of approximately 40 members and meets about once each month to discuss joint venture problems and potential solutions.[182] One complaint openly discussed in this forum was a recently passed local law that required joint ventures to pay an increased amount of money into the retirement fund of the local labor bureau. I spoke with the vice president of this organization, and he speculated that local authorities had anticipated joint venture opposition to the law and, therefore, had gone to the Bank of China to have the funds automatically removed from the joint venture accounts.[183] The Organization of Joint Ventures approached the Bank of China and had their accounts frozen so that local authorities could not continue to extract funds. Furthermore, the organization succeeded in forcing authorities to suspend the law and anticipated a battle for a permanent reversal.[184]

Recently, a battle over a social welfare requirement perceived by foreign investors to be unfair was, in fact, already being waged. The local government passed a law that required joint ventures to pay an added amount of money (the amount was not specified) into the union retirement fund.[185] The local labor bureau, the manager speculated, anticipated opposition from local joint ventures and went to the local branch of the Bank of China to extract funds from the joint venture bank accounts.[186]

The organization also acts as a consulting body for the local government.[187] In another interview, a Chinese manager explained that joint ventures can influence the policy process. Before the government announces a new policy regarding joint ventures, it normally listens to complaints and suggestions voiced by joint venture representatives, local university personnel, and government officials. The government may respond with policy changes.

Organizations established in the Tianjin Economic Development Area (TEDA) include the Industrial Commercial Association and the Foreign Investors Union.[188] The Foreign Investors Union is similar to the Organization of Joint Ventures in Wuhan. Joint venture representatives meet on a regular basis to discuss common problems and possible solutions, and may influence local authorities to respond to their concerns with law and policy initiatives. Representatives from the Policy Research Office of the Administrative Commission of TEDA attend these meetings and take notes on the problems discussed.[189] If the Policy Research Office representatives conclude that a law should be passed to address a particular problem, it will write an opinion and address it to the Administrative Commission of TEDA. Depending on the nature of the issue, the Policy Research Office will work with one of the other departments in the Administrative Commission (Industrial, Commercial, Personnel, Finance, Planning, or Technology and Science) to decide on appropriate action. The Policy Research Office then may visit one or more joint ventures to obtain details about the problem. The Research Office may develop a law in cooperation with an agency of 13 lawyers in the Administrative Bureau that addresses the complaint originally voiced at the meeting of the Foreign Investors Union.[190]

The evolution of a system of collective bargaining that allows foreign commercial interests to influence local-level policy making and implementation in China is a remarkable development in a communist nation, characterized by a political system closed to the outside world until just over a decade ago, and a notoriously perplexing and impenetrable social and political culture. China-watchers and foreign investors should monitor closely the growth of this fascinating system of collective bargaining and should study further the role of joint venture groups in policy implementation in China.

Joint Venture Bargaining Strategies: Conclusion

The importance of establishing personal relationships in China cannot be overemphasized. Establishment, however, must be followed by a long, continuous process of cultivation in order that they may flourish and yield positive benefits for all parties concerned. Successful strategies for relationship maintenance are contingent on discretion and an all-important sensitivity to Chinese cultural values.

A cursory examination of joint venture policy implementation in China reveals a legal system fraught with ambiguity that encourages free-wheeling bargaining over rules and regulations through personal contacts beyond administrative boundaries. Lawyers can play crucial roles as negotiators and consultants in these bargaining processes, but litigation represents a galaxy of unpredictability into which foreign joint venture partners are advised against entering.

Instead of engaging China's local bureaucracy individually, in fact, joint ventures have teamed up with one another to form joint venture groups that facilitate a process of collective bargaining. Interviews with group participants indicate that these organizations have proved to be effective vehicles for influencing local-level policy making and implementation. Further research should be conducted on these structures as they grow in scope and popularity throughout China.

CONCLUSION

The conflicting objectives of Chinese and foreign joint venture parties often are resolved through bargaining over implementation of joint venture rules and regulations. Foreign interests include earning profits by eventually accessing China's domestic market, achieving autonomy from the state in enterprise operations, and affecting cultural change in labor to develop a quality-conscious and productive work force. Chinese seek foreign capital, management techniques, and technology, but they also want to prevent their workers from adopting perceived harmful foreign cultural traits.

The Chinese government has drafted legislation to create a favorable environment for the foreign investor and, at the same time retain ultimate decision-making control in its own hands. Because foreigners possess wares that the government needs for modernization, they use this as leverage in bargaining that results from legal ambiguities, systemic constraints and differences in cultural values. Although ultimate power over almost all aspects of joint venture operations legally resides with Chinese authorities, the struggle for control means perpetual bargaining among a number of parties. This bargaining often leads to interesting outcomes in the form of power-sharing innovations—like "information areas" for workers who cannot be fired because of traditional Chinese values but are viewed negatively by the foreign management—that satisfy the objectives and values of both parties.

Issue areas discussed in this article include labor, taxes, and foreign exchange. An examination of the battle over labor reveals foreign and Chinese desire for control over employment decisions, the cultural differences between the two sides, and the management innovations that resulted to satisfy the conflicting views. [190] The two parties have had to struggle for control in all areas of labor relations and have developed various ways to share power. In the area of recruitment, for example, in order to preempt the state from assigning jobs to graduating college students before they have the chance to contemplate potential joint venture employment, foreign representatives from at least one foreign corporation with joint venture agreements in Guangdong have begun to recruit on college campuses, using such Western approaches as handing out literature about the corporation to students in their dormitory rooms. In hiring procedures, furthermore, foreign representatives have also been successful in implementing screening procedures (i.e., tests and interviews), despite initial Chinese opposition at the beginning of the Open Door policy and in Wuhan as late as 1991. [191]

In all areas of labor relations, it seems, foreign representatives have had to bargain with Chinese managers and local labor representatives for some control over such labor processes as recruiting, hiring, and firing. The innovations that the foreign representatives have developed often allow them to implement their management strategies without explicit violation of Chinese laws or cultural values.

A review of taxes and foreign exchange reveals how legal ambiguities invite foreigners to bargain with local officials over requirements that, at first glance, may seem impossible to meet. Innovations in these areas have also been developed; most notably, I believe, is the two-tier joint venture, which makes it possible for at least two joint ventures, with which I am familiar through interviews, to meet their foreign-exchange requirements. However, negotiations do not always resolve differences but may lead to patchwork solutions — like including contractual provisions that indicate an intention on the part of the foreign partner ultimately to export goods to earn enough foreign exchange to meet China's legal requirements when no such intention exists — that allow enterprises to continue to operate without firmly addressing the issues. This type of outcome echoes in China is reminiscent of Lampton's conclusion about Chinese bargaining—that there is often "an indeterminacy to outcomes," as "the same issues seem to rise like Lazarus on the agenda, they never stay buried." [192] Although most joint ventures in China are now able to stay in operation using a variety of devices to evade foreign-exchange requirements, which were devised through implicit bargaining between them and the Chinese government, explicitly these requirements have not been suspended and always threaten to reappear as issues of contention between the two parties throughout the joint venture term. At the very least, the foreign-exchange issue is a potential bargaining chip for the Chinese; for now, however, it is an inconvenient rule that the Chinese have agreed to overlook in many cases as long as the foreign parties operate in good faith and at least pay lip service to the Chinese request that they will eventually meet the requirements of the foreign-exchange regulations.

Throughout the course of the joint venture term, attitudes among Chinese and foreigners change. Foreign managers become more sensitive to the cultural values of the Chinese and adapt their behavior accordingly, and the Chinese gain appreciation for novel approaches to management that compete with their own ideas of how things should be run. The two sides often agree to compromise their foreign-investment objectives as well as aspects of their value systems as a result of the bargaining process.

5

The Primacy of *Guanxi* (Personal Relationships) and Other Sources of Variation

INTRODUCTION

The most important source of variation in bargaining between the joint venture and local policy implementers is the nature of the personal relationships that the enterprise has. In China, accomplishing goals through networking and "*guanxi*" (relationships) in order to bypass administrative and bureaucratic channels is a widespread practice with a very long history.[1] One observer defined several types of these relationships in business, kinship relations, neighborly relations, and social relations.[2] In business, as well as society in general, in order to bypass legal and bureaucratic obstacles (often referred to as proceeding through the "back door" [*houtai*]), "network building is used (consciously or unconsciously) by Chinese adults as a cultural strategy in mobilizing resources for goal attainment."[3] Since the beginning of the Open Door in 1979, the role of such interpersonal relations has increased in popularity in the commercial sector despite the construction of a legal framework and official policies designed to diminish and condemn the practice:

> During this rapid transition stage when the socialist universalistic values are cast into doubt and the market is not yet fully opened, *guanxi* blossoms to play a new instrumental role for people to achieve what is normally denied them through normal channels.[4]

Thus, when a foreign joint venture partner attempts to obtain raw materials for production outside official administrative channels and must utilize the strategy of bargaining with another enterprise for the necessary documentation (*piwen*) to acquire the desired goods, a personal relationship with someone in that enterprise must be established in order to close the deal.[5] Often, the foreign partner will have to rely on Chinese within the joint venture to use their own personal contacts to make contact with another enterprise. One vivid example from my own findings is the Sino-European joint venture that had prepared to produce a product for sale to a local ministry; despite impending time constraints, no meeting could be established with the ministry because no one at the joint venture had a personal contact who could make the appropriate arrangements with the necessary personnel.[6]

Indeed, "the first rule of the game" when forming a joint venture in which a district takes a 10 percent to 40 percent share is to establish good relations with local authorities.[7] This may involve "both direct and indirect subsidies, such as keeping several district officials on the joint venture payroll as 'consultants.' "[8] If a joint venture does not compensate local authorities in one way or another, it will risk failure.

A joint venture's personal relationships influence other important variables that affect local bargaining processes. Among those that I discovered were the amount of time a joint venture has been in existence, joint venture type, and mood of the central authorities.

PERSONAL RELATIONSHIPS, JOINT VENTURE TYPE, AND LEADERSHIP "MOOD"

The *amount of time* a joint venture has been in existence can be either a positive or a negative source of variation in local joint venture bargaining processes, depending on the nature of the enterprise's relationships with relevant persons. If a joint venture begins operation without having achieved consensus concerning certain issues—most notably and most frequently the issue of foreign exchange—the issues will continue to threaten to interfere with smooth decision making and joint venture operation throughout the existence of the enterprise. In an environment where termination imperils the very existence of the joint venture, the consequent strains in the relationship between foreign and Chinese management will only serve to contaminate relationships with important entities outside the enterprise, since these affiliations are based usually on the personal contacts of the Chinese joint venture representatives. One example, in particular, demonstrates the way time can positively *and* negatively affect local joint venture bargaining.

The English Vocational Training Center in Guangzhou is a joint venture between the Guangzhou Education Bureau and a Hong Kong–based company. There are two centers. The first was established in 1979 and, in the words of one representative, was a "disaster."[9] The district bureaus, the president of the center explained, were very suspicious of the center's motivations and purposes.[10] Among the issues that arose when the center was established was a demand by the Chinese side that the Hong Kong partner pay U.S.$4,000 for a language laboratory. Valuation of the equipment, it was decided, was too high, and agreement on the matter was never reached. Furthermore, the Hong Kong partners had no choice in the location of the center or in the hiring of the office staff. The center was forced to locate in a "district teachers' college," and the office staff and personnel were chosen unilaterally by local bureaus.[11]

In 1985, a new center (where I conducted the interview upon which this case is based) was established. The partners were able to conduct screening procedures before autonomously hiring personnel and office staff and were also allowed to choose the site of the enterprise. The venture also had freedom in formulating its own syllabi, which it then used in classes.[12] The 1985 negotiations over, and establishment of, the joint venture were much easier than in 1979, because the Hong Kong partners had established and cultivated relationships with local authorities from the Education Bureau. The center established in 1985 runs smoothly, but the one founded in 1979 continues to have problems as a result of strains in relationships that were forged at the time of the venture negotiations.[13]

If one uses the time to cultivate good relations with local policy implementers, the length of time that a joint venture is in existence can be a positive source of variation in bargaining. However, if one is unable to cultivate good relationships and address issues during joint venture negotiations, the resulting strains can adversely affect a venture's ability to act autonomously from the local authorities, and issues left unanswered will continue to be a source of tension throughout the term of the enterprise. Indeed, Pomfret notes that many of China's earliest joint ventures are plagued by more problems than those established after the 1983 and 1986 legislative phases.[14] Because the Chinese and foreign sides in the early joint ventures were particularly unfamiliar with each other's expectations and often had differing interpretations of laws, contracts, and each side's general responsibilities, disagreements were frequent and issues of contention were often left unaddressed and unsolved.[15]

If a joint enterprise produces a product that China needs or is an Export-Oriented Enterprise (EOE) or a Technically-Advanced Enterprise (TAE), it is automatically entitled by law to more favorable terms than other joint ventures.[16] However, it must be noted that the outcomes of bargaining for TAE or EOE status are not always determined by whether the proposed enterprise is or is not export-oriented or technologically advanced, especially in Guangdong.[17] One manager explained that in Guangdong, it has become more and more difficult to obtain approval for joint ventures that are not high-tech.[18] If, however, one has the right contacts, one can get approval for special status (especially TAE status) even if the joint venture does not, for instance, meet the requirements for TAE status.[19] Because joint ventures have considerable autonomy in how they use their foreign exchange, they have an edge when it comes to entertaining local authorities and cultivating important relations that may facilitate achieving TAE or EOE status.[20]

Without good personal relationships, even TAEs and EOEs may find that obtaining benefits is more difficult than it otherwise would be. Earlier (Chapter Four, "The Objects of Bargaining"), I discussed the case of the joint venture manager who was unable to acquire a certain tax break because relations with the local tax authorities had been severely damaged by the way he unilaterally decided simply to stop paying the tax without engaging in any kind of negotiation or consensus-building processes with relevant Chinese parties. This manager learned that a neighboring joint venture had not been paying the same tax for several years and, therefore, decided that his joint venture should not be required to pay it. Unlike the neighboring joint venture, his joint venture was export-oriented and had earned U.S.$6.2 million in foreign exchange the previous year, which, he reported to me, represented over 75 percent of Wuhan's foreign-exchange earnings and over 15 percent of the total earnings for all of Hubei Province.[21] The neighboring joint venture produces a product for sale in China,[22] but because of its good relations with local tax authorities it had not been required to pay this particular tax for years.[23] Despite the impressive credentials of the export-oriented joint venture, the damaged relations with the local authorities made the process of bargaining for the tax break much more tedious than it otherwise would have been. Indeed, the role of maintaining good personal ties cannot be overemphasized for successful bargaining and joint venture operation in China.

Personal relationships are also extremely important in overcoming bitterness toward the outside world that may be caused by changes in the *mood of the central authorities* in Beijing. The mood of the central authorities toward reform and the outside world can be a source of variation in bargaining over joint venture rules and regulations between joint venture representatives and local policy implementers. Hostility towards foreign investment, one expert has noted, often means that government units will be more likely to interfere with the negotiating process, while a more favorable attitude "may sacrifice the emphasis on narrow domestic interests and centralize the negotiations in order to ease the way for the foreign investor."[24] It is, however, plausible to argue that the role of this variable in affecting variation of local bargaining attitudes may be two-sided, depending on how good one's personal relationships with relevant Chinese are.

The attitude of the central leadership toward foreign direct investment throughout the 1980s was largely dependent on the battle over foreign-trade policies between "reformers" and "conservatives"; when the liberalization of laws and policies vis-à-vis foreign investors seemed to reap positive economic benefits, the reformers had an edge in arguing for more positive attitudes toward the outside world, while times of economic difficulties meant that the conservatives had more success in flexing their policy-making muscle. From the beginning of the Open Door policy until the mid-1980s, for instance, the SEZs experienced numerous economic and political difficulties that led to stricter control by the center over their activities. Among the problems they experienced were that by 1984, only "10 percent of approximately 500 manufacturing operations in Shenzhen at the end of 1984 involved advanced technology," exports made up only 20 percent of the zones' output, a deficit of U.S.$542 million was accumulated, only 7 percent of the products produced met international quality standards, and the U.S.$1.3 billion in investments equalled only one-third of the government investment in infrastructure.[25] In 1986, "drastic readjustments were implemented to rein in the SEZs and turn them into foreign-exchange generators rather than foreign-exchange spenders."[26] Ultimately, in 1987, the SEZs passed laws allowing expanded foreign-trade and investment privileges, tax incentives for foreign investors, and greater access to foreign exchange; investments consequently rose by 114 percent and remained at this level throughout 1988 and 1989.[27] However, this rapid growth also encouraged bureaucratic corruption and an increase in illegal trade between the SEZs and interior regions; as provinces engineered policies to build export-oriented industry that increased foreign-exchange earnings, SEZ companies used their foreign exchange to take advantage of new SEZ laws that allowed the purchase of duty-free imports and sold them to customers in China's interior regions. These sales threatened interior host-country industries, contributed to a drop in foreign-exchange earnings, "rapidly climbing inflation, and inability to meet state production quotas."[28] Other criticisms centered around foreign purchase of land, which was perceived by conservative forces to be turning the SEZs into "foreign colonies," and an increase in pornographic materials and prostitution in the areas.[29]

The conservative backlash against reformers culminated in June 1989 with the government-ordered military breakup of student protests at Tiananmen Square in Beijing. This event marked the beginning of a period of economic retrenchment, purges of reformers in China's central leadership, like Zhao Ziyang, increased suspicion of the outside world, and greater political activity at the local levels of the Chinese political system. As far as joint ventures were concerned, the implications of this new attitude for bargaining over rules and regulations are not entirely clear. On the one hand, in line with the expectations of the observers cited at the beginning of this section, the more hostile attitude toward the outside world exhibited by the new conservative-minded leadership meant an increase in the activities of government units in joint venture negotiations and operations. Pearson, for example, documented increased pressure from joint venture party cells to conduct political study and training meetings, "increased trade union activities," and a general desire among local officials and Chinese joint venture managers to keep low profiles.[30] Because most bargaining between the joint venture and local authorities depends on the personal relationships of the Chinese joint venture managers and their contacts in local government, their collective desire to maintain low profiles had the most serious effect on bargaining under the new conservative leadership in Beijing.

On the other hand, personnel of one American MNC sent to China just one month after the June 4, 1989, crackdown at Tiananmen Square in Beijing to continue joint venture negotiations enjoyed remarkable cooperation from local negotiators who bent over backward to accommodate them while they were there. A more conservative leadership meant a more hostile attitude in Beijing toward the outside world. However, provincial and local-level officials had enough strength to weather the storm and maintain an uninterrupted influx of foreign capital investment. In fact, local officials seemed bent on continuing to build commercial ties with the outside world, despite Beijing's increasingly conservative exhortations about the negative effects of foreign influences. Ironically, this may have meant a better bargaining position for the foreign partner, as local officials often made special efforts to attract investment and assure foreigners that their investments remained safe. In the case of the American negotiating team that returned to China just one month after the Tiananmen incident, their personal contacts in local and provincial governments were crucial not only in facilitating the continuation of negotiations but also in acquiring concessions from the Chinese.[31]

PARTNER CHARACTERISTICS: LEVEL OF CHINESE GOVERNMENT, CORPORATE PERSONALITY, AND NATIONALITY OF THE FOREIGN PARTNER

Characteristics of both the Chinese and the foreign partners may also be important factors in local joint venture bargaining processes. Among those that I found to be evident were the level of government of the Chinese partner, the corporate personality of the foreign partner, and the nationality of the foreign partner.

As was illustrated earlier in the example of the multinational corporation that failed to negotiate a joint venture with the Chinese because of involvement from obstinate central authorities, the *level of government* with which a foreign party is dealing can affect the bargaining between the Chinese and foreign sides during joint venture negotiations. The level of the government of the Chinese partner can also affect bargaining over policy implementation during joint venture operation. In one case, for instance, a manager from a joint venture hotel in Beijing explained that the parent ranking (the level of government with or the entity with which the foreign corporation created the joint venture) of his hotel was city-level, while the parent ranking of a competing hotel in Beijing was state-level. As the manager of a city-level enterprise, he was constrained by a law that prohibited him from paying his employees more than 150 percent more than employees in similar state-run enterprises. The hotel with the state-level parent ranking, meanwhile, is able to deviate from the Beijing labor laws and, it was reported to me, on average pays its employees 160 percent more than comparable employees in state-run firms.[32]

Thus, depending on the level of the government of the Chinese partner, a joint venture may be bound to a more stringent legal framework that may limit the latitude that parties have to bargain over joint venture laws and policies. Furthermore, especially at the stage of negotiation and establishment of the joint venture, if central authorities are deeply involved, bargaining may be a more tedious affair than if one is dealing only with local and provincial authorities. Personal relationships with local authorities, in fact, may be crucial in impeding central interference in negotiations and operations.

The personality of the foreign management team (*corporate personality*) is also an operative factor determining bargaining outcomes at the local level. The most vivid example that I discovered was the Western general manager who decided unilaterally that he should not be required to pay a certain tax. Rather than approach relevant Chinese authorities about trying to build consensus concerning the tax break, he simply stopped payment on the tax and refused to make any more payments. He incensed the local tax authorities with his attitude, and they refused to grant him the official tax break; the manager believed he would have received it immediately if he had simply approached them with a "wine them, dine them" attitude in the first place. His failure to appreciate the role of building personal contacts to expedite administrative favors meant a long process of consensus building throughout the local political structure, all the way up to the mayor, and the tedious task of repairing relations with local tax officials who had "lost face" as a result of the conflict.

With the right kind of preparation, the personality of the foreign partner can influence positively the inevitable process of bargaining that is required in Chinese business. Many foreign executives going abroad must participate in seminars to learn about the intricacies of conducting business in the countries where they are going. These programs are aimed at "suppressing a conditioned propensity on the part of . . . personnel to think in ethnocentric or geographically nearsighted terms."[33] If the foreign manager fails to appreciate the cultural nuances of the enterprise's commercial environment, that manager no doubt will suffer needless negative consequences due to such ignorance. In the case of bargaining over the implementation of joint venture rules and regulations at the local level in China, the personality of the manager is a crucial factor determining bargaining outcomes.[34]

The personality of the foreign partner is, at least in part, determined by *nationality*. Hong Kong partners tend to have an advantage in China because of a shared language and culture, "although this is more true in neighboring Guangdong province than elsewhere."[35] Their involvement has been described as a "sham" because Hong Kong joint ventures are often established with the aim of acquiring special foreign-trade advantages, not to build a successful business.[36] Often, foreign partners listed as being from Hong Kong are, in fact, not from Hong Kong; they are from the PRC and use mythical Hong Kong partners to acquire special benefits available only to joint ventures. Taiwan and South Korean businesses, furthermore, often establish joint ventures through Hong Kong companies because they want to disguise their nationalities for political reasons.[37] The Nike corporation's Taiwan partners, for instance, "have used Hong Kong-based affiliates to spearhead their expansion into the mainland," which accounts for one-fifth of Nike's total footwear output.[38] Because of the common Asian background, these partners have a greater understanding of the nature of bargaining over joint venture rules and regulations than their Western counterparts. Indeed, as wages in Taiwan rose in the 1980s, foreign businesspersons turned to China for investment opportunities. In fact, the number of shoe companies in Taiwan fell from 1,245 to

745 from 1988 to 1992, as investors from all over Taiwan rushed across the Taiwan Strait into China's Fujian Province, demonstrating how comparatively easy it is for overseas Chinese to "transcend political borders."[39]

In my interviews and discussions with the Chinese, there was a propensity to categorize foreign investors according to nationality. Pearson found that the Chinese categorize foreign investors into two groups: "There were those who 'sincerely hope to cooperate with us and use legitimate methods to do business' and those who 'resort to dishonest means or even means in violation of China's sovereignty — such as swindle [*sic*], bribery, smuggling, infiltration, and espionage — to harm the Chinese people and [to] corrupt party members, cadres, and other people.'"[40] In fact, this echoes the opinions of one Chinese joint venture representative who spoke of "good" foreign partners and "bad" foreign partners; often, he explained, the Chinese would place a foreign investor on a continuum between these two extremes, based on the person's nationality. There was substantial respect for and desire to conduct business with investors from Australia, Canada, Europe, Japan, and the United States; this respect was not as apparent when speaking of investors from Hong Kong and the former Soviet Union. Whether these categorizations are representative of Chinese attitudes or not is very uncertain. However, informants generally agreed that the Chinese categorized foreign investors according to nationality and had separate expectations for negotiators from different countries.[41] At this time, as one observer noted, "beyond some obvious geographical generalizations such as the Hong Kong concentration on Guangdong, the Japanese in the Northeast, and the United States and European investors in Shanghai, there is very little that can definitely be said."[42] Indeed, further study in this area is needed.

GEOGRAPHIC AREA: SPECIAL ZONES AND SOUTHERN CHINA

In August 1980, Shantou, Shenzhen and Zhuhai in Guangdong Province became Special Economic Zones (SEZs) under the authority of the Administrative Committee of the Special Economic Zones of Guangdong Province.[43] The zones were established to fulfill several functions. They were expected to be vehicles for the introduction of capital, technology, and advanced management training. The imminent competition between enterprises in these zones and enterprises in Hong Kong and Macao was expected to improve enterprise efficiency and quality of production; subsequently, the enterprises in Guangdong would become the standards by which enterprises throughout China would be compared in terms of regulating production according to market demands, improving quality, producing new products, and reducing production costs. Finally, the SEZs would also serve as learning centers where Chinese enterprises could experiment with capitalism.[44]

In order to run their economies according to market principles, the SEZs pressured central authorities for substantial decision-making autonomy and freedom to draft their own special sets of regulations for foreign trade and investment. On August 26, 1980, the 15th Session of the Standing Committee of the Fifth National People's Congress adopted the "Regulations on Special Economic Zones in Guangdong Province."[45] Immediately, the zones began rapid development, with over U.S.$1.6 billion in investments by the end of 1982, which represented over half of all foreign direct investment in China at that time.[46] Primarily due to their ability to earn foreign exchange, the zones gained political strength vis-à-vis Beijing and gradually enjoyed greater autonomy "to approve foreign-investment projects, retain foreign exchange, and decide how to use funds to improve their infrastructure."[47] Economic success in these zones in the early and mid-1980s led reformers in China's leadership, most notably Hu Yaobang and Zhao Ziyang, to pressure the government to initiate the "Coastal Development Strategy," which encouraged rather than discouraged imports in China's coastal regions.[48] In 1984, the Central Committee designated 14 cities as "Open Coastal Cities," entitling them to "approve foreign-investment projects, offer various investment incentives to foreign investors, retain a larger percentage of earned foreign exchange, and import certain equipment and technology duty-free."[49]

Economic Technological Development Zones (these zones are also referred to as Areas) (ETDZs or ETDAs) were created in Dalian, Tianjin, and Guangzhou, while, ultimately, in the late 1980s, High-Technology Development Zones (HTDZs) were approved for establishment in 30 cities throughout China. In all of these areas, laws have been drafted to grant special investment incentives to foreign investors. The benefits vary from area type to area type, but the bargaining position of foreign partners is greatly enhanced by these favorable legal frameworks.[50]

In southern China, the bargaining latitude of local officials and joint venture partners is further enhanced by several factors. (1) The proximity to Hong Kong and overseas Chinese investors makes this area a prime place for bargaining over commercial rules and regulations. Overseas Chinese speak the same language, understand the "ins" and "outs" of China's complex political system and culture, and appreciate the roles of guanxi and network building in overcoming legal and bureaucratic obstacles in business relations. (2) Furthermore, Guangdong's long history as an area open to foreign influences and investment and independent of central authorities in Beijing gives it the confidence it needs to carry on negotiations without constantly worrying about approval from the center. (3) Guangdong's role as China's greatest generator of foreign exchange may also give it greater independence from the center, thereby facilitating greater latitude for bargaining over rules and regulations at the local levels.[51] (4) Proximity to Beijing is also a source of variation in bargaining over the implementation of rules and regulations. During the negotiation stage of one joint venture discussed in Chapter Three, talks broke down due to meddling from central ministry representatives.[52] However, "Beijing's presence noticeably diminishes as one moves physically away from it," hence in Guangdong there exists a more relaxed feeling about bargaining "around the law" than in areas of China closer to the center.[53] (5) If a provincial capital is also a large economic region, it approaches Beijing with greater confidence, which further encourages a "bargaining relationship."[54] The bargaining atmosphere of provincial-central relations translates into greater bargaining at local levels, especially since "post-Mao reforms encourage commercial centers to go outside administrative channels and to establish direct ties with localities through investment, contracts to purchase above quota production, and so on."[55]

Bargaining is encouraged in Guangdong due to its separate and more liberal legal framework, the proximity to overseas Chinese investors who understand how to bargain for favorable implementation of joint venture laws because of a common language and cultural background, its role as China's largest foreign-exchange earner, its great distance from Beijing, and the substantial capacity it has to bargain with Beijing and to create a bargaining atmosphere for the joint ventures at the local levels.

CONCLUSION

The variables identified in this section do not represent an exhaustive list of all factors that affect local joint venture bargaining processes; they simply represent the factors that I found to be important in determining local bargaining outcomes. These variables do not operate exclusively of one another — that is, while they may contribute to the creation of final policy outcomes, they also affect each other and at any given time may supersede each other in importance, depending on the conditions. There is one exception to this rule. Personal relationships with relevant Chinese officials, managers, suppliers, and the like are the most important of all variables that affect joint venture operations and bargaining processes. Other variables will either negatively or positively impact these negotiations, often depending on the nature of the personal relationships. For instance, the length of time a joint venture is in existence will positively impact a joint venture's ability to bargain if personal relationships with relevant local Chinese have been good and nurtured well; if, however, local relationships are damaged and remain in disrepair for any number of reasons, time will only serve to exacerbate these strains. Even if the enterprise is an export-oriented enterprise that earns whopping amounts of foreign exchange, it may have difficulty gaining the cooperation of local policy implementers to extend benefits that it is supposed to receive by law if relations between the venture and the Chinese authorities are blemished. Indeed, joint ventures that are not technologically advanced, but have good relations with local policy implementers, may have a better chance of acquiring TAE benefits than those TAEs that do not get along well with the local Chinese authorities. Bargaining can become more strained at a time when the central leadership exhibits a hostile attitude toward the outside world; again, however, if a foreign joint venture partner has good relations with local authorities, they will be more willing to attempt to deflect any negative repercussions that may result from antagonistic central policy changes.

Among other factors that may affect local joint venture bargaining are geographic location, level of government of the Chinese partner, corporate personality of the foreign partner, and the nationality of the foreign partner. The geographic location of the joint venture will determine the legal framework that will govern its operation. In SEZs, EDAs, and HTDZs, enterprises may not have to bargain as strenuously for certain benefits as they might in other areas of the country, because laws automatically extend benefits to them that are not as readily extended elsewhere. If a joint venture is located in southern China, the bargaining latitude of local officials seems to be greater than in the North, where central authorities pose a closer and more ominous presence. Furthermore, the South has a long history of interaction with the outside world and is more open to new management techniques and styles than is the rest of the country, which lacks this experience.

The personality of the foreign management team is an important determinant of joint venture success and the likelihood of bargaining successes between the foreign partner and Chinese counterparts inside and outside the enterprise. In order to assuage ethnocentric attitudes that may offend the host-country management and government representatives, foreign managers should participate in seminars and other activities designed to educate them about such matters as the concessions they should be prepared to make in their expectations and management styles in order to gain cooperation from their Chinese colleagues in management, labor, and government.

Corporate personality may be at least partially dependent on the foreign partner's nationality. At least from the Chinese perspective, expectations of the foreign partners seem to be based largely on their preconceived ideas about representatives from different foreign countries. Because the Chinese think in terms of "good" and "bad" foreign partners, possibly depending on the nationality of the foreign partner, they will already have prejudged foreigners and, no doubt, will have devised their bargaining strategies based, in part, on these preconceived notions.

6

Conclusion

INTRODUCTION

Host countries and MNCs bargain with each other over terms of investment to achieve their individual objectives. At the most general level of analysis, this bargaining occurs between the Chinese government and the foreign-investment community over national-level joint venture laws and policies. Foreigners bargain for terms that will maximize their autonomy from the state over joint venture operations and increase the probability of earning a profit and gaining access to China's potentially enormous domestic market. Chinese objectives include attracting foreign capital, advanced technology, and management techniques, and gaining access to international markets.

One of the vehicles the Chinese have encouraged to achieve their goals in foreign economic relations is the Sino-foreign joint venture. Joint ventures offer MNCs the opportunity to maintain at least limited control over their investments in Chinese industry. Through the construction of a legal framework to protect foreign investments from such dangers as nationalization of assets and extensive interference from Chinese bureaucrats, the Chinese hoped that the foreign-investment community would be more willing to invest in their economy in general and in joint ventures in particular. The legal framework, however, also placed often burdensome regulations on foreigners to inhibit them from encroaching on China's sovereignty, exploiting Chinese labor and resources, and introducing morally corrupt influences to their Chinese counterparts in business and government. Furthermore, this legal framework has always vested ultimate decision-making power in the hands of the Chinese.

Bargaining between Chinese and foreign managers and Chinese policy implementers also characterizes the final stage of implementation of joint venture laws and policies at the local level of the Chinese political system. At this stage, foreigners exert influence over their Chinese colleagues to relinquish joint venture control over various aspects of joint venture operations. The dichotomy between the "foreign side" and the "Chinese side" at this time, however, becomes diffuse, as an amalgamation of interests of Chinese and foreign managers and local policy implementors develops out of a common desire to see the ultimate success of the joint venture. Final implementation of laws and policies depends on bargaining between a variety of combinations of Chinese managers, foreign managers, local bureaucrats, and other interested parties.

WHO BARGAINS AND WHEN THEY BARGAIN

Joint venture parties bargain with each other at several different stages of the joint venture term: (1) negotiation and establishment; (2) operation; (3) dispute settlement; (4) and dissolution. As has been noted, I have concentrated only on issues in stages one and two.

In fact, bargaining occurs from the moment a joint venture is negotiated, through the term of its existence, and during the process of dissolution and distribution of assets. During negotiation, the most difficult object of bargaining is the valuation of in-kind contributions, most notably land and technology. At this stage, the foreign partner may also try to bargain with relevant Chinese authorities for TAE and/or EOE status and will realize the virtual impossibility of *explicitly* bargaining over Chinese foreign-exchange requirements. Feasibility-study costs also have been reported to be traditionally major objects of bargaining between the Chinese and foreign partners,[1] although my impression was that this has not continued to be a principal issue of contention.[2] This study has shown that after the joint venture has been established, bargaining occurs over almost all aspects of operation. Foreign and Chinese managers bargain with each other over their roles and the amount of control over operations that each will enjoy, while the joint venture as a whole often must bargain with a wide array of actors, including local officials, suppliers, and other enterprises over resources, pricing, marketing, employee recruitment, hiring, discipline, dismissal, social welfare benefits, the roles of the labor union and other structures of the CCP and government within the enterprise, joint venture status (EOE and TAE), tax breaks, and foreign-exchange requirements. Indeed, there was no disagreement with the statement of one foreign manager that in China, "everything is negotiable."[3]

Recruitment and employment of potential joint venture employees involves several actors. Foreign representatives, in one case, negotiated permission to recruit on a college campus in Guangdong Province with university administration personnel. Afterward, students wanting to work in the joint venture would bargain with a number of different people to arrange this employment opportunity. Transfers also involve a number of parties bargaining with each other. In the case of a Tianjin joint venture (discussed in Chapter Four), the local labor bureau contacted the labor bureau of a neighboring locality to arrange the transfers of several workers from that locality to the area where the joint venture was located. In another case, a state employee had to instigate an enormous process of bargaining between her managers in the state enterprise, a local joint venture, and the local labor bureau to arrange her transfer from the state enterprise to the joint venture. In yet another case, a temporary joint venture employee was successful in finalizing his permanent transfer to the joint venture after one of his Chinese managers utilized a personal relationship with someone in the local labor bureau who, in turn, contacted an acquaintance in the labor bureau of the employee's hometown to expedite the transfer of his household registration (*hukou*). Bargaining between the Chinese and foreign parties has been particularly pronounced over the introduction of screening procedures at this stage as well.

In every case of local joint venture bargaining, the foreign partner must try to co-opt support from at least some Chinese colleagues in business and government. This is accomplished by convincing the Chinese that they have a vested interest in helping the foreign partner achieve her or his immediate objective. In the area of discipline and dismissal of Chinese joint venture employees, for instance, an enormous consensus-building process involving Chinese management, the Chinese labor bureau, the joint venture labor union, and foreign management is required. It may be incumbent upon the foreign investor, in these instances, to introduce controversial management decisions that require support from relevant Chinese colleagues; sometimes, this will mean that the foreign partner will have to attempt to gain the support of some Chinese in a struggle against other Chinese. In at least one instance, for example, when a dismissed employee believed that the joint venture labor union, Chinese management, and the local labor authorities would order his reinstatement in the enterprise, these groups actually sided with the foreign manager, who wanted to bring suit against him on charges of embezzlement in a Chinese court.[4] Indeed, bargaining occurs throughout the joint venture term and involves a multitude of actors. These actors, however, do not necessarily choose sides based on nationality, but often on their perceived individual interests or the interests of the enterprise.

SOURCES OF BARGAINING

China's foreign economic and trade laws have not diminished the role of bargaining in Chinese society, but, rather, have contributed to increasing the role of bargaining throughout the 1980s and into the 1990s. There are at least four general characteristics of this evolving legal framework that explain the continued widespread practice of bargaining through personal contacts to get "around the law" (*rao-zhi-zou*). First, these laws are instruments that the state uses as mechanisms to *control* foreign investment so that it serves to further the state goals of attracting capital, technology, management training, and access to international markets. Second, a traditional preference in China for the "rule of man" (*renzhi*) over the "rule of law" (*fazhi*) has encouraged joint venture partners to utilize personal contacts to avoid China's tiresome and unreliable bureaucratic and administrative channels. Third, a substantial body of internal laws precludes foreign confidence in China's ability to create a legal framework that encourages stability and predictability. Finally, China's joint venture laws have been ambiguous, and decentralization has vested power of interpretation with local Chinese authorities who are influenced by resource-rich foreigners to implement rules and regulations in ways that favor the joint venture, regardless of central directives or objectives.

Barrett L. McCormick has argued that China's legal development is very different from the legal development of most Western nations. In America, for instance, he explains,

> law not only guarantees some rights against the state, but is used by a wide range of relatively autonomous actors and enjoys a measure of autonomy from even the most powerful actors. In contrast, before and since 1949, Chinese law has had the primary goal of strengthening the state and provided only extremely limited rights against the state [and] . . .[5] has been a means of strengthening state power, not granting rights against the state.[6]

In the area of China's foreign trade, China's evolving legal framework has, in fact, been created with the stated objectives of protecting foreign investment from the state and extending rights and benefits to foreign partners in order to attract investments in capital, technology, and advanced management training. However, as I have noted throughout this book, the Chinese have also used these laws *(including internal laws to which the foreign partner has no access)* to retain ultimate decision-making authority in their own hands and to impose requirements on foreign investors to make concessions to Chinese demands that further state goals of acquiring capital, technology, management training, and access to international markets. Respondents suggested, in fact, that Chinese insistence that foreigners attempt to settle disputes out of court through mediation and conciliation was, in part, due to a belief that the foreign partner would find it very difficult to receive a fair hearing in a Chinese court.[7] This *ad hoc* recognition of the role of law as a means of serving the interests of the state encourages bargaining over legal disputes and other issues of contention that may arise throughout the joint venture term. Indeed, McCormick explains that the nature of the Chinese law is directly responsible for the popularity of bargaining "around the law" through personal relationships throughout Chinese society:

> As long as law exists primarily to serve the political purposes of the state vis-à-vis society, society will find a legal means of representing itself vis-à-vis the state and mediating disputes within society. *The most likely recourse [is] patrimonial authority*[8]

The role of law and the consequent method of solving problems and disputes through patrimonial authority is determined not only by a totalitarian state that utilizes law as a mechanism to further its own agenda, but also by a society that has a traditional conceptual preference for the "rule of man" over the "rule of law." The debate between proponents of the "rule of man" and advocates of the "rule of law" is one that has yet to be settled and is also characterized by questions concerning such issues as " 'policy is the soul of law.' "[9]

> "Policy is the soul of law" was . . . used in the 1957 Anti-Rightist Campaign to reinforce the supremacy of policy over law in the mass struggle against class enemies. Support for comprehensive codification of law and its perfection was interpreted as a sign of an anti-Party position. Law was required to change with the revolutionary situation. Emphasis on the predictability, rather than the flexibility, of law was considered a sign of political reaction, as was the advocacy of the notion of "inheritability" which allowed for some retention of old law in China's new socialist society.[10]

The primary goal of China's evolving legal framework governing foreign investment is to achieve China's "Four Modernizations" policy; hence, one can argue that laws are superseded in importance by policies.[11] However, the

Chinese government has also found that as decentralization and legal ambiguity were supposed to give local decision makers the power to interpret laws to serve the interests of China as a whole, local policy implementers "administer justice according to ad hoc standards and informal procedures" that serve their individual interests and the interests of their localities.[12] This process tends to undermine any serious attempt to create a predictable system of laws that reduces the frequency of bargaining and the use of private personal contacts to avoid the Chinese bureaucracy. This lack of confidence in China's ability to create a predictable system of laws is further exacerbated by the large body of internal (*neibu*) regulations to which foreign analysts and businesspersons have no access.

Although one observer has argued that "it is clear that law has advanced beyond the scope of political control to serve as a social regulator and a mechanism for effective administration (economic and administrative law)," and Western legal analysts generally praise the evolution of China's legal framework for foreign investment, it is nonetheless apparent that bargaining "around the law" continues to be a hallmark of interaction in China's commercial environment.[13] This situation is the result of a political system that has traditionally used law as a means of control and a society that has operated according to standards associated with the "rule of man," not the "rule of law." It has been exacerbated by decentralization of decision-making power, which has granted substantial freedom to local bureaucrats to interpret ambiguous laws in the face of a foreign-investment community that is rich in resources that can be used to influence local decision-making processes.

System Factors: Decentralization, Bureaucracy, Pricing Structure, and the Relative Value of China's Investment Incentives

In his 1987 article on bargaining in China, Lampton identified several "systematic causes of bargaining activity."[14] The most important was the "generic problem . . . with central planning systems":[15]

> Though the scope of state planning has undergone important changes in the last eight years (with guidance planning assuming a more prominent role and mandatory planning playing a declining role), the process of moving resources in society still is a political/bureaucratic decision in considerable measure. Shortages of both needed production inputs and high-quality products, as well as the perennial scarcity of building materials and capital, mean that decision makers at all levels must decide how to allocate exceedingly scarce resources

> with few, or no, market signals. Unsurprisingly, they respond to political pressure — and frequently pecuniary opportunity. Scarcity that cannot be resolved through a market system becomes the grist for the political bargaining mill.[16]

The requirement of bargaining is associated with other features of the Chinese political system, including decision-making decentralization, bureaucracy, an irrational pricing structure, and generally substandard product quality. In his article, "The Decentralization of Peking's Economic Management and Its Impact on Foreign Investment," Feng-cheng Fu argues that local governments have taken their increased decision-making powers and acted with little regard for the directives of the central authorities in Beijing.[17] Provinces and localities have attempted to defy central regulations using a wide variety of schemes; the presence of foreign investment and joint ventures has contributed to the assortment of methods that they have at their disposal to enrich themselves at the expense of the center. Often, for instance, local authorities will turn state enterprises into joint ventures simply to take advantage of special benefits that laws offer to foreign-invested businesses:

> Recently, many hinterland provinces which are not qualified for implementing the opening-up policy have used this tactic, offering foreign investors terms for cooperation that are more preferential than normal in exchange for preferential policies and more opportunities for export trade.[18]

Furthermore, this decentralization, which encompassed an attempt to limit the number of administrative personnel and to streamline bureaucratic organizations in China's foreign economic relations and trade, has actually led to an increase in the number of China's bureaucrats: "The more efforts we exerted to reduce personnel, the more people we employed. It is inconceivable to enliven enterprises, do well in promoting lateral ties, and develop a planned commodity economy by such management system characterized by overstaffed organizations, low efficiency, and overconcentration of power."[19] Rather than simplifying procedures for foreign joint venture investors, decentralization often has served only to exacerbate the problem of bureaucratism. One observer recently assessed China's reforms in the area of its foreign economic relations thusly:

> Bureaucratic privileges and other official abuses are . . . having a detrimental effect on the opening-up policy. Excessive red tape, lack of respect for the law, and embezzlement and extortion of bribes are discouraging foreign investors.

> One joint venture contract between a ferroalloy factory in Kweichow Province and a Swedish company was approved only after it had received as many as 340 chops from different departments. Other complaints from foreign investors include excessively high rents, endless disputes during contract negotiations, too many different taxes, high labor costs, embezzlement and bribe taking by cadres, and red tape in general. Bureaucrats forced one elevator manufacturer to replace its Chinese board chairman in violation of the joint venture contract, much to the annoyance of the foreign partner. In one case, the foreign manager of a joint venture in Fukien Province said that his company's prospects depended largely on bribing cadres.[20]

Decentralization of decision-making authority, then, has been an impetus for greater bargaining between local policy implementers and joint venture representatives. Not only must joint venture representatives attempt to bargain for scarce resources with local bureaucrats, they must attempt to establish good personal relationships with relevant personnel who can bypass the bureaucratic jungle that has grown since reform began in 1979.

Reform of decision-making authority over product pricing has been one of the major objectives of China's modernization drive. The objective of reform in this area has been to decentralize authority over pricing products from the hands of administrative officials to individual enterprise managers who would then price products based on their value in relationship to supply and demand.[21] Centralized planning in China had traditionally caused serious irrationalities in the pricing of various products. Agricultural goods, sideline products, manufactured goods, housing and construction materials, transport, communications, and urban public utilities were all either seriously underpriced or overpriced, out of proportion with each other, supply and demand.[22] Characteristics of the pricing system that led to these problems included power over pricing that was solely in the hands of the central government with no guidance from individual enterprise managers, and planned prices for goods that were fixed and unlikely to be changed in line with growth in supply and demand.[23]

In 1979, price reform was introduced with the deregulation of prices for various commodities designated by the state and greater decision-making authority for local governments and individual enterprises to price their own products.[24] However, what has evolved is a "double-track price system" that is a "combination of planned readjustment and market regulation . . . for fixing the prices of energy and raw materials," with state-mandated prices for goods and products used and produced within state quotas and market prices for goods and products used and produced outside the quota system.[25] Debate over the extent to which prices should be decontrolled has arisen, with conservatives in Chinese leadership enunciating support for a pricing system that is controlled by central authorities, and reformers who support gradually decontrolling all prices.

The double-track pricing structure, decision-making decentralization, and a currency system that is made up of inconvertible *renminbi,* convertible foreign-exchange certificates, and Hong Kong dollars (especially prevalent in the South) have been major sources of bargaining between Chinese policy implementers and foreign investors. Not only has the pricing system contributed to resource shortages that lead to intense bargaining between officials and enterprises, local bureaucrats have used their independence from the central authorities in Beijing egregiously to gouge foreign investors with arbitrary price hikes. Joint ventures, in turn, have been known to use their resources to persuade suppliers and officials to bypass administrative channels to obtain the necessary resources required for joint venture production. Among the joint venture objectives of bargaining in this area have been to obtain state prices for goods needed for production, especially if the joint venture is producing for sale in China; to obtain permission to use *renminbi* to purchase domestic raw materials or negotiate a suspension of foreign-exchange requirements that the government imposes on joint ventures, especially if the enterprise is producing for sale in China; and to fight local officials who try to charge exorbitant prices for resources required for production. Problems associated with China's pricing structure are exacerbated by that country's long-standing problems with product quality. Even if the foreign investor is successful in using contacts to acquire necessary materials for production, there is no guarantee that the quality will be sufficient to meet the requirements of joint venture production or, considering China's poor distribution and delivery facilities, that the needed goods will arrive on time, if at all.

Indeed, the issue of product quality is one with which the Chinese themselves have grappled since the Open Door policy began in 1979. Experts have recognized that a fundamental requirement for successful price reform is to link prices to product quality: "An irrational practice is being exercised in present price management in which there is no difference between top- and lower-quality products."[26] Related to Pye's explanation that Chinese negotiators often simply had little understanding of the monetary value of knowledge, one Chinese observer explained that "in the past, we also emphasized the principle of giving first place to quality, but we had only a superficial understanding of its significance," and that, therefore, "all workers and staff . . . must enhance their understanding, admit the backward condition, and be resolved to change this backward state of affairs."[27]

Although the Chinese government has passed laws, promulgated policies, and sponsored events to enhance Chinese awareness concerning product quality, problems recognized in the early 1980s actually worsened by the mid-1980s. According to one observer, these problems could be attributed to "the pursuit of illegitimate profits and manufacturing in a rough and slipshod way."[28] The observer suggested that only by passing *and implementing* strict laws could the Chinese change the situation of product quality in China.[29] Despite laws,[30] policies,[31] events to bring attention to product quality,[32] and organizations established to monitor and implement quality rules and regulations,[33] product quality continued to decline throughout the 1980s.[34]

Foreign investors generally agreed that the quality of resources was worse than what they would have preferred. Although one of the attractions to invest in a joint venture in China is the country's rich resource base, obtaining needed raw materials often requires bargaining with a substantial network of personal contacts. Even if one is able to obtain the needed goods, joint venture representatives must bargain over pricing; the difficulty of this process is exacerbated by a cumbersome bureaucracy, with different parties vying for a piece of the perceived lucrative foreign investment, and the generally substandard quality of the goods that foreigners perceive to be cause for lower prices.

CONCLUSION

Although we understand that developing nations bargain with MNCs over terms of investment, it is imperative that scholars understand other facts about this process. First, indigenous cultural and systemic characteristics of the host nation will affect the terms of investment. Second, the terms of investment change after the initial agreements have been reached, contracts signed, and operations begun. Finally, if the form of foreign direct investment is a joint venture, relationships between individual foreigners and host-nation representatives will be established, and the interests of the two sides will be fused in a common desire to see the joint venture succeed. Thus, the "host side" and the "foreign side" is a dichotomy that becomes diffuse when one delves into local bargaining processes, where members from each of these groups and other interested parties negotiate with each other to achieve their own respective goals.

In line with our general understanding that developing host nations bargain with MNCs over terms of foreign direct investment, this text has demonstrated how the Chinese government has bargained with the foreign-investment community throughout the 1980s and into the 1990s over the general laws and policies that govern foreign direct investment in that country. Beyond China's general foreign- investment policies and laws that evolved largely as a result of this bargaining process, bargaining between a multitude of self-interested parties at the local level of the Chinese political system determines final policy and law outcomes. Indeed, implementation depends on a complex and widespread process of bargaining.

Chinese and foreign joint venture parties bargain over conflicting objectives and, especially in the area of labor relations at the local level, over contending cultural and social values. Chinese and foreign parties build alliances that transcend the simplistic dichotomy of "host side" and "foreign side" that is used in many analyses; these alliances take a number of forms, depending on the issue of contention and the interests of the individual parties involved.

Bargaining in the commercial sector varies according to a number of factors, including the nature of the personal relationships that the joint venture has established; various general characteristics of the partners, including level of government of the Chinese partner, nationality of the foreign partner, and the joint venture type (TAE or EOE); and the geographic location of the joint venture (e.g., special zone or non-special zone, coastal or inland, and/or North or South). Bargaining in China is the primary process by which problems in the commercial sector are solved for a multitude of reasons. First, bargaining is endemic to Chinese society. Using personal relationships (*guanxi*) to achieve objectives through "back door" (*houtai* or *houmen*), rather than through administrative and official, channels is a process with a long and historic tradition in China. Also, despite hopes among some analysts that laws would limit bargaining beyond administrative bounds, a traditional disdain for the "rule of law" (*fazhi*) and preference for the "rule of man" (*renzhi*) in Chinese society has dulled the effect that this evolving framework was supposed to have on bargaining. Second, systematic factors have also contributed to an increase in the frequency of bargaining in China's commercial sector. Decentralization has meant that local bureaucrats are free to pursue their own interests with little regard for central concerns. Consequently, local officials are often all too happy to entertain the requests of resource-rich foreign investors for help in arranging special administrative favors in areas like resource procurement, arranging tax breaks, and offering other investment incentives. China's enormous foreign-trade bureaucracy, which has grown substantially since the beginning of the Open Door, has also encouraged joint venture representatives to try to bargain with relevant officials to bypass administrative procedures that waste time, money, and energy. Attributes of China's centrally planned economy, like its complex dual-pricing structure with multiple currencies, lead joint ventures to bargain with relevant officials over numerous monetary issues, including the value of relevant commodities, paying state or market prices for various goods and materials, and meeting stringent foreign-exchange requirements. Finally, China's long-standing problems with product quality control, lack of a substantial skilled labor population, and poor distribution and transportation facilities diminish the attraction of many of China's investment incentives, including a large resource base, cheap raw materials and supplies, and a huge and inexpensive labor population. Bargaining over the relative value of these commodities is very common.

OTHER RESEARCH AREAS

The Sino-foreign joint venture represents a veritable gold mine of research opportunities for all social scientists. Throughout my study, I developed a list of possible questions that scholars should consider as potential areas for further research.

1. The first question that could be investigated more closely is the role of the Sino-foreign joint venture in the implementation of Chinese government policies. It has been a stated objective of the government to use foreign joint venture expertise to help in its modernization drive; one policy area, for instance, that the government had hoped would benefit from foreign input is enterprise-management reform. In a recent discussion with a foreign expert who has studied Chinese environmental policy, the subject of the role of the Sino-foreign joint venture in implementing central policies on environmental concerns was discussed.[35] Generally, it was thought that Chinese state industries might not exhibit the concern or have the technological wherewithal to meet Beijing's environmental goals and that foreigners might positively influence this situation. What, then, is the role of the Sino-foreign joint venture in assisting China in its drive to protect its environment?
2. In the first chapter, Biersteker, it was noted, explained that proponents of foreign direct investment by MNCs in developing host nations believe that foreign corporations can be "agents of change" that contribute to the host nation's drive toward modernization.[36] Scholars should attempt to assess the effect that the joint venture has had on China's social develop-

ment. This study has touched on this subject—for instance, demonstrating that neotraditional relationships are not as evident in joint ventures as they are alleged to be in state enterprises. Pearson has also begun a more in-depth look at this issue and has argued that, in fact, Sino-foreign joint ventures are helping to "break the bonds of dependence."[37] More research is needed on the following question: To what extent has the Sino-foreign joint venture been an agent of social change in China?

3. Interference by local CCP bureaucrats has been a major impediment to the implementation of policies like enterprise-management reform. Although they exerted some influence during the period following the June 4, 1989, incident at Tiananmen in Beijing, the role of party bureaucrats in joint venture operations and implementation of joint venture rules and policies has not been examined very closely. What, then, is the role of the party in joint venture operations and policy implementation? Have party bureaucrats been a positive or a negative influence on the Sino-foreign joint venture, and what factors determine their roles?
4. No study has concentrated solely on the joint venture labor union. Although this study has argued that joint venture labor unions are generally nondisruptive and complacent, there has been evidence that they have exerted their influence to some degree after the conservatives took power in Beijing in 1989.[38] What are the functions of joint venture labor unions, and how have they evolved since 1979?
5. Chapter Five of this study explored sources of variation in bargaining processes at the local level of the Chinese political system. The factors explored merely represent a tentative list and should be studied more closely to determine the relative importance of each. One particularly interesting question to be answered is, "What are the differences in bargaining between different geographical locations in China (e.g., North versus South, special zones versus non-special zones, inland versus coastal)? Other sources of variation should also be discovered and investigated in more in-depth fashion.
6. Finally, this study uncovered the beginning of a system of collective bargaining between local joint venture groups and the Chinese government. I discovered that these groups have been successful in making demands on local governments to respond to problems that they are experiencing. Much more research on these groups is needed to discover their relative importance on policy making and implementation in China and the other roles that they play on behalf of Sino-foreign joint ventures.

APPENDIX

Rules, Regulations, and Laws

1979 “Provisional Regulations on Foreign Exchange Control of the People’s Republic of China”

1979 “The Law of the People’s Republic of China on Joint Ventures Using Chinese and Foreign Investment" (Joint Venture Law)

1980 Income Tax Law of the PRC Concerning Joint Ventures Using Chinese and Foreign Investment—Joint Venture Income Tax Law Foreign Enterprise Income Tax Law (FEITL)

1980 “Regulations on Labor Management in Joint Ventures Using Chinese and Foreign Investment” (1980 Labor Regulations)

1980 The Foreign Land-Use Measures of 1980

1980 “Regulations on Special Economic Zones in Guangdong Province”

1981 “Provisional Regulations on Wages in the Enterprises in the Special Economic Zones in Guangdong Province”

1983 “Implementing Act for the Law of the People’s Republic of China on Joint Ventures Using Chinese and Foreign Investment” (1983 Implementing Act)

1983 “Rules for the Implementation of Exchange Control Regulations”

1984 “Provisions for the Implementation of the Regulations on Labor Management in Joint Ventures Using Chinese and Foreign Investment”

1984 “The Patent Law of the People’s Republic of China”

1985 Import Technology Law of the PRC

1985 "Regulations for the Administration of Technology Import Contracts"

1986 Implementing Regulations for the 1986 Provisions

1986 Land Management Law

1986 "Provisions for the Encouragement of Foreign Investment"

1986 "Provisions of the Ministry of Labor and Personnel on Employment, Wages, and Welfare in Foreign-Invested Enterprises"

1986 "Regulations on Foreign Currency Balance of Equity Joint Ventures" (Foreign-Exchange Balancing Provisions)

1987 "Implementing Rules of the Ministry of Foreign Economic Relations and Trade for Examination and Confirmation of Export Enterprises and Technically Advanced Enterprises with Foreign Investment"

1987 "Interim Provisions Concerning Ideological and Political Work for Chinese Staff and Workers in Chinese-Foreign Equity and Cooperative Joint Ventures"

1988 "Detailed Rules for the Implementation of the Regulations on the Administration of Technology Import Contracts"

1988 "Measures for the Implementation of the Responsibility System" for Directors of Research Institutes Owned by the Whole People of Xinjiang Uygur Autonomous Region"

1988 "Sample Articles of Association for Joint Ventures Using Chinese and Foreign Investment"

1988 Ministry of Labor and Personnel "Opinion on Further Implementation of the Right of Autonomy of Enterprises with Foreign Investment in the Hiring of Personnel"

1990 "Interim Regulations of the PRC on the Sale and Transfer of Land-Use Rights in State-Owned Land in the Cities and Towns" (the Land Conveyance Regulations)

1990 "Interim Regulations of the PRC Concerning Administration of Investing, Developing, and Managing Sizeable Land Areas by Foreign Investors" (the Land Development Regulations)

1991 "Detailed Rules and Regulations for the Implementation of the Income Tax Law

1991 Income Tax Law of the PRC for Enterprises with Foreign Investment and Foreign Enterprises (popularly known as the Unified Income Tax Law)

NOTES

Chapter 1

1. For an explanation of the hard core of a theory, see Imre Lakatos, "Falsification and the Methodology of Scientific Research Programmes," in Imre Lakatos and A. Musgrave, eds. *Criticism and the Growth of Knowledge*(Cambridge: Cambridge University Press, 1978), pp. 9–196.
2. On the motivations of foreign investors and host nations, see Wolfgang G. Friedmann and George Kalmanoff, *Joint International Business Ventures* (New York: Columbia University Press, 1961), pp. 125–155. See also Wolfgang G. Friedmann and Jean Pierre Beguin, *Joint International Business Ventures in Developing Countries: Case Studies and Analysis of Recent Trends* (New York: Columbia University Press, 1971), pp. 2–11. Although the motivations identified in the literature vary, the motives included as the basis of this analysis are common to all of the writings.
3. For a straightforward summary of the "bargaining" and "Marxist-Dependencia" schools, see Joseph M. Grieco, "Between Dependency and Autonomy: India's Experiencewith the International Computer Industry," *International Organization,* vol. 36, no. 3 (Summer 1982), pp. 609–632.
4. Analysis of the "conventional" and "critical" schools appears in Thomas J. Biersteker, *Distortion or Development? Contending Perspectives on the Multinational Corporation* (Cambridge: MIT Press, 1978), pp. 1–68.
5. See Stephen J. Kobrin, "Testing the Bargaining Hypothesis in the Manufacturing Sector in Developing Countries," *International Organization,* vol. 41, no. 4 (Autumn 1987), pp. 611–613. This argument is also proposed in Theodore H. Moran, *Multinational Corporations and the Politics of Dependence: Copper in Chile* (Princeton: Princeton University Press, 1974). Also see Fred C. Bergsten, Thomas Horst, and Theodore H. Moran, *American Multinationals and American Interests* (Washington, D.C.: Brookings Institute, 1978).
6. Biersteker, *Distortion or Development?,* p. 1.
7. Conventional theorists argued that MNCs would manufacture products of higher quality than domestically produced goods, raise the prices of domestic factors of production, contribute to keeping down inflation ("because cost increases reduce the

sale of exports"), promote competition, contribute capital to the national economy in the form of taxes, reduce the gap between rich and poor through the transfer of capital and income distribution, and act as agents of change, "altering traditional value systems, social attitudes, and behavior patterns." (See Biersteker, *Distortion or Development?,* pp. 2–3). Among the benefits that joint ventures were supposed to offer: (1) Both sides would share risk in an uncertain environment; (2) local talent would be cultivated through training in the joint venture; (3) host-country laws are generally designed to make joint ventures the most (if not the only) attractive form of foreign direct investment; (4) joint ventures symbolized equality between the host nation and the MNC; (5) the symbol of equality reduced host suspicion of foreign motives; (6) the joint venture facilitated modernization through technology transfers, as well as management training.(See Friedmann and Beguin, *Joint International Business Ventures in Developing Countries,* p. 4).

8. See, for instance, Dennis J. Encarnation and Louis T. Wells Jr., "Sovereignty en Garde: Negotiating with Foreign Investors," *International Organization* vol. 39, no. 1 (Winter 1985), pp. 47–78. In this article, the authors numerous variables that affect the strength of host countries, including host government attitude toward foreign investment,"industry salience," (p. 60), level of decision-making decentralization, and "the competitive strategies of host countries." For a discussion of the effects of corporate personality on bargaining between hosts and MNCs, see Raymond Vernon, *Sovereignty at Bay* (New York: Basic Books, Inc., 1971), pp. 113–150. On the effect of government system on bargaining between hosts and MNCs, see Margaret M. Pearson, *Joint Ventures in the People's Republic of China: The Control of Foreign Direct Investment under Socialism* (Princeton: Princeton University Press, 1991); specifically, this author tests the hypothesis that socialist states are better able to control the terms of foreign direct investment than nonsocialist states. Among the works that have considered FDI in individual nations are Biersteker, *Distortion or Development?,* 1978, who considers FDI in Nigeria; Pearson, *Joint Ventures in the PRC,* on China; Grieco, "Between Dependency and Autonomy" on India; Moran, 1973, *Multinational Corporations and the Politics of Dependence: Copper in Chile* on Chile; and Peter Evans, *Dependent Development: The Alliance of Multinational, State, and Local Capital in Brazil* (Princeton: Princeton University Press, 1979).
9. Numerous legal analyses have addressed China's legal framework regulating foreign investment; an excellent example is Michael J. Moser, ed. *Foreign Trade,Investment, and the Law in the People's Republic of China* (Hong Kong: Oxford University Press, 1984). A comprehensive treatment of the Open Door policy and its repercussions for China's bargaining position vis-à-vis foreign investors appears in Samuel P. Ho and Ralph W. Huenemann, *China's Open Door Policy: The Quest for Foreign Technology and Capital* (Vancouver: University of British Columbia Press, 1984). Lucian Pye cites the mood of central authorities

as a factor believed by many foreign investors to affect the negotiating styles of Chinese negotiators (although he believes that sudden changes in the mood of Chinese negotiators usually can be attributed to deep-seated psychological factors rather than central-leadership mood); see Lucian Pye, *Chinese Commercial Negotiating Style* (Cambridge: Oelgeschlager, Gunn, and Hain, 1982).

10. This criticism appears in Encarnation and Wells, "Sovereignty en Garde," p. 51.
11. The most serious obstacle for foreign investors in China has been foreign-exchange requirements of the Chinese government. See Margaret M. Pearson, "The Erosion of Controls over Foreign Capital in China, 1979–1988," *Modern China,* vol. 17, no. 1 (January 1991), pp. 112–150. These problems were largely due to awkward pricing, which is a recurrent theme in Western analyses of China's Open Door policy since 1979; see, for instance, Richard Pomfret, *Investing in China: Ten Years of the 'Open Door' Policy* (London: Harvester/Wheatsheaf, 1991), pp. 23–33. On the challenges that China's dual pricing poses for foreigners, see Henny Sender, "Two-Price China," *Far Eastern Economic Review,* vol. 156, no. 24 (June 17, 1993), pp. 64–65. Interference with reform policies by local bureaucrats in China has been very well-documented; see, for instance, Huang Yasheng, "Web of Interests and Patterns of Behavior of Chinese Local Economic Bureaucracies and Enterprises during Reforms," *The China Quarterly,* no. 123 (September 1990), pp. 431–458, who argues that bureaucratic interference is still prevalent in China in the form of "what Kornai calls the 'tenacity of bureaucracy' —the paradoxical phenomenon of bureaucracies to proliferate themselves at the very time when their functions are supposed to decline." Chinese xenophobia and its "counter theme," zenophilia, are discussed in Pye, *Chinese Commercial Negotiating Style.*
12. For a critique of Anglo-Western legal analyses of Chinese law, see Barrett L. McCormick, *Political Reform in Post-Mao China* (Ann Arbor: University Microfilms International Dissertation Information Service, 1985), especially pp. 201–239.
13. See, for example, the following: John W. Lewis, *Leadership in Communist China* (Ithaca: Cornell University Press, 1963); Franz H. Schurmann, *Ideology and Organization in Communist China* (Berkeley: University of California Press, 1966); A. Doak Barnett, *Cadres, Bureaucracy, and Political Power in Communist China* (New York: Columbia University Press, 1967).
14. See, for instance, Franz Schurmann, *Ideology and Organization in Communist China, 2nd ed.,* (Berkeley: University of California Press, 1968).
15. See, for instance, Lowell Dittmer, "Bases of Power in Chinese Politics: A Theory of Analysis of the Fall of the Gang of Four," *World Politics,* vol. 31, no. 1 (October 1978), pp. 26–60.
16. Dorothy Solinger and David Bachman argued that there were three factions in the Chinese political system. See Dorothy Solinger, *Chinese Business Under Socialism* (Berkeley: University of California Press, 1984); see David Bachman, "Dif-

fering Visions of China's Post-Mao Economy: The Ideas of Chen Yun, Deng Xiaoping, and Zhao Ziyang," *Asian Survey,* vol. 26, no. 3 (March 1986), pp. 292–321.

17. See, for instance, the following: Lucian Pye, *The Spirit of Chinese Politics* (Cambridge: MIT Press, 1968); Richard Solomon, *Mao's Revolution and the Chinese Political Culture* (Berkeley: University of California Press, 1971); Andrew J. Nathan, "A Factionalism Model for CCP Politics," *The China Quarterly,* no. 53 (January–March 1973), pp. 34–66.
18. See David M. Lampton, ed. *Policy Implementation in Post-Mao China,* (Berkeley: University of California Press, 1987); Kenneth Lieberthal and Michael Oksenberg, *Policy Making in China: Leaders, Structures, and Processes* (Princeton: Princeton University Press, 1988); an important recent contribution is Kenneth G. Lieberthal and David M. Lampton, eds. *Bureaucracy, Politics, and Decision Making in Post-Mao China* (Berkeley: University of California Press, 1992).
19. Steven M. Goldstein, "Reforming Socialist Systems: Some Lessons of the Chinese Experience," *Studies in Comparative Communism,* vol. 21, no. 2 (Summer 1988), pp. 221–237. Please note that this phrase was not used by the author to convey his view, but rather to represent the views he believed to be held commonly by other scholars at this time.
20. See David M. Lampton, *Health, Conflict, and the Chinese Political System* (Ann Arbor: University of Michigan, Center for Chinese Studies, 1974).
21. See Joel Glassman, "Change and Continuity in Chinese Communist Education Policy," *Contemporary China* vol. 2, no. 2 (September 1978), pp. 847–890.
22. On water, the one-child policy, and election campaigns, see Lampton, White, and McCormick, respectively, in Lampton, ed. *Policy Implementation in Post-Mao China.*
23. Melanie Manion, "Policy Implementation in the People's Republic of China: Authoritative Decisions Versus Individual Interests," *Journal of Asian Studies,* vol. 50, no. 2 (May 1991), p. 275.
24. Please see Zhongyun Zi, "The Relationship of Chinese Traditional Culture to the Modernization of China: An Introduction to the Current Discussion," *Asian Survey,* vol. 27, no. 4 (April 1987), pp. 442–458, which discusses central characteristics of Chinese political culture that affect China's modernization. I found the article particularly useful in understanding debate between a positive school of thought that favors the view that Chinese cultural characteristics can be adapted to new conditions to play a positive role in China's modernization and a negative school of thought that contends that traditional Chinese culture has "become, on balance, a burden for China today as the country marches on to a modern society." (pp. 450–451)
25. Bargaining appears to be an inherent characteristic of Chinese culture and society in David M. Lampton, "Chinese Politics: The Bargaining Treadmill," *Issues and*

Studies vol. 23, no. 3, (March 1987), pp. 11–41. Also see David M. Lampton, "A Plum for a Peach: Bargaining, Interest, and Bureaucratic Politics in China," in Lieberthal and Lampton, *Bureaucracy, Policy, and Decision Making,* pp. 33–58, which is a revised and updated version of his 1987 *Issues and Studies* article on bargaining.

26. The importance of Confucian values in the economic development of many Asian nations is discussed in the following: David I. Steinberg, "The Confucian Backdrop: Setting the Stage for Economic Development," in Lee A. Tavis, ed. *Multinational Managers and Host Government Interactions* (Noter Dame, Ind.: University of Notre Dame Press, 1982), pp. 73–90.
27. On the negative impact of traditional Chinese culture on China's modernization, see Zi, "The Relationship of Chinese Traditional Culture." See especially pp. 448–452.
28. See Lampton, "Chinese Politics."
29. Examples are Interviews #2 and #36, 1990–1991.
30. For a consideration of Sino-foreign joint ventures in historical context, see David G. Brown, *Partnership with China: Sino-Foreign Joint Ventures in Historical Perspective* (Boulder: Westview Press, 1986). For an analysis of joint ventures in the context of the Open Door policy, see Ho and Huenemann, *China's Open Door Policy.* The role of joint ventures in terms of U.S.-China relations in general is discussed in Eugene K. Lawson, ed., *U.S.-China Trade: Problems and Prospects* (New York: Praeger, 1989). On the role of joint ventures in the context of socialist state development strategies, see Pearson, *Joint Ventures in the PRC.*
31. Interview #32, 1990–1991. Also, for a discussion of neotraditional relationships in Chinese industry, see Andrew G. Walder, *Communist Neotraditionalism: Work and Authority in Chinese Industry* (Berkeley: University of California Press, 1986). For contending views on the utility of the concept of neo-traditionalism, see the following articles: Brantley Womack, "An Exchange of Views about Basic Chinese Social Organization; Review Essay: Transfigured Community: Neo-Traditionalism and Work Unit Socialism," *The China Quarterly,* no. 126, (June 1991), pp. 313–333, and Andrew G. Walder, "A Reply to Womack," *The China Quarterly,* no. 126, (June 1991), pp. 333–339. The views of my informant are echoed in Margaret M. Pearson, "Breaking the Bonds of 'Organized Dependence: Managers in China's Foreign Sector," *Studies in Comparative Communism,* vol. 25, no. 1 (March, 1992).
32. Baocheng Han, "Wuhan: Enterprises Compete and Thrive," *Beijing Review,* vol. 31, no. 3 (January 18–24, 1988), pp. 24–27.
33. Interview #7, 1990–1991. Since 1991, this situation has changed dramatically as the foreign-investment community has responded with great zeal to Wuhan's economic reforms.
34. Interview #36, 1990–1991.

35. Paul Mooney, "At China's Crossroads," *Far Eastern Economic Review,* vol. 155, no. 46 (November 19, 1992), p. 66.
36. Ibid.
37. Ibid.
38. The East Lake High-Technology Development Zone focuses "on optical communications, bioengineering, laser technology, and the development of raw materials." The Wuhan Economic Development Zone specializes "in the production of automobiles and spare parts," with a joint venture between Peugot and the Number 2 Auto Works as the foundation of the zone. The Yangluo Economic and Technology Zone serves "as a container-transfer center. It has bonded areas offering preferential tax rates, an industrial commercial area, and a power plant." Ibid., p. 67.
39. Ibid.
40. Ibid.
41. "Infrastructure Improved in Wuhan," *The Xinhua Overseas General News Service* (November 2, 1993).
42. "Overseas Investment Flows into Wuhan," *The Xinhua General Overseas News Service* (August 19, 1993).
43. "Wuhan Becomes Hot Spot for Foreign Investment," *The Xinhua General Overseas News Service* (September 18, 1992).
44. "Central China City Improves Investment Environment," *The Xinhua General Overseas News Service* (March 16, 1993).
45. "Infrastructure Improved in Wuhan," *The Xinhua General Overseas News Service* (November 2, 1993).
46. "Wuhan Makes Progress in Producing Optic Fiber Cables," *The Xinhua General Overseas News Service* (January 15, 1993).
47. Ibid.
48. "Wuhan Gives Enterprises More Freedom," *The Xinhua General Overseas News Service* (November 22, 1992).
49. Ibid.
50. "Wuhan Upgrades Old Industrial Enterprises with Foreign Investment," *The Xinhua General Overseas News Service* (December 9, 1992).
51. See Mooney, "At China's Crossroads," pp. 66–67.
52. "Wuhan Builds 'City of Cars,'" *The Xinhua General Overseas News Service* (December 28, 1992).
53. According to one article, at the end of 1993 in Wuhan there were 2,023 foreign-funded projects with a total contractual investment of U.S.$2.7 billion. In the first eleven months of 1993, 1,023 foreign-funded projects were established with a total investment of U.S.$1.2 billion. See "Foreign Investors Flock to Wuhan," *The Xinhua General Overseas News Service* (December 24, 1993).

54. Hanyang, Wuhan's oldest section, claims "eight sites of historical and cultural relics listed as important spots under state and provincial protection, such as Guiyuan Temple and Qintai Park." See "Wuhan Builds Modern Tourist Town," *The Xinhua General Overseas News Service* (December 12, 1992).
55. "Wuhan Opens International Futures Market," *The Xinhua General Overseas News Service* (December 9, 1993).
56. See Mooney, "At China's Crossroads," p. 68.
57. For a discussion of the importance and difficulty of differentiating between the Chinese government and the CCP in the study of Chinese politics, see Lieberthal and Oksenberg, *Policy Making in China,* pp. 21–22.
58. For a discussion of the importance of internal laws and the difficulty of analyzing Chinese law without access to these laws, see Michael J. Moser, "Introduction," in Moser, ed. *Foreign Trade, Investment, and the Law.* Also, Lieberthal discusses many different types of internal documents and their respective implications for the policy process in Kenneth Lieberthal, *Central Documents and PolitburoPolitics in China* (Ann Arbor: University of Michigan, Center for Chinese Studies, 1978). The quote is from interview #7, 1990–1991.
59. A classic analysis that portrays how localities gain power to pursue their own interests in lieu of central objectives is Audrey Donnithorne, "China's Cellular Economy: Some Economic Trends Since the Cultural Revolution," *China Quarterly,* vol. 13, no. 52, (October–December 1972), pp. 605–619.
60. See Lampton, "Chinese Politics." Also see Lieberthal and Oksenberg, *Policy Making in China,* pp. 406–410, on the evolution of a system of policy making and implementation based on bargaining among bureaucrats and other interested parties.
61. See Ronald C. Keith, "Chinese Politics and the New Theory of 'Rule of Law,'" *The China Quarterly,* no. 121 (March 1991), pp. 109–118; the author summarizes the debate among Chinese regarding the "rule of man" versus the "rule of law"; he concludes that a combination of the two perspectives is evolving and is conceptually popular among Chinese intellectuals and legal scholars. For a more pessimistic perspective on the role of the "rule of law" in contemporary Chinese society, see Te-sheng Chen, "The Interaction between Economic and Political Reform in Mainland China, 1978–1989," *Issues and Studies,* vol. 26, no. 2 (February 1990), pp. 13–34. See also "Rule of Law, not Rulers," *Far Eastern Economic Review* (February 4, 1994), p.5, which is an editorial that speculates on the negative repercussions if Hong Kong's strong and effective legal framework will be undermined by Mainland China and its ways of conducting business when it takes over in 1997.
62. Interview #36, 1990–1991.
63. Susan Shirk, "The Politics of Industrial Reform," in Elizabeth Perry and Christine Wong, eds. *The Political Economy of Reform in Post-Mao China* (Cambridge: Harvard University Press, 1985), pp. 195–219.

Chapter 2

1. See, for instance, Pearson, *Joint Ventures in the PRC,* pp. 58–65.
2. Ibid., pp. 59–60.
3. Weizao Deng and Zheshi Jiang, "Growth of the Multinationals," *Beijing Review,* vol. 24, no. 16, (April 20, 1981), pp. 16–17.
4. Ibid., p. 16.
5. Ibid., p. 20.
6. Chongwei Ji, "China's Utilization of Foreign Funds and Relevant Policies," *Beijing Review,* vol. 24, no. 16 (April 20, 1981), pp. 16–17. Creating jobs for the millions of Chinese that are added to the workforce every year is a major challenge to Beijing's leadership. On the impact of China's population on its moderniztion program, see, for instance, Liu Zheng, Song Jian and Others, eds. *China's Population: Problems and Prospects* (Beijing: New World Press, 1981), especially pp. 77–110 and pp. 119–128; also see "Providing Jobs for China's Hundreds of Millions," *China Reconstructs,* vol. 35, no. 2 (February 1986), pp. 12–14.
7. Jianzhang He, "Newly Emerging Economic Forms," *Beijing Review,* vol. 24, no. 21 (May 25, 1981), pp. 16–17.
8. Ibid., p. 17. Also see Muqiao Xue, *China's Socialist Economy* (Beijing: Foreign Languages Press, 1981), pp. 39–44. This chapter, "The Socialist Transformation of the Handicrafts and Small Businesses under Individual Ownership," explains the role of handicrafts and small businesses in China's modernization, as well as their roles in historical perspective since 1949.
9. Ibid. A concise description of the functions of foreign capital in China's economy also appears in Meizhen Yao, *Guoji Touzi Fa (International Investment Law)* (Wuchang, PRC: Wuhan University Press, 1989), p. 120.
10. See Pearson, *Joint Ventures in the PRC,* 1991, pp. 38–63. Pearson traces China's determination to remain self-reliant in its interaction with the outside commercial arena to the "late-nineteenth-century intellectual movement that called for China's self-strengthening against foreign aggression through selective use of foreign ideas and goods," and follows it through its stated objectives during the Open Door policy. (p. 38) This strategy, she explains, came to be known as the *ti-yung* formula, "which called for Chinese learning as the essence (*ti*) of modernization, but for incorporation of foreign learning for practical use."(p. 38)
11. Chongwei Ji, "China's Utilization of Foreign Funds," p. 18.
12. Ibid.
13. Ibid., p. 19. For a reference to other major organizations involved in China's foreign trade and their responsibilities, see "Organizations Involved in Invest-

ment," *The China Business Review,* vol. 15, no. 2 (March–April, 1988), pp. 34–35. A more detailed discussion of "the players" (p. 38) in China's foreign-trade bureaucracy, including CITIC, before and after the beginning of administrative reform in this area in 1979 appears in Ho and Huenemann, *China's Open Door Policy,* pp. 38–47.

14. See Chongwei Ji, "China's Utilization of Foreign Funds," pp. 19–20.
15. Ibid.
16. Priorities in this area are found in China's "Three Guarantees and Three Restrictions," which "guarantee the construction of projects included in the plan, productive projects, and key projects while restricting projects that are outside the plan, nonproductive and non-key projects." This phrase is quoted from the following: Wanming Gu and Li Li, "Expanded Use of Extra-Budgetary Funds" (text). Beijing *Xinhua Domestic Service* in Chinese (January 17, 1988). Translation by the Foreign Broadcast Information Service. (FBIS–CHI–88–018; January 28, 1988). See Ming Bu, "China's Financial Relations with Foreign Countries," *Beijing Review,* vol. 24, no. 16 (April 20, 1981); in this article, the author outlines the principles that will govern China's borrowing practices as follows: (1) the project must meet feasibility requirements; (2) the loans should be low-interest and/or interest-free; (3) "the loans are granted on the basis of mutual benefit and equality, are not detrimental to our sovereignty and conform to international practice;" (4) loans are accepted based on China's ability to repay them. (p. 22)
17. Chongwei Ji, "China's Utilization of Foreign Funds," pp. 19–20.
18. Guang Han, "Capital Construction: Achievements and Problems," *Beijing Review,* vol. 25, no. 13 (March 29, 1982), p. 19.
19. Ibid.
20. Education Department of *Hongqi,* "On China's Economic Relations with Foreign Countries," *Beijing Review,* vol. 25, no. 22 (May 31, 1982), p. 14.
21. Guang Han, "Capital Construction," p. 20.
22. Ibid.
23. Education Department of *Hongqi,* "On China's Economic Relations," p. 15.
24. Ibid., p. 14.
25. Ibid., p. 15. See also p. 16 in Muhua Chen, "Prospects for China's Foreign Trade in 1983," *Beijing Review,* vol. 26, no. 6 (February 7, 1983), pp. 14–17, stressing the need to improve the quality of raw materials and primary products that made up almost half of China's exports.
26. Rongji Zhu, "On Technological Progress and Technological Imports," (text). Beijing *Gongren Ribao* in Chinese (September 12, 1983). Translation by the Foreign Broadcast Information Service. *FBIS Daily Report-China,* September 22 1983, (FBIS–CHI–83–185 pp. K2–K7).
27. Ibid., pp. K5–K6.

28. The "Four Modernizations" is a famous policy pronounced by Zhou Enlai at the 10th National People's Congress of the Chinese Communist Party. The objectives of the policy are to modernize China's industry, agriculture, technology, and national defense. For historical background to China's technology-import practices, see Stanley B. Lubman, "Technology Transfer to China: Policies, Law and Practice," in Moser, ed. *Foreign Trade, Investment, and the Law*, pp. 84–102. The author discusses four "waves" of technology imports from 1952 through the beginning of the Open Door policy.
29. Jiarui Cao, "The Present Condition of and Problems in China's Technology Import Practices (Part One)" (text). Hong Kong *Liaowang Overseas Edition* in Chinese (May 5, 1986). Translation by the Foreign Broadcast Information Service. *FBIS Daily Report-China,* May 16, 1986, p. K5.
30. Ibid.
31. Ibid., p. K6.
32. Ibid.
33. Rongji Zhu, "On Technological Progress," p. K6.
34. Pearson, *Joint Ventures in the PRC,* p. 147.
35. Ibid., pp. 147–152.
36. Ibid.
37. On problem areas in China's science and technology research and development systems, see Lubman, "Technology Transfer to China."
38. Cao, "The Present Condition," pp. 14–15.
39. Ibid.
40. Ibid. Also see Pearson, *Joint Ventures in the PRC,* p. 150.
41. Rongji Zhu, "On Technological Progress," p. K7.
42. Cao, "The Present Condition," p. K9.
43. Anonymous, "China, Thailand, Indonesia among Countries Criticized for Inadequate Protection of Intellectual Property," *East Asian Executive Reports,* vol. 13, no. 3 (March 15, 1991), pp. 18–21.
44. Sandy Henry, "Limited Protection," *Far Eastern Economic Review,* vol. 153, no. 29 (July 18, 1991), pp. 61–62.
45. On the issue of industrial-property rights before 1949, see Gene T. Hsiao, *The Foreign Trade of China: Policy, Law, and Practice* (Berkeley: University of California Press, 1977), pp. 128–134. Hsiao explains that although China had adopted a copyright law in 1928, a trademark law in 1930, and a patent law in 1944, the legislation was very loose and did not serve the purpose of protecting industrial-property rights effectively. On technology transfer to the PRC, see Pearson, *Joint Ventures in the PRC,* 1991, pp. 145–153.
46. For an excellent description and legal analysis of China's patent legislation from 1984–1987, see Jeanette L. Pinard and Chun-cheng Lian, "Patent Protection under Chinese Law," *Journal of Chinese Law,* vol. 1, no. 1 (Spring 1987), pp. 69–91.

47. "The Patent Law of the PRC" is translated in *The China Business Review,* vol. 12, no. 1 (January–February 1985), pp. 54–57. On the effects of this legislation, see Pearson, *Joint Ventures in the PRC,* p. 152.
48. The "Implementing Rules of the Ministry of Foreign Economic Relations and Trade for Examination and Confirmation of Export Enterprises and Technologically Advanced Enterprises with Foreign Investment" appears in *China Economic News,* (February 23, 1987), pp. 5–7. See Pearson, *Joint Ventures in the PRC,* footnotes 160 and 161, p. 281.
49. "Copyright Law Set for June 1991 Implementation" (text). Beijing *Xinhua* in English (January 3, 1991). In *FBIS Daily Report-China,* December 30, 1990, (FBIS–CHI–002; p. 17).
50. Peirong Zhuo, "Publication of Intellectual Rights Journal Marked" (text). *Beijing Xinhua Domestic Service* in Chinese (January 22, 1991). Translation by the Foreign Broadcast Information Service. *FBIS Daily Report-China,* January 24, 1991 (FBIS–CHI–91–016; pp. 22–23).
51. "7.3 Copyright," *Business International, China Hand* (March 1, 1993). Please see this article for a detailed description of recent copyright legislation in China.
52. Ibid., p. 23.
53. Recognition and discussion of China's failure to follow the law and China's lack of institutions to implement laws appear in the following: "Commentary on Copyright Protection" (text). In Chinese (August 9, 1991). Translation by the Foreign Broadcast Information Service. *FBIS Daily Report-China,* August 12, 1991 (FBIS–CHI–91–155; pp. 48–49). The reference to China's property-rights law court is from the following: "New Court Handles Intellectual Property Issues," (text). Beijing *China Daily (Business Weekly)* in English (September 8, 1991). *FBIS Daily Report-China,*September 10, 1991 (FBIS–CHI–91–175).
54. Ibid. For a pessimistic view of recent intellectual-property-rights legislation in China, as well as recommendations for improvement, see the following: Morton David Goldberg and Jesse M Feder, "China's Intellectual Property Legislation," *The China Business Review,* vol. 18, no. 5 (September–October 1991), pp. 8–11. For a report on copyright protection for Chinese authors, please see "Copyright as Individual Property," *China News Analysis,* no. 1445 (October 15, 1991), pp. 1–9.
55. Sheng Mu, "Science and Technology White Paper: A Guide to China's Policies on Science and Technology" (text). Hong Kong *Liaowang Overseas Edition* in Chinese, (September 8, 1986). Translation by the Foreign Broadcast Information Service. *FBIS-Daily Report-China,*September 18, 1986 (FBIS–CHI–86; pp. 14–15).
56. Jian Song, "Industries Employing New High Technologies Must Be Oriented to the World" (text). Beijing*Guangming Ribao* in Chinese (December 27, 1991). Translation by the Foreign Broadcast Information Service. *FBIS Daily Report–China,* January 18, 1991 (FBIS–CHI–91–013; pp. 35–37).

57. "Responsibility System for Researchers Published" (text). Urumqi *Xinjiang Ribao* in Chinese (August 25, 1991). Translation by the Foreign Broadcast Information Service. *FBIS Daily Report-China,* September 17, 1991 (FBIS–CHI–180; pp. 60–62).
58. James C.F. Wang, *Contemporary Chinese Politics*(Englewood Cliffs: Prentice Hall Inc., 1985), p. 222.
59. Ibid.
60. Hong Ma, *New Strategy for China's Economy*(Beijing: New World Press, 1983), p. 118.
61. Michael Goldberg, "Management Skills for the New Mandarins," *Far Eastern Economic Review,* vol. 134, no.45 (November 6, 1986), pp. 30-31.
62. Hong Ma, *New Strategy for China's Economy,* p. 118.
63. "Enterprises Demand More Power," *Beijing Review,* vol. 29, no. 24 (June 16, 1986), p. 6. In addition to demanding more authority over economic decision making, enterprise managers often complained about responsibilities that had little to do with enterprise operation, including handling social welfare benefit distribution, day care for children, housing, and even marriage arrangements; see Qiu-yuan Tian, *Dalu de Changzhang yu Xianggang de Laoban* (*Mainland Managers and Hong Kong Bosses*) (Liaoning: People's Republic of China: Liaoning University Press, 1989); see, especially, pp. 3–5.
64. Kevin J. O'Brien and James Z. Lee, "Chinese Enterprise Reform: A Factory-Level Perspective." Paper Presented at the Annual Meeting of the Midwest Political Science Association, April 5–7, 1990, Chicago, Ill., pp. 12–15. This paper appears as Kevin J. O'Brien, "Bargaining Success of Chinese Factories," *The China Quarterly,* vol. 33, no. 132 (December 1992), pp. 1086–1100.
65. Goldberg, "Management Skills for the New Mandarins," pp. 30-31.
66. Ibid.
67. Much has been written about the cultural differences between Chinese and foreign (especially Western) management styles. Among those writings I have found helpful are the following:

    A) A general analysis of the difficulties in bringing Western management techniques to China through the joint venture appears in Pearson, *Joint Ventures in the PRC,* pp. 177–182.

    B) Edwin C. Nevis, "Using an American Perspective in Understanding Another Culture: Toward a Hierarchy of Needs for the PRC," *Journal of Applied BehavioralScience,* vol. 19, no. 3 (March 1983), pp. 249–264.

    C) On the difficulty of negotiating labor contracts that satisfy foreign and Chinese concerns, see Jamie P. Horsely, "Chinese Labor," *The China Business Review,* vol. 11, no. 3 (May–June 1984), pp. 16–25.

    D) On contending with the communist power structure, economy, and cultural differences, see Jonathon M. Zamet and Murray E. Bovarnick, "Employee Relations for Multinational Corporations in China," *Columbia Journal of World Business,* vol. 21, no. 1 (Spring 1986), pp. 13–19.

E) The effects of conflicting cultural values on negotiations between Chinese and foreign parties are discussed in the following: 1) Pye, *Chinese Commercial Negotiating Style;* (2) Paul E. Schroeder, "The Ohio-Hubei Agreement: Clues to Chinese Negotiating Practices," *The China Quarterly,* no. 91, (September 1982), pp. 486–491; (3) Oded Shenkar and Simcha Ronen, "The Cultural Context of Negotiations: The Implications of Chinese Interpersonal Norms,"*Journal of Applied Behavioral Science,*vol. 23, no. 2 (1987) pp. 263–275.

F) *Management International Review* (*MIR*) featured several articles on human resource management in the PRC. I have found the following particularly interesting: (1) Yorem Zeira and Oded Shenkar, "Interactive and Specific Parent Characteristics: Implications for Management and Human Resources in International Joint Ventures," *MIR,* vol. 30, Special Issue (1990), pp. 7–23; (2) Inga S. Baird, Marjorie A. Lyles, and Robert Wharton, "Attitudinal Differences between American and Chinese Managers regarding Joint Venture Management," *MIR,* vol. 30, Special Issue (1990), pp. 53–68; (3) Henry W.

68. See Pearson, *Joint Ventures in the PRC,* pp. 318–320.
69. Ibid., pp. 183–191. Also, for a focused view of the effects of the June 4, 1989, Tiananmen incident on the roles of CCP cells and labor unions in joint ventures, see "Party and Politics in Joint Ventures," *The China Business Review,* vol. 17, no. 6 (November–December 1990), pp. 38–40.
70. See Michael J. Moser, "Foreign Investment in China: the Legal Framework," in Moser, ed. *Foreign Trade, Investment, and the Law,* pp. 126–128.
71. Ibid.
72. Ibid.
73. Ibid.
74. Ibid. Also see Pearson, *Joint Ventures in the PRC,* pp. 318–320.
75. Ibid., Moser, "Foreign Investment in China."
76. Ibid. Also, for an excellent description of these processes, see Richard H. Holton, "Human Resource Management in the People's Republic of China," *MIR,* vol. 30, Special Issue (1990), pp. 121–136; these values are also discussed by Steinberg in "The Confucian Traveler."
77. See Holton, "Human Resource Management."
78. Ibid.
79. See Walder, *Communist Neotraditionalism.* On the importance of the work unit for personal connections, see especially pp. 21–27 and pp. 59–84; on layoffs and expulsions in Chinese society, see pp. 72–74.
80. See Holton, "Human Resource Management," p. 131.

81. See Hong Ma, *New Strategy for China's Economy,* p. 118.
82. An excellent treatment of Chinese xenophobia appears in Pye, *Chinese Commercial Negotiating Style,* especially pp. 81–84.

Chapter 3

1. Pearson uses this dichotomy throughout her analysis, *Joint Ventures in the PRC.* The justification for using this dichotomy appears in a discussion on pp. 21–25. On domestic determinants of Chinese foreign policy, I have found the following helpful: Pearson, *Joint Ventures in the PRC,* pp. 20–28; Kenneth Lieberthal,"Domestic Politics and Foreign Policy," in Harry Harding, ed. *China's Foreign Relations in the 1980's* (New Haven: Yale University Press, 1984), pp. 43–70; Susan Shirk, "The Domestic Political Dimensions of China's Foreign Economic Relations," in Samuel S. Kim, ed. *China and the World: Chinese Foreign Policy in the Post-Mao World* (Boulder: Westview Press, 1984), pp. 57–81; David Bachman, "Domestic Sources of Chinese Foreign Policy," in Samuel S. Kim, ed. *China and the Outside World: New Directions in Chinese Foreign Relations* (Boulder: Westview Press, 1989), pp. 31–54.
2. See Jerome Alan Cohen, "Equity Joint Ventures: Twenty Pitfalls That Every Company Should Know About," *The China Business Review,* vol. 9, no. 6 (November–December 1982), pp. 23–30. This article identifies and briefly discusses all of these issues. Similarly, Jerome Alan Cohen and Jamie P. Horsley, "The New Joint Venture Regulations," *The China Business Review,* vol. 10, no. 6 (November-December 1983), pp. 44–48, which is a follow-up to Cohen's 1982 publication, discusses how the 1983 Implementing Act addressed each of these issues. I also recommend Jo Ann Swindler, "The New Legal Framework for Joint Ventures in China:Guidelines for Investors," *Law and Policy in International Business,* vol. 16, no. 3 (1984), pp. 1005–1050, which discusses legal adjustments made in the 1983 legislation. Legislation passed in 1986 and 1987 ("Provisions of the State Council for the Encouragement of Foreign Investment" and the 1987 implementing regulations for these provisions) also addressed many of these issues. I recommend Farhad Simyar and Kamal Argheyd, "China: Crossroad to Fame or Failure?" *Business Quarterly,* vol. 51, no. 3 (November 1986), pp. 30–38; Jerome Alan Cohen and Ta-kuang Chang, "New Foreign Investment Provisions, *The China Business Review,* vol. 17, no. 6 (January–February 1987), pp. 11–15; Lucille A. Barale, "China's Investment Implementing Regulations," *The China Business Review,* vol. 18, no. 2 (March–April 1988), pp. 19–23. On lending to joint ventures, see Moser, "Foreign Investment in China: The Legal Framework,"

in Moser, ed. *Foreign Trade, Investment, and the Law,* pp. 122–123, and p. 129. On profit distribution, see pp. 133–134; see also Franklin D. Chu, "Banking and Finance in the China Trade," in Moser, ed. *Foreign Trade, Investment, and the Law,* pp. 229–265. On dispute settlement and dissolution, much has been written. The literature that I have perused includes Jerome Alan Cohen, "The Role of Arbitration in Economic Cooperation with China," in Moser, ed. *Foreign Trade, Investment, and the Law,* pp. 296–319; "PRC Disputes, Part Three: Going For Litigation as a Last Resort," *Business China,* vol. 17, no. 5 (September 10, 1990), pp. 132–133; John Frisbie and David Ben Kay, "Jont Venture Dissolution," *The China Business Review* vol. 17, no.6, (November–December 1990), pp. 42–45.

3. Lincoln Kaye, "Uncertain Patrimony," *Far Eastern Economic Review,* vol. 155, no. 43 (October 29, 1992), pp. 10–12.
4. Ibid., p. 10.
5. Ibid.
6. Lincoln Kaye, "Deng by a Whisker," *Far Eastern Economic Review,* vol. 155, no. 45 (November 12, 1992), p. 41.
7. A Correspondent in Peking, "Aims Are High, Funds Are Low," *Far Eastern Economic Review,* vol. 155, no. 45 (November 12, 1992), pp. 44–46.
8. Tai Ming Cheung, "Pushing the Pendulum," *Far Eastern Economic Review,* vol. 155, no. 14 (April 9, 1992), p. 46.
9. Lincoln Kaye, "Role Reversal," *Far Eastern Economic Review,* vol. 156, no. 21 (May 27, 1993), pp. 10–11.
10. Ibid., p. 10.
11. Ibid., p. 11.
12. Henny Sender, "By the Horns," *Far Eastern Economic Review,* vol. 156, no. 29 (July 22, 1993), p. 81.
13. Ibid., pp. 81–82.
14. Henny Sender, "No Bed of Roses," *Far Eastern Economic Review,* vol. 156, no. 31 (August 5, 1993), p. 64.
15. Ibid., p. 64.
16. Carl Goldstein, "Full Speed Ahead," *Far Eastern Economic Review,* vol. 156, no. 42 (October 21, 1993), p. 66.
17. Louise de Rosario, "Politics in Command," *Far Eastern Economic Review,* vol. 156, no. 47 (November 25, 1993), pp. 14–15.
18. For a list of main objectives of this austerity campaign, please see "Get Off Our Backs," *Far Eastern Economic Review,* vol. 156, no. 28 (July 15, 1993), p. 69.
19. Ibid., p. 15.
20. Moser, "Foreign Investment in China," p. 125.
21. See Cohen, "Equity Joint Ventures," p. 23.
22. Moser, "Foreign Investment in China," p. 125.

23. See Cohen, "Equity Joint Ventures," 1982.
24. Cohen and Horsley, "New Joint Venture Regulations," pp. 44–48.
25. Pearson, *Joint Ventures in the PRC,* uses the term "shadow management" in her discussion of Chinese joint venture management. The quote is from Moser, "Foreign Investment in China," p. 125.
26. Cohen and Horsley, "New Joint Venture Regulations," p. 41. The Ministry of Foreign Economic Relations and Trade (MOFERT) "was established in 1982 through a merger of four ministry-level bodies-the Ministry of Foreign Trade, the Ministry of Foreign Economic Relations (responsible for China's foreign aid), the State Import and Export Commission, and the State Foreign Investment Control Commission." Generally, it is said to be "'responsible for the study and implementation of foreign economic and trade policies, for the administration of trade matters, for laws and regulations on foreign economic relations, and for coordination of activities relating to foreign economic relations.'" See A. Doak Barnett, *The Making of Foreign Policy in China: Structure and Process* (Boulder: Westview Press, 1985), p. 94. For a more detailed description, see pp. 93–96.
27. Pearson, *Joint Ventures in the PRC,* pp. 171–172.
28. Pearson explains in some detail the strategies that the Chinese government used to prevent its citizens from imitating their foreign colleagues in the joint ventures. (See, for instance, *Joint Ventures in the PRC,* pp. 122–125). Also see John Gennard, "The Impact of Foreign-Owned Subsidiaries on Host-Country Labor Relations: The Case of the United Kingdom," in Robert J. Flanagan and Arnold R. Weber, eds. *Bargaining without Boundaries: The Multinational Corporation and International Labor Relations* (Chicago: The University of Chicago Press, 1974), pp. 77–102; see, especially, pp. 80–85. Gennard argues that among variables that may encourage disruption by foreign-owned subsidiaries of host-country labor relations "is the extent to which foreign multinationals operate styles of management in industrial relations which are very different from those of British companies." (p. 81) This possible cause of conflict "has been reduced by the tendency for most foreign-owned subsidiaries to employ British managers in industrial relations." (p. 84) Foreign multinationals, it seems, have to adapt their management approaches to the unique characteristics of the host-country environments where their enterprises are located.
29. Cohen, "Equity Joint Ventures," p. 26. Originally, joint ventures were not allowed to pay their Chinese employees more than 150 percent more than they would be paid in comparable positions in the state sector. Subsequent to the 1986 Provisions, however, the Ministry of Labor and Personnel removed this cap. Localities, including Shanghai, however, undermined these attempts to grant more autonomy to joint ventures by instituting limits in local legislation.(See Joel L. Greene, "FIEs Face New Labor Obstacles," *The China Business Review,* vol. 18, no. 1 (January–February 1991), pp. 8–9.

30. Moser, "Foreign Investment in China," p. 126.
31. Ibid.
32. A striking example of Chinese aversion to employee dismissals was explained to me by a joint venture hotel manager in Beijing. This manager discovered that one of the employees in the hotel had been stealing. After the chairperson of the labor union was consulted and agreed that the employee should be dismissed, the manager fired her. However, the manager discovered that for the same crime in the past, employees had never been fired or even severely disciplined. (See Interview #34, 1990–1991).
33. Moser, "Foreign Investment in China," p. 126.
34. Ibid., p. 128. Moser explains that the labor plan is intended to ensure that joint venture labor needs are satisfied locally in a coordinated manner. If joint venture labor needs cannot be satisfied locally, the joint venture may obtain permission from the local labor bureau to go outside the localities. With regard to conditions under which an employee may be dismissed, Moser explains, "the [1984] law prohibits dismissal where workers and staff members are undergoing medical treatment due to a work-related ailment or are in the hospital." (p. 128) Joint ventures are also not permitted to dismiss women "who are six months pregnant or more or are on maternity leave." (p. 128)
35. See Cohen and Chang, "New Foreign Investment Provisions," pp. 11–15. The 1986 Provisions clarified many issues that concerned foreign investors; specifically, those concerning wage and welfare benefits were "designed to eliminate the payment of subsidies for heat, cooking oil, grain allowance, and other items that make up an estimated 20 percent of the current labor costs for foreign- invested enterprises." (p. 12)
36. Ibid.
37. See Barale, "China's Investment Implementing Regulations," p. 20.
38. Ibid.
39. Joint ventures still had to contend with other domestic rules and regulations that, for instance, govern the movement of Chinese citizens from one area of the country to another, as is explained in the section on "recruitment" in Chapter Two of this book. The difficulties gaining approval for transfers and the "hidden costs" of such transfers are discussed at some length in Greene, "FIEs Face New Labor Obstacles," *The China Business Review,* vol. 21, no. 1 (January–February 1991), pp. 8–12.
40. See Barale, "China's Investment Implementing Regulations," pp. 20–21.
41. See Greene, "FIEs Face New Labor Obstacles," pp. 8–9.
42. Ibid., p. 9.
43. For an explanation of how decentralization can exacerbate "long-standing problems in Chinese industry (for example, irrational prices, supply shortages, over-

payment of workers)," see Shirk, "The Politics of Industrial Reform," cited in Daniel Kelliher, "The Political Consequences of China's Reforms," *Comparative Politics,* vol. 18, no. 4 (July 1986), pp. 480–481.

44. Lampton, "Chinese Politics," p. 13.
45. On general energy-pricing policies in China, see Bruce Reynolds, "China in the International Economy," in Harry Harding, ed. *China's Foreign Relations in the 1980s* (New Haven: Yale University Press, 1984), pp. 71–106; Pearson reported frequent energy failures in joint ventures in *Joint Ventures in the PRC.* Also see Pomfret, *Investing in China,* who writes that "the critical shortage of energy is a frustration for all producers in China and, although some favored joint ventures are guaranteed electricity supplies, most have to accept days without energy or to expect brownouts or energy failure." (p. 132) An excellent analysis of China's energy problems and potential solutions to those problems is Carl Goldstein, "China's Generation Gap," *Far Eastern Economic Review,* vol. 155, no. 23 (June 11, 1992), pp. 45–51. On the role foreign firms are playing in contributing to solving China's energy problems, please see Carl Goldstein, "Charged Up," *Far Eastern Economic Review,* vol. 156, no. 15 (April 15, 1993), p. 63.
46. On distribution and transportation problems, see Kemp, *Investing in China: Where, How, and Why?* (London: The Economist Publications, Ltd., 1987): "Distribution of supplies is largely centralized, and allocations are still made according to the state planning system. Shortages of materials frequently occur. A number of foreign investors have expressed the view that it is very important for a joint venture to be considered a high priority investment and for the foreign managers to be on good terms with relevant officials, in order to ensure a consistent allocation of materials and supplies.

    "Although the supplier may be able to produce on schedule, goods can often be held up in transportation. This applies to domestic goods and raw materials, particularly those that have to be sent from inland provinces on the limited road, rail, and inland waterway systems, as well as to imported goods which may suffer delays at port. It is not uncommon for supplies to be several weeks late, thus holding up the production process and adding significantly to costs. In extreme cases, the difficulty in procuring supplies and raw materials may make all the difference between success or failure of a venture. A joint venture established in Guangdong to build yachts ultimately failed because arrival of the components and materials it had intended to purchase in China was delayed by between six and nine months."(p. 82)
47. See Pearson, *Joint Ventures in the PRC,* pp. 112–116.
48. See Lampton, "Chinese Politics." Also see Pearson, *Joint Ventures in the PRC,* pp. 191–198. On the prevalence of corruption in modernizing nations, see Samuel P. Huntington, *Political Order in Changing Societies* (New Haven: Yale University Press, 1968), pp. 59–71. On the frequency of corruption that encompasses "gouging"

by local officials, see Alan P.Liu, "The Politics of Corruption in the People's Republic of China," *American Political Science Review,* vol. 77, no. 3 (September 1983), pp. 602–621. The Chinese also recognized the problem of corruption; see, for instance, "We Must Persistently Grasp Things with Two Hands When Carrying Out Socialist Modernization" (text). Beijing *Renmin Ribao* in Chinese (September 17, 1983). Translation by the Foreign Broadcast Information Service. *FBIS Daily Report-China,* September 19, 1983 (China PRC National Affairs; pp. K1–K3). The problem was also associated with China's long-standing problem of bureaucratism; see, for example, the following concerning this phenomenon: Jiwen Zhong, "Overcoming Bureaucratism Is an Important Task in Reforming the Political Structure — Studying Comrade Deng Xiaoping's Article 'On the Reform of the System of the Party and State Leadership'" (text). Beijing *Renmin Ribao* in Chinese (August 4, 1987). Translation by the Foreign Broadcast Information Service. *FBIS Daily Report-China,* August 7, 1987 (FBIS-China National Affairs; pp. K22–K26); for insight into the history of bureaucratism, see Baozhu Li, "'Bureaucrat Profiteering' in China's History" (text). Beijing *Renmin Ribao* in Chinese (November 7, 1988). Translation by the Foreign Broadcast Information Service. *FBIS Daily Report-China,* November 15, 1988 (FBIS–CHI–88–220; pp. 35–39). On the freedom of local bureaucrats to behave largely without regard for the center, see Yasheng Huang, "Web of Interests and Patterns of Behavior of Chinese Local Economic Bureaucracies and Enterprises during Reform," *The China Quarterly,* no. 123 (September1990), pp. 431–458. An excellent article on the sources of corruptionin China is Helena Kolenda, "One Party, Two Systems: Corruption in the People's Republic of China and Attempts to Control It," *Journal of Chinese Law,* vol. 4, no. 2 (Fall 1990), pp. 187–232. On a recent anti-corruption drive that led to the arrests of 46,800 government officials, see Hong Chang, "Over 46,800 Corrupt Officials Punished in 1990" (text). Bejing *China Daily* in English (January 26,1991). *FBIS Daily Report-China*, January 29, 1991 (FBIS–CHI–91–019; pp. 38–42). A general overview of the 1991 government anti-corruption campaign is given by Zhiguo An, "Anti-corruption Struggle Continues," *Benjing Review*, vol. 34, no. 31 (August 5–11, 1991), pp. 4–5. A recent article on the role of corruption in economic crimes that I also found helpful in understanding how widespresad the phenomenom is in China is Jean-Louis Rocca, "Corruption and Its Shadow: An Anthropological View of Corruption in China," *The China Quarterly*, no. 130, June 1992, pp. 402–416.

49. See Pearson, *Joint Ventures in the PRC,* pp. 112–116, on joint-venture resource-procurement restrictions.
50. Ibid. Joint ventures, Pearson explains, also could be affected adversely by changes in the plan. She explains, for example, that "the draft production plan of the Hitachi joint venture to produce television sets was reviewed routinely by both provincial and central organs after the board of directors had approved it. At one point in the

first phase, central authorities unilaterally revised the plan to cut production volume by over half to reflect a new central directive to decrease national production of television sets." (p. 113)

51. Ibid., pp. 113–114.
52. Ibid., p. 114.
53. Ibid.
54. Ibid., p. 115.
55. Ibid.
56. Barry Naughton, "Economic Directions for the 1990s," *The China Business Review,* vol. 18, no. 3 (May–June 1991), p. 10.
57. An overheated economy in the first six or seven months of 1988 was blamed for an inflation rate that reached 18.5 percent and remained at 17.8 percent throughout much of 1989; see Ping Li, "Price Reform: The Progressive Way," *Beijing Review,* vol. 35, no. 18 (May 4–10, 1992), pp. 18–21.
58. Naughton, "Economic Directions for the 1990s," p. 10.
59. See Cohen, "Equity Joint Ventures."
60. The total value of each side's contribution is "registered capital" (*zhuce ziben*). This term is defined as "the total amount of the capital contribution subscribed by the parties to the joint venture, which is registered with the Chinese authorities at the time the venture is formally established." (See Moser, "Foreign Investment in China," pp. 120–121).
61. Ibid. Also see Pearson, *Joint Ventures in the PRC,* p. 166; and Schroeder, "The Ohio-Hubei Agreement."
62. Eugene K. Lawson, "Introduction," p. 13.
63. Pye, *Chinese Commercial Negotiating Style,* p. 36–37.
64. Cohen, "Equity Joint Ventures," p. 24.
65. Pye, *Chinese Commercial Negotiating Style,* p. 38.
66. Terrance W. Conley and Paul W. Beamish, "Joint Ventures in China: Legal Implications," *Business Quarterly,* vol. 51, no. 1 (November 1986), p. 40.
67. In January 1983, the Ministry of Finance "provided that the withholding tax rate would be halved to 10 percent, and certain transactions made wholly exempt, 'where the technology is advanced and the terms preferential,' in certain cases." See Lubman, "Technology Transfer to China."
68. See Perry Keller, "Liberating the Land," *The China Business Review,* vol. 15, no. 2 (March–April 1988), p. 41.
69. Ibid.
70. Ibid., p. 40.
71. Ibid.
72. Ibid.
73. Ibid., p. 41.

74. Pitman B. Potter, "China's New Land Development Regulations," *The China Business Review,* vol. 18, no. 6 (November–December 1991), pp. 12–15.
75. Ibid., p. 13.
76. Ibid.
77. Cohen, "Equity Joint Ventures," p. 27.
78. Ibid.
79. "For domestic sales, ventures are ordinarily to rank their products according to quality, set their prices according to state-set prices for that product quality, and receive payment in *renmibi*." The prices must be approved by local pricing authorities; during this process, joint venture representatives may ask them to take into consideration the international market price for the product in question.(Ibid.).
80. See "Regulations of Wuhan Municipal Government on the Rapid Construction of East Lake High-Technology Development Zone," *Wuhan Local Laws,* pp. 329–335.
81. Ibid.
82. Interview #2, 1990–1991.
83. Ibid.
84. For a comprehensive overview of Chinese tax policies, please see Michael J. Moser and Winston K. Zee, *China Tax Guide* (Oxford: Oxford University Press, 1987).
85. See Cohen, "Equity Joint Ventures." Under the Joint Venture Income Tax Law, if an enterprise "chooses to reinvest some of its profits in China for five years . . . 40 percent of the income taxes paid on the reinvested amount may be refunded as an investment incentive." (p. 28). On the Joint Venture Income Tax Law, see Moser and Zee, *China Tax Guide,* pp. 38–52. On the provision granting a tax reduction to enterprises with advanced technology, see Swindler, "The New Legal Framework," p. 1021, footnote 98.
86. For instance, the individual withholding income tax on foreign and Chinese employees was not addressed in the original legislation. Reportedly, Chinese employees who received a salary of more than 800 *yuan* per month would be taxed under the Individual Income Tax Law and joint ventures that withhold the tax would be paid 1 percent commission of the tax withheld as compensation for acting as a withholding agent. Other taxes that often had to be addressed in individual joint venture contracts because the language of the legislation was too general and open to too many interpretations included customs duties, the Industrial and Commercial Consolidated Tax, "which is similar to a sales tax that is imposed at every stage in the transfer of goods from their production through marketing channels, and which varies in its rate depending on the type of goods taxed," the Buildings and Land Tax, and the Transport License Tax.(Cohen, "Equity Joint Ventures," pp. 29–30).

    For a more detailed treatment of the implementation of customs regulations during the early 1980s, please see Michael J. Moser, "Introduction," pp. 20–26, and

Moser and Zee, *China Tax Guide,* pp. 75–86. A detailed analysis of the implementation of the Individual Income Tax Law is found in Timothy A. Gelatt and Richard D. Pomp, "China's Tax System: An Overview and Transactional Analysis," in Moser, ed., pp. 37–41, and Moser and Zee, pp. 18–37. On the Industrial and Commercial Tax, see Gelatt and Pomp, "China's Tax System," pp. 41–42. On the Joint Venture Income Tax Law and the Foreign Enterprise Income Tax Law, see Gelatt and Pomp, "China's Tax System," pp. 42–45 and pp. 45–50 respectively.

87. Swindler, "The New Legal Framework," p. 1033.
88. Ibid.
89. Ibid. See footnote 186.
90. Ibid.
91. Cohen and Chang, "New Foreign Investment Provisions," p. 12.
92. See Barale, "China's Investment Implementing Regulations," pp. 19–23; after initial tax breaks, the author explains, the 1986 Provisions cut income tax by 50 percent for EOEs that export over 70 percent of output per year, while TAEs receive three additional years of a 50 percent income tax reduction with refunds paid retroactively to 1986 to enterprises that prepaid taxes that are now exempt. (p. 21) Enterprises that reinvest profits with a duration of five or more years can obtain a refund on tax paid on the amount invested. This benefit can be extended to any foreign-invested enterprise. Beforehand, such a refund was limited to only 40 percent of the tax paid and available only to equity joint ventures. (p. 22)
93. For the foreign reaction to the law, see Joyce Peck, "Standardizing Foreign Income Taxes," *The China Business Review,* vol. 18, no. 5 (September–October, 1991), pp. 12–15. The quote is from page 12 of this article. The Chinese reaction is from the following article: "Gu Ming Explains New Income Tax Law" (text). Beijing *Xinhua* in English (April 3, 1991). Translation by the Foreign Broadcast Information Service. *FBIS Daily Report-China,* April 4, 1991 (FBIS–CHI–91–065; pp. 31–32). The citation appears on page 32 of the article.
94. See "The Income Tax Law of the People's Republic of China for Enterprises with Foreign Investment and Foreign Enterprises," *Beijing Review,* vol. 34, no. 25 (June 24–30, 1991), pp. 27–31.
95. Peck, "Standardizing Foreign Income Taxes," p. 12.
96. Ibid.
97. Ibid.
98. Ibid., p. 13.
99. Ibid.
100. Ibid. Under the new law, the author explains, "profits distributed from an equity joint venture, cooperative joint venture, or wholly foreign-owned enterprise to another such enterprise in China will be exempt from withholding tax." (p.13) Tax exemptions are available for the first and second profit-making years with a

50 percent cut in years three, four, and five. (p. 13) Under earlier legislation, only TAEs and EOEs received refunds for reinvestment; the new law extends a 40 percent tax refund for reinvested profits. (p. 14)

101. Ibid., p. 14. It should be noted that to gain approval for filing a single return, one unit in the company must take responsibility for all management and accounts of the others, which is an enormous task that often, reportedly, will not be worth the effort. For oil and gas businesses, the news is good because "the law allows profits and losses from upstream and downstream operations to be included in the same tax return, as long as the activities are in the same line of business." (p. 14)
102. Ibid.
103. Xiaobin Yang, "New Tax Law Favors Foreign Enterprises," Beijing Review, vol. 34, no. 18 (May 6–12, 1991), p. 31.
104. Peck, "Standardizing Foreign Income Taxes," p. 14.
105. Ibid.
106. Carl Goldstein, "The Inspector Calls," *Far Eastern Economic Review,* vol. 156, no. 26 (July 1, 1993), p. 72.
107. Ibid.
108. Ibid.
109. Pearson, "The Erosion of Controls," p. 115.
110. "The Law of the People's Republic of China on Joint Ventures using Chinese and Foreign Investment" appears in Franklin Chu, Michael J. Moser, and Owen Nee, eds. *Commercial, Business and Trade Laws: People's Republic of China,* (Dobbs Ferry, New York: Oceana Publications, 1982).
111. John Frisbie, "Balancing Foreign Exchange," *The China Business Review* (March–April 1988), p. 24.
112. Pearson, "The Erosion of Controls," p. 122.
113. See "The Implementing Act for the Law of the PRC on Joint Ventures using Chinese and Foreign Investment, *Beijing Review,* vol. 31, no. 4 (August 22, 1983), pp. 25–26.
114. Enterprises were deemed qualified to purchase joint-venture-produced goods with foreign exchange if they met the following conditions:(1) If the products were ones that China needed and would otherwise have to be imported; (2) If the products could not be produced by another Chinese enterprise;(3) If the domestic enterprise was purchasing domestic work. See Pearson, "The Erosion of Controls," p. 123.
115. Ibid., p. 124.
116. Ibid., p. 127; also see Pomfret, *Investing in China,* pp. 61–65.
117. Yinghui Wang, "Yin Jieyan Says the Foreign-Exchange Control Structure Reform Goal Is to Turn *Renminbi* into a Convertible Currency" (text). Beijing *Jingji Cankao Bao* in Chinese (February 16, 1993). Translation by the Foreign Broadcast Information Service. *FBIS Daily Report-China,* March 5, 1993 (FBIS–CHI–93–042; pp. 30–31).

118. John Frisbie and Richard Brecher, "A Tough Balancing Act," *The China Business Review,* vol. 20, no. 6 (November–December 1993), pp. 9–13.
119. Ibid., p. 9.

Chapter 4

1. On foreign objectives and motivations for investing in China, see Kemp, *Investing in China,* pp. 65–91.
2. Pearson, *Joint Ventures in the PRC,* p. 244, footnote 48.
3. Ibid., p. 28.
4. Kemp, *Investing in China,* p. 72.
5. Article Ten, "Chapter Two: Employment, Dismissal, and Resignation of the Staff and Workers," in "Provisions of Labor and Personnel Management for Sino-foreign Joint Ventures in Wuhan" (promulgated by the Wuhan Municipal Government on December 26, 1988), *Wuhan Local Laws and Regulations,* p. 320.
6. Interview #42, 1990–1991.
7. Ibid.
8. Ibid.
9. Ibid.
10. Ibid.
11. Ibid.
12. Ibid.
13. Article Seven, *Wuhan Local Laws and Regulations,* p. 319.
14. Ibid.
15. Interview #3, 1990–1991.
16. Ibid.
17. Ibid.
18. Ibid.
19. Ibid.
20. Ibid.
21. Interview #28, 1990–1991.
22. Ibid.
23. Interview #32, 1990–1991.
24. Interview #34, 1990–1991.
25. Ibid.
26. Ibid.
27. Interview #18, 1990–1991.
28. Ibid.

29. Interview #7, 1990–1991.
30. Ibid.
31. Ibid.
32. Ibid.
33. "Provisions of Labor and Personnel Management for Sino-Foreign Joint Ventures in Wuhan," (promulgated December 26, 1988) *Wuhan Local Laws and Regulations,* pp. 318–319.
34. Interview #5, 1990–1991.
35. Ibid.
36. Interview #18, 1990–1991.
37. Ibid.
38. Interviews #5, #18, #22, 1990–1991.
39. Article Six, "Provisions of Labor and Personnel Management for Sino-Foreign Joint Ventures in Wuhan," *Wuhan Local Laws and Regulations,* p. 319.
40. Interview #5, 1990–1991.
41. Ibid.
42. Ibid.
43. Ibid.
44. See, for example, Thomas N. Thompson, "How Not to Do Business with China," *The China Business Review* (January–February 1985), pp. 10–13; see especially pp. 10–11.
45. Interview #36, 1990–1991.
46. Moser, "Law and Investment in the Guangdong Special Economic Zones," in Michael J. Moser, ed. *Foreign Trade, Investment, and the Law,* p. 159.
47. Interview #15, 1990–1991.
48. Ibid.
49. Interview #23, 1990–1991.
50. Ibid.
51. Interview #5, 1990–1991.
52. Ibid.
53. Ibid.
54. Ibid.
55. Ibid.
56. Ibid.
57. Interview #7, 1990–1991; unlike the term *jiegu,* which means "arbitrary removal or layoff characteristic of capitalism," *kaichu* "is an administrative punishment meted out in response only to flagrant abuses of factory rules or to lawbreakers and political dissidents. For an explanation of Chinese terminology used in employee dismissals, see Walder, *Communist Neotraditionalism,* pp. 68–76. See especially p. 74 for an explanation of the term *kaichu.*

58. Interview #7, 1990–1991.
59. Ibid.
60. Ibid.
61. Ibid.
62. Ibid.
63. Ibid.
64. Lincoln Kaye, "Mayday May Day," *Far Eastern Economic Review,* vol. 155, no. 18 (May 7, 1992), p. 22.
65. Paul Mooney, "At China's Crossroads," pp. 66–67.
66. Pearson, *Joint Ventures in the PRC,* p. 174.
67. Interview #7, 1990–1991; the housing requirements that are often quite burdensome in joint ventures in China are discussed in Kathy Chase Hanna, "The New Housing Crunch," *The China Business Review,* vol. 18, no. 4 (July–August 1991), pp. 30–32.
68. Ibid.
69. Ibid.
70. Unfortunately, we did not discuss what the tradeoffs were for him to be allowed to do this.
71. Ibid.
72. Chapter Three: Wages, Welfare, and Insurance," (Articles 21 and 22), "Provisions of Labor and Personnel Management for Sino-Foreign Joint Ventures in Wuhan," *Wuhan Local Laws and Regulations,* p. 324.
73. Ibid.
74. Interview #7, 1990–1991.
75. Ibid.
76. Ibid.
77. Ibid.
78. Ibid.
79. Ibid.
80. Ibid.
81. Ibid.
82. Ibid.
83. Ibid.
84. It should be noted that Chinese state-enterprise managers also have been reported to feel burdened by responsibilities they have over the distribution of social welfare benefits. Indeed, one manager complained that he was responsible for social welfare benefits which included employee housing, child day care, marriage, and often education up to and including university-level education; it was, he explained, as though he had the responsibility of running an entire society, not just an enterprise. See Tian, *Mainland Managers,* pp. 1–5.

85. See Chapter Thirteen: "Trade Union," in "Regulations for the Implementation of the Law of the People's Republic of China on Joint Ventures using Chinese and Foreign Investment," *Beijing Review,* vol. 26, no. 41 (October 10, 1983), p. 12.
86. Pearson, *Joint Ventures in the PRC,* p. 184.
87. Interview #5, 1990–1991.
88. Ibid.
89. Ibid.
90. Ibid.
91. Interview #3, 1990–1991.
92. Ibid.
93. Ibid.
94. Lincoln Kaye, "The Price of Reform," *The Far Eastern Economic Review,* vol. 156, no. 44 (November 4, 1993), p. 13.
95. Ibid.
96. Gelatt and Pomp, "China's Tax System," p. 137.
97. Interview #18, 1990–1991; also, interviews #8 and #23, 1990–1991, made this point.
98. This tax is a combination of a commodity tax, a commodity circulation tax, a sales tax, and a chop tax. See Rong Zhijie, *Shewai Shuishou yu Guoji Shuishou* (*Foreign Taxes and International Taxes*) (Henan, People's Republic of China: Henan People's Press, 1988), pp. 37–39, for a detailed description of the tax and its function in China's economic development.
99. Interview #7, 1990–1991.
100. Ibid.
101. Ibid.
102. Ibid.
103. Ibid.
104. Ibid.
105. Ibid.
106. Ibid.
107. Ibid.
108. Ibid.
109. Ibid.
110. Ibid.
111. Ibid.
112. Interview #6, 1990–1991.
113. Ibid.
114. Ibid.
115. Ibid.
116. Ibid.

117. Ibid.
118. Ibid.
119. Ibid.
120. Ibid.
121. Ibid.
122. Ibid.
123. Frisbie, "Balancing Foreign Exchange."
124. Interview #36, 1990–1991. Also, see Frisbie and Brecher, "A Tough Balancing Act," pp. 9–13.
125. See Frisbie, "Balancing Foreign Exchange,"1988; also, Frisbie and Brecher, "A Tough Balancing Act."
126. See Frisbie and Brecher, "A Tough Balancing Act." The authors explain that for most FIEs, "swap centers are the leading means for obtaining foreign exchange."(p. 10) Approximately 25 percent of 41 surveyed use swap centers for 55 percent of their foreign-exchange needs, while 14 use the swap centers for 70 percent or more of their foreign-exchange needs (p. 10)
127. Interviews #35 and #38, 1990–1991.
128. Ibid.
129. Ibid.
130. Ibid.
131. Ibid.
132. Ibid.
133. Ibid.
134. Ibid.
135. Ibid.
136. Ibid.
137. The experience of Beijing Jeep has become the classic example of a foreign corporation's problems with China's stringent foreign-exchange requirements. See Jim Mann, *Beijing Jeep: The Short Unhappy Romance of American Business in China* (New York: Simon and Schuster, 1989).
138. Interview #36, 1990–1991.
139. Ibid.
140. Interviews #1, #2, and #21, 1990–1991.
141. Ibid.
142. Ibid.
143. Ibid.
144. Ibid.
145. Paul Epner, "Managing Chinese Employees," *The China Business Review,* vol. 18, no. 4 (July–August 1991), p. 25.
146. Interview #7, 1990–1991.

147. The Chinese security manager was present at the first interview conducted with foreign management at this particular joint venture. I later accompanied him and the family of one of the foreign managers to dinner; it was obvious from the conversation that he had become a close friend of this family.
148. Interview #35, 1990–1991.
149. See Lampton, "Chinese Politics."
150. Interview #1, 1993.
151. Interview #35, 1990–91. This was a joint venture involving a large Western multinational corporation. I have found that among major corporations with large joint venture agreements in China, management training for members of the Chinese side in the host country is usually stipulated in the joint venture contract. In fact, major MNCs seem to prefer that obligations and responsibilities of both sides be clearly stipulated in contractual agreements, leaving less room for misunderstandings due to linguistic and cultural differences.
152. It should be noted that, generally, in most Western countries, unlike China, these bureaucratic fees are set by laws, rules and/or regulations and are tax deductible.
153. In order to bring attention to the problem of corruption, publicized cases usually involve substantial amounts of money. One *China Daily* article about arrested Chinese officials, for instance, concentrated on cases involving U.S.$32,758–U.S.$172,000; see "Corrupt Officials Seized in Campaign," *China Daily* vol. 12, no. 3646 (February 17, 1993), p. 3.
154. Because the meeting was in Chinese, the bureaucrat may have assumed that I did not understand the conversation and used terminology that she otherwise might not have used.
155. I discussed with a local tax bureau representative a manager's assertion that a "wine them, dine them" approach would have increased the possibility of receiving a tax break from the local tax bureau. He responded that any tax official who responded favorably to such an approach would be dismissed. (Interview #6, 1990–1991) In retrospect, my question lacked the style that I am suggesting foreign investors adopt in dealing with Chinese colleagues. His only proper response to my question was to dismiss the manager's assertion, because the style of my questioning implied bribery and corruption. If I had suggested that efforts on the part of a joint venture to create and maintain good relations with the local tax bureau might be of benefit to all parties concerned, the tax official's response may have been different and a more fruitful exchange may have followed.
156. Interview #7 and #28, 1990–91; Interview #1, 1993. Also see Epner, "Managing Chinese Employees," pp. 24–30.
157. For a description of the changing nature of gift-giving in China, see Hai Bian, "Giving Gifts: A Poor Practice?" *China Daily,* vol. 12, no. 3646 (February 17, 1993), p. 6.

158. Indeed, it is the "historical legacy of foreign military, political, and economic encroachment in China" that encourages Chinese leaders to stress constantly China's sovereignty, internal affairs, and the need for equality and mutual benefit in economic interaction with the outside world. See Pearson, *Joint Ventures in the PRC,* pp. 38–46. See also Michael H. Hunt, "Chinese Foreign Relations in Historical Perspective," in Harry Harding, ed. *China's Foreign Relations in the 1980s* (New Haven: Yale University Press, 1984), pp. 1–42.
159. Interview #35, 1990–1991.
160. Ibid.
161. Ibid.
162. See Gordon A. Bennett, "Chinese Political Culture," *Problems of Chinese Communism,* vol. 28, no. 1 (January–February 1979), pp. 67–74.
163. Interview #35, 1990–1991.
164. Vernon, *Sovereignty at Bay,* p. 146.
165. Interview #39, 1990–1991.
166. Ibid.
167. Interview #36, 1990–1991.
168. Ibid.
169. Interview #39, 1990–1991.
170. Interview #7, 1990–1991.
171. Ibid.
172. Du Xichuan and Zhang Lingyuan, *China's Legal System: A General Survey* (Beijing: New World Press, 1987), p. 184.
173. "PRC Disputes, Part Thrcc," p. 132.
174. Interview #36, 1990–1991.
175. Interview #24, 1990–1991.
176. See "PRC Disputes, Part Three," p. 132.
177. Ibid.
178. Interview #20, 1990–1991.
179. Interview #22, 1990–1991.
180. Pearson, *Joint Ventures in the PRC,* p. 60.
181. Interview #7, 1990–1991.
182. Ibid.
183. The respondent for Interview #7, 1990–1991 is also the vice president of the joint venture group in Wuhan.
184. Ibid.
185. Ibid.
186. Ibid.
187. Interview #4, 1990–1991.
188. Interview #28, 1990–1991.

189. Ibid.
190. Ibid. Because multinationals can cause conflicts in host-country labor relations, they must devise innovations to manage the problems. On such innovations in Britain, see Gennard, "The Impact of Foreign-Owned Subsidiaries," especially pp. 85-89.
191. Interviews #1, 1990-1991 and #5, 1990-1991.
192. Lampton, "Chinese Politics," p. 41.

Chapter 5

1. The translation of *guanxi* as "relationship" is very rough. In fact, Lucian Pye asserts that *guanxi* is "a word for which there is no English equivalent." For a more detailed discussion of this concept as it relates to foreign businesspeople, see Pye, *Chinese Commercial Negotiating Style,* pp. 88–89.
2. See Ambrose Yeo Chi King, "*Kuan-hsi* and Network Building: A Sociological Interpretation," *Daedalus,* vol. 120, no. 2, (Spring 1991), p. 77. This typology was taken from D.R. DeGlopper, "Doing Business in Lukang," in Arthur P. Wolf, ed. *Studies in Chinese Society* (Stanford: Stanford University Press, 1978), pp. 314–15.
3. King, *"Kuan-hsi and Network Building,"* p. 79.
4. Ibid., p. 80.
5. This process was discussed in the "Bargaining Strategies" section of Chapter Four.
6. It should be noted that in a later conversation with a Chinese manager from this same joint venture, I related this case to him. His response was that personal relationships were important all over the world, not just in China, and that the foreign partner who related the experience of trying to arrange a meeting with a local ministry was probably overstating the importance of finding a personal contact in the ministry before the meeting could be arranged.
7. Henny Sender, "Be Sure to Bring Money," *Far Eastern Economic Review,* vol. 156, no. 32 (August 12, 1993), pp. 72–73.
8. Ibid.
9. Interview #17, 1990–1991.
10. Ibid.
11. Ibid.
12. Ibid.
13. Ibid.
14. See Pomfret, *Investing in China,* pp. 46–54.
15. Ibid.
16. The benefits were identified most recently in the 1991 legislation.

17. The theme of this sort of bargaining being most apparent in Guangdong was stressed through all my interviews.
18. Interview #24, 1990–1991.
19. See the "Implementing Rules of the Ministry of Foreign Economic Relations and Trade for Examination and Confirmation of Export Enterprises and Technologically Advanced Enterprises with Foreign Investment," *China Economic News,* (February 23, 1987), pp. 5–7.
20. Interview #24, 1990–1991.
21. Interview #7, 1990–1991. This joint venture was made up of two operating units: one unit exports 80 percent of its products, while the other exports 100 percent of its products.
22. A representative from the neighboring joint venture indicated that it would soon begin exporting to other countries.
23. Interview #7, 1990–1991.
24. Encarnation and Wells, "Sovereignty en Garde," pp. 60–61.
25. Pearson, *Joint Ventures in the PRC,* p. 158.
26. Lawrence C. Reardon, "The SEZs Come of Age," *The China Business Review,* vol. 18, no. 6 (November–December 1991), p. 17.
27. Pearson, *Joint Ventures in China,* 1991, p. 158.
28. Reardon, 1991, pp. 15–16.
29. Ibid.
30. See Pearson, "Party and Politics in Joint Ventures,"*The China Business Review,* vol. 17, no. 6 (November–December 1990), pp. 38–40.
31. Interview #35, 1990–1991. For instance, the Chinese officially admitted that all blame for delays to begin production rested with the Chinese side; furthermore, they agreed to pay the foreign partner for the delays with interest.
32. Interview #34, 1990–1991.
33. Vernon, *Sovereignty at Bay,* p. 146.
34. Among the pieces that I have found helpful in understanding this issue are: Chapter Four: "Personality of the Multinational Enterprise" in Vernon, *Sovereignty at Bay,* pp. 113–150; also see Pye, *Chinese Commercial Negotiating Style.*
35. Pomfret, *Investing in China,* p. 109.
36. Ibid., p. 110. Also see Zigeng Dai, "What We Should Say About 'False Joint Ventures'" (text). Beijing *Guangming Ribao* in Chinese (April 4, 1993). Translation by the Foreign Broadcast Information Service. *FBIS Daily Report China,* May 4, 1993 (FBIS–CHI–93–084; pp. 30–31).
37. Ibid.
38. Mark Clifford, "The China Connection," *Far Eastern Economic Review,* vol. 155, no. 44 (November 5, 1992), p. 60.
39. Ibid.
40. Pearson, *Joint Ventures in the PRC,* p. 123.

41. Interviews #31 and #33, 1990–1991.
42. Pomfret, *Investing in China,* p. 112.
43. For an excellent treatment of the process of establishing these zones and their respective legal frameworks, see Moser, "Law and Investment," pp. 143–177.
44. See Dixin Xu, "China's SEZs," *Beijing Review,* vol. 50, (December 14, 1981), pp. 14–17.
45. Moser, "Law and Investment," p. 147.
46. Ibid., p. 147.
47. Pearson, *Joint Ventures in China,* p. 157.
48. Reardon, "The SEZs Come of Age," p. 15.
49. Ibid.
50. For a comparison of benefits in ETDZs, SEZs, and new investment incentives in Shanghai's Pudong New Area, see Norman P. Givant, "Putting Pudong in Perspective," *The China Business Review,* vol. 18, no. 6 (November–December 1991), pp. 30–32; see especially the table entitled "Incentives for Foreign-Invested Enterprises in China's Special Investment Zones," p. 31.
51. This proposition is in sync with Lieberthal and Oksenberg's notion that "the existing evidence . . . suggests that revenue-producing areas both have a greater claim upon the center and are the object of tighter control by the center." However, as I will argue, if the area in question is experiencing economic success, the center will have less influence than when it is experiencing an economic downturn. See Lieberthal and Oksenberg, *Policy Making in China,* p. 351.
52. Lieberthal and Oksenberg explain that centralrepresentatives tend to be more involved because of three factors: (1) "Ministries and bureaus have particular missions that they should pursue with zeal; (2) "ministers and bureau chiefs should represent and articulate the views of their units; (3) economic ministries and bureaus should seek additional investment capital so as to better carry out their mandates." See Lieberthal and Oksenberg, *Policy Making in China,* p. 29.
53. Ibid., p. 351. The informant for Interview #21, 1990–1991, used a Chinese phrase, which she translated as "around the law," several times to describe business in Guangdong.
54. Ibid., p. 352.
55. Ibid.

Chapter 6

1. See Moser, "Foreign Investment in China," p. 119. Also see Cohen, "Equity Joint Ventures," on feasibility-study costs as an issue of contention between the Chinese and foreign partners.

2. The trend, indeed, seems to be for foreign partners to undertake their own feasibility studies independently of the Chinese. (Interview #35, 1990–1991) Furthermore, Chinese searching for foreign partners may already have conducted feasibility studies for the project(s) they are proposing to undertake; in one case, foreign investors were able to secure over U.S.$200,000 in private investments and bank loans based on feasibility studies of a proposed joint venture project developed solely by the Chinese side. (Interview #43, 1990–1991)
3. Interview #2, 1990–1991.
4. Interview #7, 1990–1991.
5. McCormick, *Political Reform in Post-Mao China,* pp. 201–202.
6. Ibid., p. 104.
7. Also, see "PRC Disputes, Part Three."
8. McCormick, *Political Reform in Post-Mao China,* p. 207. I added the underlining in this quotation.
9. Keith, "Chinese Politics and the New Theory," p. 111. Please, see Zhiping Liang, "Explicating 'Law': A Comparative Perspective of Chinese and Western Legal Culture," *Journal of Chinese Law,* vol. 3, no. 1 (Summer 1989), pp. 55–94. In this article, the author has argued that the debate between proponents of the "rule of law" and proponents of the "rule of man" is misguided: "There are those who have incorrectly used 'rule of law' as the equivalent of the *'fazhi'* advocated by the pre-Qin legalists, leading to many senseless scholarly debates . . . Actually, what the legalists called *'fazhi'* only embodied the meanings of the two characters 'punishment and reward' (*xingshang*)." (pp. 80–81) The author makes a convincing argument that it is a mistake to believe that Chinese intellectuals who are reported to favor *'fazhi'* understand or have an appreciation for a western interpretation of law. Indeed, Chinese do not understand "the real and profound meaning of 'law' in Western culture [that] these differences result from difficulty of communication due to cultural differences." (p. 89) In fact, in China, "law was never perceived as a means of preserving rights, freedom, justice, since these were completely alien concepts in ancient China. Law was punishment." (p. 89)
10. Keith, "Chinese Politics and the New Theory," p. 111.
11. For an excellent discussion of the relationship between Chinese laws and policies, see Kevin J. O'Brien, *Reform without Liberalization: China's National People's Congress and the Politics of Institutional Change* (New York: Cambridge University Press, 1990), pp. 158–164; see especially pp. 158–159.
12. McCormick, *Political Reform in Post-Mao China,* p. 223.
13. A generally positive outlook on China's evolving legal system is Carlos W.H. Lo, "Deng Xiaoping's Ideas on Law," *Asian Survey,* vol. 22, no. 17, (July 1992), pp. 649–665; the quotation appears on p. 663.
14. Lampton, "Chinese Politics," pp. 12–15.

15. Ibid., p. 13.
16. Ibid.
17. Feng-cheng Fu, "The Decentralization of Peking's Economic Management and Its Impact on Foreign Investment," *Issues and Studies*, (February 1992), pp. 67–83.
18. Po-shih Ho, "An Undercurrent in Mainland China during the Eighth Five-Year Plan: Busy Making Money, Provinces Overtly Agree with, but Covertly Oppose, Policies from the Central Authorities" (text). Hong Kong *Tantai* in Chinese (February 9, 1991, pp. 7–8). Translation by the Foreign Broadcast Information Service. *FBIS Daily Report-China*, February 14, 1991, (FBIS–CHI–91–031; pp. 22–24), p. 23.
19. Chengxun Yang, "Bureaucracy and a Management System Characterized by Overconcentration of Power" (text). Beijing *Renmin Ribao* in Chinese (September 12, 1986). Translation by the Foreign Broadcast Information Service. *FBIS Daily Report-China*, September 18, 1986, pp. K11–K14.
20. Te-sheng Chen, "The Interaction between Economic and Political Reform," pp. 26–27.
21. Xue, *China's Socialist Economy See* pp. 135–162 on China's pricing system and price-reform policies.
22. Guogang Liu, "Price Reform Essential to Growth," Beijing Review, vol. 29, no. 33 (August 18, 1986), p. 14.
23. Ibid.
24. Ibid.
25. Ibid.
26. Long Ji, "Conscientiously Implement the Principle of Fixing Prices according to Quality" (text). Beijing *Renmin Ribao* in Chinese (August 19, 1983, p. 5). Translation by the Foreign Broadcast Information Service. *FBIS Daily Report-China*, August 26, 1983, pp. K10–K11.
27. Jiannan Zhou. "Reiterating the Policy of Attaching Primary Importance to Quality," (text). Beijing *Renmin Ribao* in Chinese (September 7, 1983, p. 2). Translation by the Foreign Broadcast Information Service. *FBIS Daily Report-China*, September 13, 1983, pp. K7–K10.
28. "It Is Necessary to Be Strict and Do Solid Work in Improving the Quality of Products," (text). Beijing *Renmin Ribao* in Chinese (May 14, 1985, p. 2). Translation by the Foreign Broadcast Information Service. *FBIS-Daily Report-China*, May 20, 1985, pp. K9–K10.
29. Ibid.
30. See, for instance, Edward J. Epstein, "Tortious Liability for Defective Products in the People's Republic of China," *Journal of Chinese Law*, vol. 2, no. 2 (Fall 1988), pp. 285–321, for an informative look at Chinese legislation concerning product quality. In response to substandard product quality in China, Epstein

explains, "there was a flurry of legislative activity which created new administrative measures for standardization, supervision, and licensing of a wide range of industrial products." (p. 287) These laws "offered rewards for success and threatened punishment for noncompliance, but they did not necessarily cause a manufacturer to feel the economic effects of producing poor-quality goods. Nor did these laws address the problem of supervising the supervisors; that is, making administrative authorities themselves economically responsible for quality control." (p. 287)

31. In one instance, the government issued an internal circular, "Report on Reversing the Decline in Quality of Some Individual Products," which outlined declining product quality and "increasing cases of fraud and deception and violations of law and discipline with regard to product quality." See "State Council Transmits Report on Quality" (text). Beijing *Xinhua Domestic Service* in Chinese (September 9, 1985). Translation by the Foreign Broadcast Information Service. *FBIS Daily Report-China,* September 18, 1985, pp. K19–K21. This passage is from p. K20.
32. Events have included conferences on quality control and awards ceremonies during "Quality Months." On these conferences, see, for instance, Daxiang Ge, "Zhang Jingfu Speaks at Quality Control Conference," (text). Beijing *Xinhua Domestic Service* in Chinese (June 19, 1985). *FBIS Daily Report-China,* June 21, 1985, pp. K16–K17. "Quality Months" were discussed in Fengchu Huang, "Zhang Jingfu Stresses Quality in Production" (text). Beijing *Xinhua Domestic Service* in Chinese (September 15, 1983). Translation by the Foreign Broadcast Information Service. *FBIS Daily Report-China,* September 20, 1983, pp. K9–K10.
33. For instance, the China Import and Export Consumer Goods Inspection Center, which was set up in 1988 in Shanghai by the China Import and Export Commodities Inspection Company, the General Society of Surveillance of Switzerland, and the Mitsui Company Ltd. of Japan "to ensure the quality of imports and exports." See "Commodity Inspection Center Set Up in Shanghai" (text). Beijing *Xinhua* in English (May 1988). *FBIS Daily Report-China,* May 19, 1988 (FBIS–CHI–88–097, pp. 54–55). Also, in 1988, China established the Bureau of Technical Supervision "to exercise technical supervision over the country's standardization of weights and measurements and quality control." See "Bureau of Technical Supervision Established" (text). Beijing *Xinhua* in English (July 19, 1988). *FBIS Daily Report-China,* July 20, 1988, p. 35.
34. According to one article, "the state spot-checked 679 domestic products of 40 varieties from 497 enterprises. Only 8 varieties were 100 percent qualified." See "Song Jian Speaks at Opening," (text). Beijing *China Daily* in English (July 20, 1988, p. 2). *FBIS Daily Report-China,* July 20, 1988, pp. 35–36.
35. Interview #44, 1992.

36. For a discussion of joint ventures as agents of change, please see Kathryn Rudie Harrigan, *Strategies for Joint Ventures* (Lexington, Mass.: Lexington Books 1985), pp. 377–384.
37. Pearson, "Breaking the Bonds."
38. Pearson, "Party and Politics."

LIST OF REFERENCES

"73 Copyright." *Business International, China Hand* (March 1, 1993).

A Correspondent in Beijing, "Aims Are High, Funds Are Low." *Far Eastern Economic Review,* vol. 155, no. 45 (November 12, 1992), pp. 44–46.

An, Zhiguo. "Anti-Corruption Struggle Continues." *Beijing Review,* vol. 34, no. 31 (August 5–11, 1991), pp. 4–5.

Anonymous, "China, Thailand, Indonesia among Countries Criticized for Inadequate Protection of Intellectual Property." *East Asian Executive Reports,* vol. 13, no. 3 (March 15, 1991).

Bachman, David. "Differing Visions of China's Post-Mao Economy: The Ideas of Chen Yun, Deng Xiaoping, and Zhao Ziyang." *Asian Survey,* vol. 26, no. 3 (March 1986), pp. 292–321.

———. "Domestic Sources of Chinese Foreign Policy," in Samuel S. Kim, ed. *China and the Outside World: New Directions in China's Foreign Relations.* Boulder: Westview Press, 1989, pp. 31–54.

Baird, Inga S., Marjorie A Lyles, and Robert Wharton. "Attitudinal Differences between American and Chinese Managers regarding Joint Venture Management." *Management International Review,* vol. 30, Special Issue, (1990), pp. 53–68.

Barale, Lucille A. "China's Investment Implementing Regulations." *The China Business Review,* vol. 15, no. 2 (March–April 1988), pp. 19–23.

Barnett, A. Doak. *Cadres, Bureaucracy, and Political Power in Communist China.* New York: Columbia University Press, 1967.

Bennett, Gordon. "Chinese Political Culture." *Problems of Chinese Communism,* vol. 28, no. 1 (January–February 1979), pp. 67–74.

Bergsten, Fred C., Thomas Horst, and Theodore H. Moran. *American Multinationals and American Interests.* Washington, D.C.: Brookings Institute, 1978.

Bian, Hai. "Giving Gifts: A Poor Practice?" *China Daily,* vol. 12, no. 3646 (February 17, 1993), p. 6.

Biersteker, Thomas J. *Distortion or Development? Contending Perspectives on the Multinational Corporation.* Cambridge: MIT Press, 1978.

Brown, David G. *Partnership with China: Sino-foreign Joint Ventures in Historical Perspective.* Boulder: Westview Press, 1986.

"Bureau of Technological Supervision Established" (text). Beijing *Xinhua* in English (July 19, 1988). *FBIS Daily Report-China,* July 20, 1988 (FBIS–CHI–88–139; p. 35).

Cao, Jiarui. "The Present Condition of and Problems in China's Technology Import Practices (Part One)" (text). Hong Kong *Liaowang Overseas Edition* in Chinese (May 5, 1986). Translation by the Foreign Broadcast Information Service. *FBIS Daily Report-China,* May 16, 1986 (FBIS–CHI–1986; pp. K5–K9).

Casati, Christine. "Satisfying Labor Laws and Needs." *The China Business Review,* vol. 18, no. 4 (July–August 1991), pp. 16-22.

"Central China City Improves Investment Environment," *The Xinhua General Overseas News Service* (March 16, 1993).

Chen, Gan and Xiaobing Yang. "Lawyers With New Acceptance in China." *Beijing Review,* vol. 31, no. 28 (July 11–17, 1988), pp. 18–22.

Chen, Muhua. "Prospects for China's Foreign Trade in 1983," *Beijing Review,* vol. 26, no. 6 (February 7, 1983), pp. 14–17.

Chen, Te-sheng. "The Interaction Between Economic and Political Reform in Mainland China, 1978–1989." *Issues and Studies* vol. 26, no. 2 (February 1990), pp. 13–34.

Cheng, Lucie and Arthur Rossett. "Contract with a Chinese Face: Socially Embedded Factors in the Transformation from Hierarchy to Market, 1978–1989." *Journal of Chinese Law,* vol. 5, no. 2 (Fall 1991), pp. 143–244.

Cheung, Tai Ming. "Pushing the Pendulum." *Far Eastern Economic Review,* vol. 155, no. 45 (April 9, 1992), p. 46.

Chu, Franklin D. "Banking and Finance in the China Trade," in Michael J. Moser, ed. *Foreign Trade, Investment, and the Law in the People's Republic of China.* Hong Kong: Oxford University Press, 1984, pp. 229–265.

Chu, Franklin D., Michael J. Moser, and Owen Nee, eds. *Commercial, Business, and Trade Laws: People's Republic of China.* Dobbs Ferry, N.Y.: Oceana Publications, 1982.

Clifford, Mark. "The China Connection," *Far Eastern Economic Review,* vol. 155, no. 44 (November 5, 1992), p. 60.

Cohen, Jerome Alan. "Equity Joint Ventures: Twenty Potential Pitfalls That Every Company Should Know About." *The China Business Review,* vol. 9, no. 6 (November–December 1982), pp. 23–30.

Cohen, Jerome Alan and Ta-kuang Chang. "New Foreign Investment Provisions." *The China Business Review,* vol. 14, no. 1 (January–February 1987), pp. 11–15.

Cohen, Jerome Alan and Jamie P. Horsley. "The New Joint Venture Regulations." *The China Business Review,* vol. 9, no. 6 (November–December 1983), pp. 44–48.

Cohen, Jerome Alan and Stuart Valentine. "Foreign Direct Investment in the People's Republic of China: Progress, Problems, and Proposals." *Journal of Chinese Law,* vol. 1, no. 2 (Fall 1987), pp. 161–216.

"Commentary on Copyright Protection" (text). In Chinese (August 9, 1991). Translation by the Foreign Broadcast Information Service. *FBIS Daily Report-China.* August 12, 1991 (FBIS–CHI–91–155; pp. 48–49).

"Commodity Inspection Center Set Up in Shanghai," (text). Beijing *Xinhua* in English (May 19, 1988). *FBIS Daily Report-China,* May 19, 1988 (FBIS–CHI–88–097; pp. 54–55).

Conley, Terrance W. and Paul Beamish. "Joint Ventures in China: Legal Implications." *Business Quarterly,* vol. 51, no. 1 (November 1986).

"Copyright Law Set for 1991 Implementation" (text). Beijing *Xinhua* in English (January 3, 1991). *FBIS Daily Report-China,* December 30, 1990 (FBIS–CHI–90–002; p. 17).

"Corrupt Officials Seized in Campaign," *China Daily,* vol. 12, no. 3646 (February 17, 1993), p. 3.

Dai, Zigeng. "What We Should Say About 'False Joint Ventures'" (text). Beijing *Guangming Ribao* in Chinese (April 4, 1993). Translation by the Foreign Broadcast Information Service. *FBIS Daily Report-China,* May 4, 1993 (FBIS–CHI–93–084; pp. 30–31).

Deng, Weizao and Zheshi Jiang. "Growth of the Multinationals." *Beijing Review,* vol. 24, no. 7 (February 16, 1981), pp. 16–20.

De Rosario, Louise. "Politics in Command." *Far Eastern Economic Review,* vol. 156, no. 47 (November 25, 1993), pp. 14–15.

Dittmer, Lowell. "Bases of Power in Chinese Politics: A Theory of Analysis of the Gang of Four." *World Politics,* vol. 31, no. 1 (October 1978), pp. 26–60.

Du, Xichuan and Lingyuan Zhang. *China's Legal System: A General Survey.* Beijing: New World Press, 1987.

Education Department of *Hongqi.* "On China's Economic Relations with Foreign Countries." *Beijing Review,* vol. 25, no. 22 (May 31, 1982), pp. 13–15.

Encarnation, Dennis J. and Louis T. Wells, Jr. "Sovereignty en Garde: Negotiating with Foreign Investors." *International Organization* vol. 39, no. 1 (Winter 1985), pp. 47–78.

"Enterprises Demand More Power." *Beijing Review,* vol. 29, no. 24 (June 16, 1986), p. 6.

Epner, Paul. "Managing Chinese Employees." *The China Business Review,* vol. 18, no. 4 (July–August 1991), pp. 24–30.

Epstein, Edward J. "Tortious Liability for Defective Products in the People's Republic of China." *Journal of Chinese Law* vol. 2, no. 2 (Fall 1988), pp. 285–381.

Evans, Peter. *Dependent Development: The Alliance of Multinational, State, and Local Capital in Brazil.* Princeton: Princeton University Press, 1979.

Finder, Susan. "Like Throwing an Egg against a Stone? Administrative Litigation in the People's Republic of China." *Journal of Chinese Law,* vol. 3, no. 2 (Summer 1989), pp. 1–29.

Flanagan, Robert J. and Arnold R. Weber, eds. *Bargaining without Boundaries: The Multinational Corporation and International Labor Relations.* Chicago: The University of Chicago Press, 1974.

"Foreign Investors Flock to Wuhan." *The Xinhua General Overseas News Service* (December 24, 1993).

Friedman, Wolfgang G. and George Kalmanoff. *Joint International Business Ventures.* New York: Columbia University Press, 1961.

Friedman, Wolfgang G. and Jean Pierre Beguin. *Joint International Business Ventures in Developing Countries: Case Studies and Analysis of Recent Trends.* New York: Columbia University Press, 1971.

Frisbie, John. "Balancing Foreign Exchange." *The China Business Review,* vol. 15, no. 2 (March–April 1988), pp. 24–28.

Frisbie, John and Richard Brecher. "A Tough Balancing Act." *The China Business Review,* vol. 20, no. 6 (November 12, 1993), pp. 9–13.

Frisbie, John and David Ben Kay. "Joint Venture Dissolution." *The China Business Review,* vol. 17, no. 6 (November–December 1990), pp. 42–45.

Fu, Feng-cheng. "The Decentralization of Peking's Economic Management and Its Impact on Foreign Investment." *Issues and Studies,* (February 1992), pp. 67–83.

Ge, Daxiang. "Zhang Jingfu Speaks at Quality Control Conference" (text). Beijing *Xinhua Domestic Service* in Chinese (June 19, 1985). Translation by the Foreign Broadcast Information Service. *FBIS Daily Report-China,* June 21, 1985, pp. K16–K17.

Gelatt, Timothy A. and Richard D. Pomp. "China's Tax System: An Overview and Transactional Analysis," in Michael J. Moser, ed. *Foreign Trade, Investment, and the Law in the People's Republic of China.* Hong Kong: Oxford University Press, 1984, pp. 36–83.

Gellhorn, Walter. "China's Quest for Legal Modernity." *Journal of Chinese Law,* vol. 1, no. 1 (Spring 1987), pp. 1–32.

Gennard, John. "The Impact of Foreign-Owned Subsidiaries on Host Country Labor Relations: The Case of the United Kingdom," in Robert J. Flanagan and Arnold R. Weber, eds., *Bargaining without Boundaries: The Multinational Corporation and International Labor Relations.* Chicago: The University of Chicago Press, 1974, pp. 77–102.

"Get Off Our Backs." *Far Eastern Economic Review,* vol. 156, no. 28 (July 15, 1993), p. 69.

Givant, Norman P. "Putting Pudong in Perspective." *The China Business Review,* vol. 18, no. 6 (November–December 1991), pp. 31–32.

Glassman, Joel. "Change and Continuity in Chinese Communist Education Policy." *Contemporary China,* vol. 2, no. 2 (September 1978), pp. 847–890.

Goldberg, Michael. "Management Skills for the New Mandarins." *China Reconstructs.*

Goldberg, Morton David and Jesse M. Feder. "China's Intellectual Property Legislation." *The China Business Review,* vol. 18, no. 5 (September–October 1991), pp. 8–11.

Goldstein, Carl. "Charged Up." *Far Eastern Economic Review,* vol. 156, no. 15 (April 15, 1993), p. 63.

Goldstein, Carl. "The Inspector Calls." *Far Eastern Economic Review,* vol. 156, no. 26 (July 1, 1993), p. 72.

Goldstein, Carl. "Full Speed Ahead." *Far Eastern Economic Review,* vol. 156, no. 42 (October 21, 1993), pp. 66–68.

Goldstein, Steven M. "Reforming Socialist Systems: Some Lessons of the Chinese Experience." *Studies in Comparative Communism,* vol. 21, no. 2 (Summer 1988), pp. 221–237.

Greene, Joel L. "FIEs Face New Labor Obstacles." *The China Business Review,* vol. 18, no. 1 (January–February 1991), pp. 8–12.

Grieco, Joseph M. "Between Dependency and Autonomy: India's Experience with the International Computer Industry." *International Organization,* vol. 36, no. 3 (Summer 1982), pp. 609–632.

Gu Ming Explains New Income Tax Law" (text). Beijing *Xinhua* in English (April 3, 1991). Translation by the Foreign Broadcast Information Service. *FBIS Daily Report-China.* (FBIS–CHI–91–065; pp. 31–32).

Gu, Wanming and Li Li. "Expanded Use of Extra-Budgetary Funds" (text). Beijing *Xinhua Domestic Service* in Chinese (January 17, 1988). Translation by the Foreign Broadcast Information Service. *FBIS Daily Report-China.* (FBIS–CHI–88–018).

Han, Baocheng. "Wuhan: Enterprises Compete and Thrive." *Beijing Review,* vol. 31, no. 3 (January 18–24, 1988), pp. 24–27.

Han, Guang. "Capital Construction: Achievements and Problems," *Beijing Review,* vol. 25, no. 22 (March 29, 1982), pp. 17–20.

Hanna, Kathy Chase. "The New Housing Crunch." *The China Business Review,* vol. 18, no. 4 (July–August 1991), pp. 30–32.

Harrigan, Kathryn Rudie. *Strategies for Joint Ventures.* Lexington, Mass.: Lexington Books, 1985.

He, Jianzhang. "Newly Emerging Economic Forms." *Beijing Review,* vol. 24, no. 21 (May 25, 1981), pp. 15–18.

Henry, Sandy. "Limited Protection." *Far Eastern Economic Review,* vol. 153, no. 29 (July 18, 1991), pp. 61–62.

Ho, Po-shih. "An Undercurrent in Mainland China During the Eighth Five-Year Plan: Busy Making Money, Provinces Overtly Agree With, But Covertly Oppose Policies from the Central Authorities" (text). Hong Kong *Tangtai* in Chinese (February 9, 1991, pp. 7–8). Translation by the Foreign Broadcast Information

Service. *FBIS Daily Report-China,* February 14, 1991 (FBIS–CHI–91–031; pp. 22–24).

Ho, Samuel P. and Huenemann, Ralph W. *China's Open Door Policy: The Quest for Foreign Technology and Technology and Capital.* Vancouver: University of British columbia Press, 1984.

Holton, Richard H. "Human Resource Management in the People's Republic of China." *Management International Review* vol. 30, Special Issue (1990), pp. 121–136.

Hong, Chang. "Over 46,000 Corrupt Officials Punished in 1990" (text). Beijing *China Daily* in English (January 26, 1991) *FBIS Daily Report-China,* January 29, 1991 (FBIS–CHI–91–019; pp. 38–42).

Horsley, Jamie P. "Chinese Labor." *The Chinese Business Review,* vol. 11, no. 3 (May–June 1984), pp. 16–25.

Hsiao, Gene T. *The Foreign Trade of China: Policy, Law, and Practice.* Berkeley: University of California Press, 1977.

Huang, Fengchu. "Zhang Jingfu Stresses Quality in Production" (text). Beijing *Xinhua Domestic Service* in Chinese (September 15, 1983). Translation by the Foreign Broadcast Information Service. *FBIS Daily Report-China,* September 20, 1983, pp. K9–K10.

Huang, Yasheng. "Web of Interests and Patterns of Behavior of Chinese Local Economic Bureaucracies and Enterprises During Reforms." *The China Quarterly,* no. 123 (September 1990), pp. 431–458.

Hunt, Michael H. "Chinese Foreign Relations in Historical Perspective," in Harry Harding, ed. *China's Foreign Relations in the 1980's.* New Haven: Yale University Press, 1984, pp. 1–42.

Huntington, Samuel P. *Political Order in Changing Societies.* New Haven: Yale University Press, 1968.

"The Implementing Act for the Law of the People's Republic of China on Joint Ventures Using Chinese and Foreign Investment." *Beijing Review,* vol. 26, no. 4 (August 22, 1983), pp. 25–26.

"Implementing Rules of the Ministry of Foreign Economic Relations and Trade for Examination and Confirmation of Export Enterprises and Technologically Advanced Enterprises with Foreign Investment." *China Economic News* (February 23, 1987), pp. 54–57.

"Income Tax Law of the People's Republic of China for Enterprises with Foreign Investment and Foreign Enterprises." *Beijing Review,* vol. 34, no. 25 (June 24–30, 1991), pp. 27–31.

"Infrastructure Improved in Wuhan." *The Xinhua General Overseas News Service* (November 2, 1993).

Ireland, Jill. "Finding the Right Management Approach." *The China Business Review,* vol. 18, no. 1 (January–February 1991), pp. 14–17.

"It Is Necessary to Be Strict and Do Solid Work in Improving the Quality of Products" (text). Beijing *Renmin Ribao* in Chinese (August 19, 1983, p. 5). Translation by the Foreign Broadcast Information Service. *FBIS Daily Report-China,* August 26, 1983, pp. K10–K11.

Jackson, Sukhan. "Reform of State Enterprise Management in China." *The China Quarterly,* vol. 27, no. 107 (September 1986), pp. 405–428.

Ji, Chongwei. "China's Utilization of Foreign Funds and Relevant Policies." *Beijing Review,* vol. 24, no. 16 (April 20, 1981), pp. 15–20.

Ji, Long. "Conscientiously Implement the Principle of Fixing Prices according to Quality" (text). Beijing *Renmin Ribao* in Chinese (August 19, 1983, p. 5). Translation by the Foreign Broadcast Information Service. *FBIS Daily Report-China,* August 26, 1983, pp. K10–K11.

Kaye, Lincoln. "Deng by a Whisker." *Far Eastern Economic Review,* vol. 155, no. 45 (November 12, 1992), p. 41.

———. "May Day." *Far Eastern Economic Review,* vol. 155, no. 45 (November 12, 1992), p. 41.

———. "Role Reversal." *Far Eastern Economic Review,* vol. 156, no. 22 (May 27, 1993), pp. 10–11.

———. "The Price of Reform." *Far Eastern Economic Review,* vol. 156, no. 44 (November 4, 1993), p. 13.

———. "Uncertain Patrimony." *Far Eastern Economic Review,* vol. 155, no. 43 (October 29, 1992), pp. 10–12.

Keith, Ronald C. "Chinese Politics and the New Theory of Rule of Law." *The China Quarterly,* vol. 32, no. 121 (March 1991), pp. 109–118.

Keller, Perry. "Liberating the Land." *The China Business Review,* vol. 15, no. 2 (March–April 1988), pp. 40–44.

Kelliher, Daniel. "The Political Consequences of China's Reforms." *Comparative Politics,* vol. 18, no. 4 (July 1986), pp. 480–481.

Kemp, Lynette. *Investing in China: Where, How and Why?* London: The Economist Publications Ltd., 1987.

King, Ambrose Yeo Chi. "*Kuan-hsi* and Network-Building: A Sociological Interpretation." *Daedalus,* vol. 120, no. 2 (Spring 1991), pp. 63–84.

Kobrin, Stephen J. "Testing the Bargaining Hypothesis in the Manufacturing Sector in Developing Countries." *International Organization* vol. 41, no. 4 (Autumn 1987), pp. 609–638.

Kolenda, Helen. "One Party, Two Systems: Corruption in the People's Republic of China and Attempts to Control It." *Journal of Chinese Law* vol. 4, no. 2 (Fall 1990), pp. 187–232.

Lakatos, Imre. "Falsification and the Methodology of Scientific Research Programmes," in Imre Lakatos and A. Musgrave, eds. *Criticism and the Growth of Knowledge*. Cambridge: Cambridge University Press, 1978, pp. 91–196.

Lampton, David M. "Chinese Politics: The Bargaining Treadmill." *Issues and Studies,* vol. 23, no. 3 (March 1987), pp. 11–41.

———. "A Plum for a Peach: Bargaining, Interest, and Bureaucratic Politics in China," in Kenneth G. Lieberthal and David M. Lampton, eds., *Bureaucracy, Politics, and Decision Making in Post-Mao China.* Berkeley: University of California Press, 1992, pp. 33–58.

———. *Health, Conflict, and the Chinese Political System.* Ann Arbor: University of Michigan, Center for Chinese Studies, 1974.

———. ed. *Policy Implementation in Post-Mao China.* Berkeley: University of California Press, 1987.

———. "Water: Challenge to a Fragmented Political System," in David M. Lampton, ed. *Policy Implementation in Post-Mao China.* Berkeley: University of California Press, 1987, pp. 157–189.

Lane, Henry W. and Paul Beamish. Cross-Cultural Cooperative Behavior in Joint Ventures in LDCs." *Management International Review* vol. 30, Special Issue 1990, pp. 87–102.

Lawson, Eugene K., ed. *U.S.-China Trade: Problems and Prospects.* New York: Praeger, 1989.

———. "Introduction," in Eugene K. Lawson, ed., *U.S.-China Trade: Problems and Prospects.* New York: Praeger, 1989.

Lewis, John W. *Leadership in Communist China.* Ithaca: Cornell University Press, 1963.

Li, Ping. "Price Reform: The Progressive Way." *Beijing Review,* vol. 35, no. 18 (May 4–10, 1992), pp. 18–21.

Liang, Zhiping. "Explicating 'Law': A Comparative Perspective of Chinese and Western Legal Culture." *Journal of Chinese Law,* vol. 3, no. 1 (Summer 1989), pp. 55–94.

Lieberthal, Kenneth. *Central Documents and Politburo Politics in China.* Ann Arbor: University of Michigan, Center for Chinese Studies, 1978.

———. "Domestic Politics and Foreign Policy" in Harry Harding, ed. *China's Foreign Relations in the 1980's* (New Haven: Yale University Press, 1984, pp. 43–70.

Lieberthal, Kenneth G. and David M. Lampton, eds. *Bureaucracy, Politics, and Decision Making in Post-Mao China.* Berkeley: University of California Press, 1992.

Lieberthal, Kenneth and Michel Oksenberg. *Policy Making in China: Leaders, Structures, and Processes.* Princeton: Princeton University Press, 1988.

Liu, Alan P. "The Politics of Corruption in the People's Republic of China." *American Political Science Review* vol. 77, no. 3 (September 1983), pp. 602–621.

Liu, Guogang. "Price Reform Essential to Growth," vol. 29, no. 33 (August 18, 1986), p.14.

Liu, Zheng, Jian Song and Others. *China's Population: Problems and Prospects.* Beijing: New World Press, 1981.

Lo, Carlos W.H. "Deng Xiaoping's Ideas on Law." *Asian Survey,* vol. 22, no. 17 (July 1992), pp. 649–665.

Lubman, Stanley. "Technology Transfer to China: Policies, Law, and Practice," in Michael J. Moser, ed. *Foreign Trade, Investment, and the Law in the People's Republic of China.* Hong Kong: Oxford University Press, 1984, pp. 85–106.

Ma, Hong. *New Strategies for China's Economy.* Beijing: New World Press, 1983.

Manion, Melanie. "Policy Implementation in the People's Republic of China: Authoritative Decisions Versus Individual Interests." *Journal of Asian Studies,* vol. 50, no. 2 (May 1991), pp. 253–279.

Mann, Jim. *Beijing Jeep: The Short Unhappy Romance of American Business in China.* New York: Simon and Schuster, 1989.

McCormick, Barrett L. *Political Reform in Post-Mao China.* Ann Arbor: University Microfilms International Dissertation Information Service, 1985.

Ming, Bu. "China's Financial Relations with Foreign Countries." *Beijing Review,* vol. 24, no. 16 (April 20, 1981), pp. 21-23.

Mooney, Paul. "At China's Crossroads." *Far Eastern Economic Review,* vol. 155, no. 46 (November 19, 1992), p. 66.

Moran, Theodore H. *Multinational Corporations and the Politics of Dependence: Copper in Chile.* Princeton: Princeton University Press, 1974.

Moser, Michael J. "Foreign Investment in China: The Legal Framework," in Michael J. Moser, ed. *Foreign Trade, Investment, and the Law in the People's Republic of China.* Hong Kong: Oxford University Press, 1984, pp. 106-141.

———. "Introduction," in Michael J. Moser, ed. *Foreign Trade, Investment, and the Law in the People's Republic of China.* Hong Kong: Oxford University Press, 1984.

———. "Law and Investment in the Guangdong Special Economic Zones," in Michael J. Moser, ed. *Foreign Trade, Investment, and the Law in the People's republic of China.* Hong Kong: Oxford University Press, 1984, 143–177.

———, ed. *Foreign Trade, Investment, and the Law in the People's Republic of China.* Hong Kong: Oxford University Press, 1984.

Moser, Michael J. and Winston K. Zee. *China Tax Guide.* Oxford: Oxford University Press, 1987.

Mu, Sheng. "Science and Technology White Paper: A Guide to China's Policies on Science and Technology" (text). Hong Kong *Liaowang Overseas Edition* in Chinese (September 8, 1986). Translation by the Foreign Broadcast Information Service. *FBIS Daily Report-China,* September 18, 1986 (FBIS–CHI–86–181; pp. K24–K28).

Nathan, Andrew J. "A Factionalism Model for CCP Politics," *China Quarterly* vol. 14, no. 53 (January–March 1973), pp. 34–66.

Naughton, Barry. "Economic Directions for the 1990s." *The China Business Review*, vol. 18, no. 3 (May–June 1991), pp. 8–12.

Nevis, Edwin C. "Using an American Perspective in Understanding Another Culture: Toward a Hierarchy of Needs for the People's Republic of China." *Journal of Applied Behavioral Science* vol. 19, no. 3 (March 1983), pp. 249–264.

Newman, William H. *Birth of a Successful Joint Venture*. Lanham, MD.: University Press of America, 1992.

O'Brien, Kevin J. "Big Success of Chinese Factories." *The China Quarterly* vol. 33, no. 132 (December 1992), pp. 1086–1100.

———. *Reform without Liberalization: China's National People's Congress and the Politics of Institutional Change*. New York: Cambridge University Press, 1990.

O'Brien, Kevin J. and James Z. Lee. "Chinese Enterprise Reform: A Factory-Level Perspective." Paper Presented at the Annual Meeting of the Midwest Political Science Association, April 5–7, 1990, Chicago, Illinois.

"Organizations Involved in Investment." *The China Business Review*, vol. 13, no. 2 (March–April 1988), pp. 34–35.

"Overseas Investment Flows into Wuhan." *The Xinhua General Overseas News Service* (August 18, 1992).

"The Patent Law of the People's Republic of China." *The China Business Review* vol. 12, no. 1 (January–February 1985), pp. 54–57.

Pearson, Margaret M. "Breaking the Bonds of Dependence: Managers in China's Foreign Sector." *Studies in Comparative Communism*, vol. 25, no. 1 (March 1992).

———. *Joint Ventures in the People's Republic of China: The Control of Foreign Direct Investment Under Socialism*. Princeton: Princeton University Press, 1991.

———. "Party and Politics in Joint Ventures." *The China Business Review*, vol. 18, no. 2 (November–December 1990), pp. 38–40.

———. "The Erosion of Controls over Foreign Capital in China, 1979–1988." *Modern China* vol. 17, no. 1 (January 1991), pp. 112–150.

Peck, Joyce. "Standardizing Foreign Income Taxes." *The China Business Review*, vol. 18, no. 5 (September–October 1991), pp. 12–15.

Pinard, Jeanette and Lian Chun-cheng. "Patent Protection under Chinese Law." *Journal of Chinese Law*, vol. 1, no. 1 (Spring 1987), pp. 69–91.

Pomfret, Richard. *Investing in China: Ten Years of the 'Open Door' Policy*. London: Harvester/Wheatsheaf, 1991.

Potter, Pitman B. "China's New Land Development Regulations." *The China Business Review*, vol. 18, no. 6 (November–December 1991), pp. 12–15.

"PRC Disputes, Part Three: Going for Litigation as a Last Resort." *Business China*, vol. 17, no. 5 (September 10, 1990), pp. 132–133.

"Providing Jobs for China's Hundreds of Millions." *China Reconstructs,* vol. 35, no. 6 (February 1986), pp. 12–14.

"Provisions of Labor and Personnel Management for Sino-foreign Joint Ventures in Wuhan" (promulgated by the Wuhan Municipal Government on December 26, 1988), *Wuhan Local Laws and Regulations.*

Pye, Lucian. *Chinese Commercial Negotiating Style.* Cambridge: Oelgeschlager, Gunn, and Hain, 1982.

———. *The Dynamics of Chinese Politics.* Cambridge: Oelgeschlager, Gunn, and Hain, 1981.

———. *The Spirit of Chinese Politics.* Cambridge: MIT Press, 1968.

Reardon, Lawrence C. "The SEZs Come of Age." *The China Business Review,* vol. 18, no. 6 (November–December 1991), pp. 14–20.

"Regulations for the Implementation of the Law of the PRC Joint Ventures Using Chinese and Foreign Investment." *Beijing Review,* vol. 26, no. 41 (October 10, 1983), pp. 1–16.

"Responsibility System for Researchers Published" (text). Urumqi *Xinjiang Ribao* in Chinese (August 25, 1991). Translation by the Foreign Broadcast Information Service. *FBIS Daily Report-China,* September 17, 1991 (FBIS–CHI–180; pp. 60–62).

Reynolds, Bruce. "China in the International Economy," in Harry Harding, ed. *China's Foriegn Relations in the 1980's.* New Haven: Yale University Press, 1984, pp. 71–106.

"Regulations of the Wuhan Municipal Government on the Rapid Construction on the Rapid Construction of the East Lake High Technology Development Zone," *Wuhan Local Laws,* pp. 329–335.

Rocca, Jean-Louis. "Corruption and Its Shadow: An Anthropological View of Corruption in China." *The China Quarterly,* no. 91 (September 1982), pp. 486–491.

Rong, Zhi-jie. *Shewai Shuishou yu Guoji Shuishou* (*Foreign Taxes and International Taxes*). Henan, People's Republic of China: Henan People's Press, 1988.

Schroeder, Paul E. "The Ohio-Hubei Agreement: Clues to Chinese Negotiating Practices." *The China Quarterly,* no. 91 (September 1992), pp. 486–491.

Schurmann, Franz. *Ideology and Organization in Communist China.* Berkeley: University of California Press, 1966.

Schurmann, Franz. *Ideology and Organization in Communist China.* 2nd ed. Berkeley: University of California Press, 1968.

Sender, Henny. "Be Sure to Bring Money." *Far Eastern Economic Review,* vol. 156, no. 32 (August 12, 1993), p. 73.

———. "By the Horns." *Far Eastern Economic Review,* vol. 156, no. 29 (July 22, 1993), p. 81.

———. "No Bed of Roses." *Far Eastern Economic Review,* vol. 156, no. 31 (August 5, 1993), p. 64.

———. "Two-price China." *Far Eastern Economic Review,* vol. 156, no. 24 (June 17, 1993), pp. 64–65.

Shenkar, Oded and Simcha Ronen. "The Cultural Context of Negotiations: The Implications of Chinese Interpersonal Norms." *Journal of Applied Behavioral Science* vol. 23, no. 2 (1987), pp. 263–275.

Shirk, Susan. "The Domestic Political Dimensions of China's Foreign Economic Relations," in Samuel S. Kim, ed. *China and the World: Chinese Foreign Policy in the Post-Mao Era.* Boulder: Westview Press, 1984.

———. "The Politics of Industrial Reform," in Elizabeth J. Perry and Christine Wong, eds., *The Political Economy of Reform in Post-Mao China.* Cambridge: Harvard University Press, 1985, pp. 195–219.

Simyar, Farhad and Kamal Argheyd. "China: Crossroads to Fame or Failure?" *Business Quarterly,* vol. 51, no. 1 (1986), pp. 30–38.

Solinger, Dorothy. *Chinese Business under Socialism.* Berkeley: University of California Press, 1984.

Solomon, Richard. *Mao's Revolution and the Chinese Political Culture.* Berkeley: University of California Press, 1971.

Song, Jian. "Individuals Employing New High Technologies Must Be Oriented to the World" (text). Beijing *Guangming Ribao* in Chinese (December 27, 1991). Translation by the Foreign Broadcast Information Service. *FBIS Daily Report-China,* January 18, 1991 (FBIS–CHI–91–013; pp. 35–37).

"State Council Transmits Report on Quality" (text). Beijing *Xinhua Domestic Service* in Chinese (September 9, 1985). Translation by the Foreign Broadcast Information Service. *FBIS Daily Report-China,* September 18, 1985, (CHI–85–181; pp. K19–K21).

Steinberg, David I. "The Confucian Backdrop: Setting the Stage for Economic Development," in Lee A. Tavis, ed., *Mulinational Managers and Host Government Interactions.* Notre Dame, Ind.: University of Notre Dame Press, 1982, pp. 73–90.

Swindler, Jo Ann. "The New Legal Framework for Joint Ventures in China: Guidelines for Investors." *Law and Policy in International Business,* vol. 16, no. 3 (1984), pp. 1005–1050.

Tavis, Lee A., ed. *Multinational Managers and Host Government Interactions.* Notre Dame, Ind.: University of Notre Dame Press, 1982.

Thompson, Thomas N. "How Not to Do Business with China." *The China Business Review,* vol. 12, no. 1 (January–February 1985), pp. 10–13.

Tian, Qiu-yuan. *Dalude Changzhang yu Xianggangde Laoban* (*Mainland Managers and Hong Kong Bosses*). Liaoning, People's Republic of China: Liaoning University Press, 1989.

Vernon, Raymond. *Sovereignty at Bay.* New York: Basic Books, Inc., 1971.

———. *Storm over the Multinationals.* Cambridge: Harvard University Press, 1977.

Walder, Andrew G. "A Reply to Womack." *China Quarterly,* vol. 32, no. 126 (June 1991), pp. 334–339.

———. *Communist Neo-Traditionalism: Work and Authority in Chinese Industry.* Berkeley: University of California Press, 1986.

———. "Local Bargaining Relationships and Urban Industrial Finance," in Kenneth G. Lieberthal and David M. Lampton, eds. *Bureaucracy, Politics and Decision Making in Post-Mao China.* Berkeley: University of California Press, 1992. pp. 308–333.

———. "Organized Dependency and Cultures of Authority in Chinese Industry." *Journal of Asian Studies* vol. 43, no. 1 (November 1983), pp. 51–76.

Wang, James C.F. *Contemporary Chinese Politics.* Englewood Cliffs: Prentice Hall Inc., 1985.

Wang, Yinghui. "Yin Jieyan Says the Foreign Exchange Control Structure Reform Goal Is to Turn *Renminbi* into a Convertible Currency" (text). Beijing *Jingji Cankao Bao* in Chinese (February 16, 1993). Translation by the Foreign Broadcast Information Service. *FBIS Daily Report-China,* March 5, 1993 (FBIS–CHI–93–042; pp. 30–31).

"We Must Persistently Grasp Things with Two Hands When Carrying Out Socialist Modernization" (text). Beijing *Renmin Ribao* in Chinese (September 17, 1983). Translation by the Foreign Broadcast Information Service. *FBIS Daily Report-China,* September 19, 1983, pp. K1–K3.

White, Tyrene. "Implementing the 'One-Child-per-Couple' Population Program in Rural China: National Goals and Local Politics," in David M. Lampton, ed. *Policy Implementation in Post-Mao China.* Berkeley: University of California Press, 1987, pp. 284–320.

Womack, Brantley. "Review Essay: Transfigured Community: Neo-traditionalism and Work Unit Socialism." *China Quarterly,* vol. 32, no. 126 (June 1991), pp. 313–333.

"Wuhan Becomes Hot Spot for Foreign Investment." *The Xinhua General Overseas News Service* (September 18, 1992).

"Wuhan Builds 'City of Cars.'" *The Xinhua General Overseas News Service* (December 28, 1992).

"Wuhan Builds Modern Tourist Town." *The Xinhua General Overseas News Service* (December 12, 1992).

"Wuhan Gives Enterprises More Freedom." *The Xinhua General Overseas News Service* (November 22, 1992).

"Wuhan Makes Progress in Producing Optic Fiber Cables," *The Xinhua General Overseas News Service* (January 15, 1993).

"Wuhan Opens International Futures Market." *The Xinhua General Overseas News Service* (December 9, 1993).

"Wuhan Upgrades Old Industrial Enterprises with Foreign Investment." *The Xinhua General Overseas News Service* (December 9, 1992).

Xu, Dixin. "China's SEZs." *Beijing Review,* vol. 24, no. 50 (December 14, 1981), pp. 14–17.

Xue, Muqiao. *China's Socialist Economy.* Beijing: Foreign Languages Press, 1981.

Yang, C. Chengxun. "Bureaucracy and a Management System Charaxterized by Overconcentration of Power" (text). Beijing *Renmin Ribao* in Chinese (September 12, 1986). Translation by the Foreign Broadcast Information Service. *FBIS Daily Report-China,* September 18, 1986, pp. K11–K14.

Yang, Xiaobin. "New Tax Law Favors Foreign Enterprises." *Beijing Review,* vol. 34, no. 18 (May 6–12, 1991).

Yao, Meizhen. *Guoji Touzi Fa* (*International Investment Law*). Wuchang, Wuhan, People's Republic of China: Wuhan University Press, 1989.

Zamet, Jonathan and Murray E. Bovarnick. "Employee Relations for Multinational Companies in China." *Columbia Journal of World Business,* vol. 21, no. 1 (Spring 1986), pp. 13–19.

Zeira, Yorem and Oded Shenkar. "Interactive and Specific Parent Characteristics: Implications for Management and Human Resources in International Joint Ventures." *Management International Review,* vol. 30, Special Issue, 1990, pp. 7–23.

Zhang, Feifei. "Use Law as a Weapon to Protect Copyrights." (text). Beijing *Xinhua Domestic Service* in Chinese (August 9, 1991). Translation by the Foreign Broadcast Information Service. *FBIS Daily Report-China,* August 12, 1991 (FBIS–CHI–91–155; pp. 48–49).

Zhong, Jiwen. "Overcoming Bureaucratism Is an Important Task in Reforming the Political Structure-Studying Comrade Deng Xiaoping's Article 'On the Reform of the Party and State Leadership" (text). Beijing *Renmin Ribao* in Chinese (August 4, 1987). Translation by the Foreign Broadcast Information Service. *FBIS Daily Report-China,* November 15, 1988 (FBIS–CHI–88–220; pp. 35–39).

Zhou, Jiannan. "Reiterating the Policy of Attaching Primary Importance to Quality" (text). Beijing *Renmin Ribao* in Chinese (September 7, 1983, p. 2). Translation by the Foreign Broadcast Information Service. *FBIS Daily Report-China,* September 13, 1983, pp. K7–K10.

Zhou, Yuan. "New Court Handles Intellectual Property Issues" (text). Beijing *China Daily (Business Weekly)* in English (September 8, 1991). *FBIS Daily Report-China,* September 10, 1991 (FBIS–CHI–91–175; pp. 55–56).

Zhu, Rongji. "On Technological Progress and Technological Imports," (text). Beijing *Gongren Ribao* in Chinese (September 12, 1983). Translation by the Foreign Broadcast Information Service. *FBIS Daily Report-China,* September 22, 1983, pp. K2–K7.

Zhuo, Peirong. "Publication of Intellectual Rights Journal Marked" (text). Beijing *Xinhua Domestic Service* in Chinese (January 22, 1991). Translation by the Foreign Broadcast Information Service. *FBIS Daily Report-China,* January 24, 1991 (FBIS–CHI–91–016; pp. 22–23).

Zi, Zhongyun. "The Relationship of Chinese Traditional Culture to the Modernization of China." *Asian Survey,* vol. 27, no. 4 (April 1987), pp. 444–458.

INDEX